HAWAIIAN STREET NAMES

The Complete Guide to O'ahu Street Names

— updated with 5,000 street names —

Compiled by Rich Budnick
Translated by Duke Kalani Wise

Preface by Rev. Abraham Akaka
Introduction by Samuel H. Elbert

HAWAIIAN
STREET NAMES

The Complete Guide to O'ahu Street Names

Published by

Aloha Press
934 Wainiha
Honolulu, HI 96825

alohapress@att.net

Library of Congress Catalog Card Number 87-082281
        Budnick, Rich and Wise, Duke Kalani
        Hawaiian Street Names
        ISBN NO. 0-944081-00-2

Book Cover Design by Richard Mishina, John Prichett, Debra Castro

Many illustrations are used with permission from Guava Graphics

Table of Contents

People ask, "What do the Hawaiian street names mean?"
So we compiled this book to find out.

Preface

The teamwork of Rich Budnick and Duke Kalani Wise has produced a valuable book.

Through the years of my ministry, many people asked me for the meanings of Hawai'i street names and Hawai'i place names. This book will provide help to all who seek answers to these questions.

Readers will find insight and pleasure in this book, and gain a deeper understanding and appreciation of our islands and people, from ancient to modern times.

I am grateful to Budnick and Wise for producing this gracious guide. In addition to translating the names of Hawaiian streets, they are helping to communicate and perpetuate a passion and an aloha for this special island state, located in the heart of the Pacific.

As "Ala Hele – the way to go," this book will enrich any book shelf in and beyond Hawai'i.

Rev. Abraham Kahikina Akaka
Pastor Emeritus,
Kawaiaha'o Church
Honolulu, Hawai'i

Introduction

Hawaiian Street Names is the first and only book to translate 5,000 Hawaiian street names of Oʻahu. In addition, nearly 100 Hawaiian place names are translated.

This book reveals who or what our streets are named for, and why. Readers will learn the accomplishments of important people; the beneficial uses of plants, trees and flowers; and the descriptive names that ancient Hawaiians gave to the winds, rain, and the sea – honored today with street names.

What emerges from our street names is a sense of Hawaiʻi history, folklore, language, land usage, people, and culture.

Curious? Look up your Hawaiian street name in this book. Have you ever wondered what inspired someone to give your street its special Hawaiian name?

Professor T. Blake Clark compiled an impressive history of our earliest street names in a 1939 report for the Hawaiian Historical Society entitled, "Honolulu's Streets." He wrote:

"The history of the islands are well preserved in our Honolulu streets…They are a people's creation... Let us hope that our Lanes and Ways will continue to reflect the charm, the color, and the variety of life in Honolulu."

Honolulu's first street names were divided among Hawaiian and English words. In 1850, during the reign of King Kamehameha III, the Privy Council (king's cabinet), adopted 35 street names.

To date, 17 of those original names have survived the passage of time:

Beretania	Mauna Kea	Queen
Fort	Merchant	Richards
Hotel	Mission	School
Kīna'u	Nu'uanu	Smith
King	Punchbowl	Victoria
Marin		Young

Honolulu's first street names were printed on wooden sign posts, in both English and Hawaiian. People routinely ignored the English names, and spoke the more familiar Hawaiian words.

Many Hawaiian street names are based on Hawaiianized English words created during the last two centuries, since contact with the Western world.

More than 120 O'ahu streets are named for the original land awardee or land grantee. The original land awardee lived on the land prior to the 1848 Great Mahele. The land grantee purchased government land after the Great Mahele, when private property ownership was first granted. Extensive research by Duke Kalani Wise found the names of land awardees and land grantees recorded on maps and land documents.

This book reveals how many streets are named:

407 for geographic and topographic locations (e.g., land sections, land divisions, mountains, valleys, streams, etc.)
189 for foliage (e.g., flowers, plants, trees, shrubs, vines)
171 for people
157 for stars, planets and galaxies
92 for fish and birds
27 for mythological gods and goddesses
23 for winds and rain

Streets in many communities carry an identifiable theme. Some communities with identifiable street name themes are:

- 'Ewa Beach: Hawaiian legends and ocean-related
- Hawai'i Kai: island place names
- Kahala: birds
- Kahalu'u: names begin with Hui (Group of...)
- Kapolei: names of stars
- Mililani: stars, days, nights

- Pauoa Valley and Waialua: names of land awardees
- Pearl City: street names begin with Ho'o (To...)
- Salt Lake: street names begin with Ala (Road...)
- Waikīkī: Hawaiian royalty and other people
- Waimānalo: place names and fish
- Waipahu: street names are plantation-related

Until recent decades, most street names were selected by land developers and realtors. Street names today are chosen by city officials and yes, land developers and realtors, with final approval from City Hall. Too often, "nice sounding words" from a Hawaiian dictionary are selected or combined into new street names. This practice tends to ignore historic themes or nearby landmarks.

Research of city documents revealed more than 100 street names misspelled, and hundreds more translated erroneously. Officials in the City Department of Land Utilization readily admit to this problem. Yet, when a spelling error is discovered, they say it is easier to change the translation than to change the spelling. This policy ignores the significance of community themes.

How to Spell, Speak
and Use Hawaiian Words

Diacritical markings help people to spell, speak, and use Hawaiian words correctly. Without diacritical markings, it may be difficult to distinguish many words.

What does the word **pau** mean? It depends.   **Pau** can be four words. **Pau** means *finished, ended.* **Pa'u** is *soot, smudge, or drudgery.* **Pa'ū** means *moist, damp.* **Pā'ū** is *a skirt worn by female horseback riders.*

Contemporary spelling and pronunciation alter the pronunciation and meaning of a word such as **Ha'ikū**. **Ha'ikū** is both an O'ahu and Maui community, and the *name of a flower*, but **haiku** is a Japanese word, *a style of Japanese poetry.*

The English language doesn't employ special pronunciation or spelling markings, yet phonetic guides appear in English dictionaries. In contrast, many other languages use some kind of markings. Spanish places the accent (´) for stress, as in **José,** *Joe*. German adopts the umlaut (¨), as in **über**, *over*. French uses four diacritical marks on vowels, as in **élève,** *pupil,* **crêpe,** *a French pancake,* and **Noël,** *Christmas*. Arabic employs the hamzah as a glottal stop to differentiate meaning.

Few people today are familiar with the Hawaiian language, except for a couple dozen popular words and phrases that can be found in any booklet sold to tourists.

When words are consistently misspelled and misspoken, the language changes and erodes. This is particularly true of the Hawaiian language. Lifelong Hawai'i residents routinely dismiss the correct pronunciation and spelling of Hawaiian words, and proclaim: "That's how we say it! That's how we spell it!"

As if to reply, a 1976 pamphlet prepared for the Hawaii Bicentennial Commission by Kalani Meinecke, a University of Hawai'i instructor of the Hawaiian language, asserts:

"Today the Hawaiian language is in danger of being distorted beyond recognition, and its rhythmic and phonetic beauty lost forever...The greatest factors contributing to the (distortion) of the language are the mispronunciation, misuse, and misspelling of the common Hawaiian words, names, and expressions which occur everyday in Hawai'i nei."

Street Names Preserve
the Hawaiian Language

Our street names help to preserve the Hawaiian language for future generations. Since 1954, city law has established four criteria for naming streets:

1. The Hawaiian names, words or phrases must be "appropriate" to cultural, scenic, and topographic features.
2. There must be no duplication in spelling or similarity in sound from existing street names.
3. Street names can not exceed 18 spaces (to fit on the street sign).
4. Street names must be spelled with diacritical markings.

On February 19, 1962, the Honolulu City Council approved a resolution to require Hawaiian names for all streets.

In a "hit-and-miss" fashion, O'ahu now has 138 streets with the same Hawaiian name in two or more communities. (Once I mistakenly addressed a letter to a street named **Ala Loa** in 'Ewa Beach, without realizing that I should have mailed it to **Alaloa** Street in Kāne'ohe).

There are 33 duplicative Hawaiian street names honoring people or topographic sites.

For instance, Honolulu has two streets named **Kamuela**. The Place is named for Samuel 'Aikanaka Dowsett. The Avenue is named for Samuel Wilder King, the governor. Here is another example: **Lanihuli** means *changing heaven*. The Street and Place in Lā'ie are named for an ancient *mo'o god*, while the Drive in Honolulu is named for an O'ahu mountain peak.

Mauna Kea, the Hawai'i Island volcano, means *white mountain*. But the Honolulu street is named for the steamship, "Mauna Kea" which formerly docked at the foot of Mauna Kea Street. The steamship was probably named for the mountain.

Many streets carry the same names – in different languages. In Mānoa, there is Rainbow Drive and **Ānuenue** Street. Each is a translation of the other. One day, I wanted to turn the car at Rainbow, but I must have been thinking in two languages. I turned instead, at Ānuenue.

Hawaiian Street Names is a book the average person will enjoy. There is something in it for everyone. The translations are informative, interesting, and readable.

Best of all, this book answers the question, "What does my street name mean?"

Foreword

A good way to show respect for another culture is to try to speak its words as a native speaker does. To pronounce Hawaiian street names as Hawaiians do is to respect Hawaiian culture, and to honor Hawaiians.

Here we have an excellent guide to the 4,300 Hawaiian street names of Oʻahu.

Rich Budnick had the foresight to realize that a book such as this would help people learn to appreciate the Hawaiian language. He enlisted the assistance of Duke Kalani Wise who is a Hawaiian of a distinguished family, and a University of Hawaiʻi graduate who majored in the Hawaiian Language and Anthropology. Wise is extremely knowledgeable about Hawaiian culture, and the pronunciation of the language. He is an able speaker of the Hawaiian language.

These authors have shown great care and accuracy with two all-important diacritical marks...the glottal stop, a break shown by the apostrophe (ʻ); and the macron (ˉ), which has two functions: it is used on all long vowels, and on one-syllable words and particles that are always stressed.

Why are these signs so important?

I have written extensively on this subject, and will summarize briefly here.

Words with and without glottal stops have different meanings:

- **ʻai**, *to eat;* **ai**, *sexual intercourse.*
- **awa**, *harbor, milkfish;* **ʻawa**, *a plant with roots that supply a tranquilizing, nonalcoholic, bitter drink.*
- **kai**, *sea;* **kaʻi**, *to lead.*

And different words that seem similar, except for the macron:

- **wahine**, *woman*; **wāhine**, *women*.
- **kāne**, *male*; **kane**, *a skin disease*.
- **hūnā,** *to hide*; **huna,** *tiny bit*.

Single syllable words with and without an initial glottal stop:

- **o**, *of*; **'o**, *a grammatical subject of a sentence*. Single syllable words with and without macrons:
- **ī**, *to say*; **i**, *at*.
- **nō**, *to leak, very*; **no**, *of, for*.

And words with both a glottal stop and none at all:

- **Lāna'i**, *name of an island*; **lanai**, *porch*.
- **māka'i**, *policeman*; **makai**, *towards the sea*.

A pronunciation mistake that might be embarrassing is: **Kūhiō**, the name of our former prince and Congressman. It literally means, *to stand (and) lean*. Quite a difference from **kūhio**, *to fart silently*.

Someone must have complained about the Alapa'i Street sign, as it first appeared, without the glottal stop. A few days later, I was pleased that a glottal stop had been inserted.

Eventually people may find that these unusual diacritical marks add a touch of elegance to the street signs.

In my opinion, this is the most complete and authoritative guide to O'ahu street names, and the only book that includes so many meanings.

So I would say to the reader, **'Imi ā loa'a**! *Discover and learn!*

Samuel H. Elbert
Mānoa

Acknowledgements

Duke Kalani Wise deserves special tribute for his scholarly devotion to excellence. His patient and careful research is responsible for separating hear-say from fact. His linguistic expertise and knowledge of Hawaiian history, culture, street names and community themes are evident throughout this book.

I also thank University of Hawai'i Professor Emeritus **Samuel H. Elbert,** the eminent author of numerous books on Hawaiian and Polynesian languages. He read the manuscript, contributed helpful suggestions, and permitted the authors to adopt translations from his books.

I appreciate the generous encouragement and support of **Raymond Pua**, Honolulu City Clerk, and I wish to acknowledge the assistance of these city officials: **Bob Moore**, Department of Land Utilization, **Phil Simon**, Public Works Department, and **Dennis Silva**, Department of Planning and Permitting.

Further acknowledgements to: **Lee Winters**, University of Hawai'i Professor Emeritus; **Esther Mo'okini**, author and Hawaiian Language Lecturer, Kapi'olani Community College; **Lee Wild**, Mission Houses Museum; and **Stanley Kī'ope Raymond**, Office of Hawaiian Affairs.

Also: **Gordon Pi'iānāi'a**, Kamehameha Schools; **A. Grove Day,** author; **John Clere**, EMIC Graphics; also **Wilmer Morris, Joan Osborne, Wil Hokama**, and especially **Kelli McCormack, Bill Souza, Debra Castro, John Pritchett**, and **B.J. Wade**.

Finally, I thank my wife, **Min-Tzu**, for understanding that a book, like a journey, takes time to complete.

Words You Need to Know

Ahupua‘a – Land division, extending from uplands to the sea.

Endemic plants – Plants that grow only in Hawai‘i.

House of Nobles – Modeled after Britain's House of Lords. Ali‘i and other high-ranking people were appointed by the monarch.

Kanaloa – God of the ocean.

Kāne – God of creation. Ancestor of chiefs and commoners.

Kapu – Taboo; sacred; keep out.

Kava (‘awa) – A plant, used as a narcotic drink in ceremonies, and medicinally, to ease pain.

Kū – God of war, agriculture, and fishing.

Kuhina Nui – Prime minister, premier. Hawai‘i had six Kuhina Nui: Ka‘ahumanu (1819-1832), Kīna‘u (1832-1839), Kekāuluohi (1839-1845), John Young II (Keoniana, 1845-1854), Kamāmalu (1855-1863), and Mataio Kekūanao‘a (1863-1864) – all women, except John Young.

Land awardee – A person who lived here before the Great Mahele.

Land grantee – A person who owned land after the Great Mahele.

Lua – A type of hand-to-hand fighting. Fighters broke and dislocated bones, and inflicted severe pain by pressing on nerve centers. Specific lua holds were given names.

Mo‘o (god) – Supernatural lizard (guardian). Reptile of any kind.

Native plants – Plants that grow in Hawai‘i, and elsewhere.

Pele – Lava flow, volcano, eruption. The volcano goddess.

Poi board – Board used for beating taro to make poi.

Privy Council – King's Cabinet of advisors.

Tapa (kapa) – Cloth or clothes made from tree bark, usually māmaki or wauke bark, pounded smooth.

Tī (kī) – A plant in the Lily family. Its leaves were used for house thatch, food wrappers, hula skirts, and sandals. Its roots were baked for food or distilled for brandy.

1848 Great Mahele – A law that allowed people to own property. Land was assigned: one-third to the king, one-third to the government, and one-third to private landowners. Previously, the king owned all the land. The Great Mahele was adopted under pressure from foreigners who wanted to own land.

Hawaiian Community Names

'Āhuimanu – Bird cluster. Named for an O'ahu land section, which is the same as Āhuimanu.

'Aiea – Four species of endemic shrubs and trees in the Tomato family. Named for an O'ahu land division.

'Aikahi – Eat scrape (as the sides of a poi bowl; to eat all). Named for an O'ahu land section.

'Āina Haina – Hind's land. Named for Robert Hind (1863-1938). Part-Hawaiian rancher and dairy farmer on Hawai'i Island, and Territorial Senator (1917-1938). Son of a sugar planter. The Hind-Clarke Dairy was located nearby.

'Āinakoa – Land of soldiers.

Ala Moana – Ocean road.

'Ālewa – Suspended (on a height). Named for an O'ahu land section.

Āliamanu – Bird salt-pond. (Many vegetarian birds eat salt). Named for an O'ahu crater.

Ali'i Shores – Chief, chiefess, king, queen, noble.

'Ewa Beach – Crooked, out-of-shape, imperfect. Figuratively: unjust. Named for an O'ahu district.

Haha'ione – Sand broken. Named for an O'ahu valley.

Ha'ikū – Haughty, conceited. Named for an O'ahu valley.

Hālawa – Curve, as a road or along the beach. Named for an O'ahu land division.

Hale'iwa – House (of) frigate bird.

Hau'ula – Red hau tree. Named for an O'ahu land division.

Hawai'i – Definition not known. A similar name is found in Polynesia: Havaiki (New Zealand, North Marquesas), 'Avaiki (Cook Islands), and Savai'i (Samoa).

Hawai'i Kai – Sea Hawai'i. Kai is short for Kaiser. Named for Henry J. Kaiser (1882-1967). He developed this 6,000 acre area in 1959, and also built the Hilton Hawaiian Village. One of the world's richest men. An industrialist, he founded numerous corporations, including Kaiser Aluminum, Kaiser Steel, Kaiser Cement, and Kaiser Foundation Medical Health Care.

Hawai'i Loa – 1) Distant Hawai'i. 2) Long Hawai'i. Named for an O'ahu mountain ridge.

He'eia – Definition not known. Named for an O'ahu land division.

Honolulu – Protected bay.

Honouliuli – Dark bay.

Iwilei – Collarbone. Named for an O'ahu land section.

Ka'a'awa – The 'a'awa. 'A'awa: certain wrasse fishes, common on coral reefs. A popular and tasty fish. Named for an O'ahu land division.

Iwilei

Kahala – The hala (pandanus tree). The hala tree is known for its slanting aerial roots and pineapple-shaped fruits. Its tough, pliable hala leaves (lau hala) are woven into floor and sleeping mats, baskets, fans, sandals, and pillows. The fleshy ends of unripe fruits are strung in leis. Named for an O'ahu land section.

Kahalu'u – Diving place.

Kahana – Definition not known.

Kahuku – The projection. Named for an O'ahu land division.

Kailua – Two seas. An O'ahu land division, named for Kawainui and Ka'elepulu, two fishponds, formerly lagoons that were open to the sea.

Kaimukī – The tī oven. Named for an O'ahu land section.

Kahalu'u

Kaka'ako – Definition not known. Named for an O'ahu land section.

Kalāheo – The proud day. Named for an O'ahu land section.

Kalama – The lama (tree).

Kalihi – The edge; the boundary. Named for an O'ahu land division.

Kāne'ohe – Bamboo husband. Legend says that a woman compared her husband's cruelty to the cutting edge of a bamboo knife. Named for an O'ahu land division.

Kapālama – The lama (wood) fence. The fence surrounding a house of ali'i women was considered a kapu sign. Named for an O'ahu land division.

Kapolei – Beloved Kapo (sister of Pele). A cone (166 feet high) on the southeast slope of the Wai'anae mountain range.

Kawailoa – The big water. Named for an O'ahu land section.

Kawela – The heat. Named for an O'ahu land division.

Keolu – Definition not known. Named for an O'ahu land section.

Koko – Blood. Named for an O'ahu canoe landing and promontory.

Kokokahi – One blood.

Koko Kai – Sea blood, blood water.

Kō 'Olina – Fulfillment of joy.

Kuilima – To go arm in arm, to hold hands; arm in arm.

Kuli'ou'ou – Sounding knee. Named for an O'ahu land section.

Kunia – Burned. Named for an O'ahu land section.

Lāʻie – ʻIe leaf.
Lanikai – Sea heaven, marine heaven.
Lualualei – Definition not known. Named for an Oʻahu land division.
Māʻili – Pebble; pebbly, full of pebbles.
Mākaha – Fierce. Named for an Oʻahu land division.
Makakilo – Observant, watchful eyes; to watch with great attention. Named for an Oʻahu crater.
Makiki – Type of stone used for adzes, and as weights for octopus lures. Named for an Oʻahu land section.
Mānoa – Vast. Named for an Oʻahu valley.
Māpunapuna – Bubbling spring. Named for an Oʻahu land section and former fishpond.
Maunalani – Heavenly mountain. Modern name of an Oʻahu land area.
Maunalua – Two mountains. Named for an Oʻahu land section.
Maunawili – Twisted mountain. Named for an Oʻahu land section.
Mililani – To praise, exhalt.
Moanalua – Two encampments. Named for an Oʻahu land division.
Mōʻiliʻili – Pebble lizard.
Mokulēiʻa – Isle (of) abundance.
Nānākai – Observing seaward.
Nānākuli – Look at knees. Named for an Oʻahu land division.
Niu – The coconut, the world's best known palm. Hawaiians used all parts of the tree for food, fiber, oil, and building materials. Its leaves were shaped into fans, baskets, brooms, and musical instruments. Its husk was used for containers and hula rattles. Its milk and meat were forbidden to ancient Hawaiian women. Niu was the official tree of Hawaiʻi Territory (1930-1959).
Nuʻuanu – Cool heights. Named for an Oʻahu valley.
Oʻahu – Definition not known.
Pālama – Lama (wood) enclosure. Short for Kapālama: an Oʻahu land division.

Niu

Pālolo – Sticky clay. Named for an Oʻahu valley.
Pauoa – Definition not known. Named for an Oʻahu valley.
Punaluʻu – Diving spring (water). Named for an Oʻahu land division.
Pūpūkea – White shell. Named for an Oʻahu land division.
Puʻuloa – Long hill. Hawaiian name for Pearl Harbor.
Puʻunui – Big hill. Named for Oʻahu land sections.
Wahiawā – Place of noise (refers to sound of rough seas).
Waiāhole – Āhole (fish) water. Named for an Oʻahu land division.
Waiʻalae – Mudhen water. Named for an Oʻahu valley.
Waiʻalae Iki – Little Waiʻalae.
Waiʻalae Nui – Big Waiʻalae.
Waialeʻe – Definition not known.

Waialua – Definition not known. Named for an Oʻahu district.

Waiʻanae – Mullet (fish) water. Named for an Oʻahu district and a land division within that district.

Waiau – Swirling water of a current. Named for an Oʻahu land division.

Waiʻauʻau – Bathing water.

Waiheʻe – Squid liquid, octopus water. Named for an Oʻahu land division.

Waikalani – Water (of) the chief.

Waikāne – Water (of) Kāne. Kāne: one of the four major Hawaiian gods. God of creation. Ancestor of chiefs and commoners. Named for an Oʻahu land division.

Waikīkī – Spouting water. Said to be named for swamps (later drained to create the Ala Wai Canal); also the name of a chicken.

Waimānalo

Wailupe – Kite water. Named for an Oʻahu valley.

Waimalu – Sheltered water.

Waimānalo – Drinkable water. Named for an Oʻahu gulch.

Waimea – Reddish water. Named for an Oʻahu land division.

Waipahu – Drum water. Said to have been originally Waipahū: bursting water. Named for an Oʻahu land section.

Waipiʻo – Arched water. Named for an Oʻahu land division.

Hawaiian Street Names

A'aahi St./Pl. (Mililani) – Shoot of sandalwood.
'A'aha Pl. ('Ewa Beach) – Net used to carry a calabash. Net was made of sennit or olonā cord (rope). See Olonā.
'A'ahu Pl. (Mililani) – Clothing.
'A'ahuali'i St./Pl. (Kapolei) – Regal attire, a royal robe.
Aakahi Gulch Rd. (Lā'ie) – Should be 'A'akāki'i: strike at waist. Named for an O'ahu gulch.
'A'ala Dr./Walk (Kailua, Wai'anae) – Fragrant.
'A'ala St./Pl. (Honolulu) – Fragrant. Named for an O'ahu land section.
Aalapapa Dr./Pl./Way (Kailua) – Should be 'Āla'apapa: probably, a long cloud formation. Named for an O'ahu land section.
'A'aliamanu Pl. (Honolulu) – Wattles (a fleshy lobe that hangs from the beak or chin) of a bird. Probably should be Āliamanu: bird salt-pond. Vegetarian birds eat salt.
'A'ali'i St./Pl. (Honolulu, Pearl City) – Endemic hardwood shrubs and trees. Their wood was shaped into digging sticks, spears, and weapons. Their leaves yield red dye. The pretty fruit clusters are combined with ferns to make leis.
'A'ama Pl. ('Ewa Beach) – A large black crab. Its discarded red shell is often seen on shoreline rocks.
'A'āmaka St./Pl. (Pearl City) – To stare or glare with wide-open eyes, as in desire, fear, or intent to frighten.
'A'amanu St. (Pearl City) – Bag for carrying birds, made of coconut or pandanus leaves.
Aamomi St. (Pearl City) – Should be 'A'amoni: purse.
'A'aniu Lp./Pl. (Pearl City) – Cloth-like covering at base of coconut frond.
'A'api Pl./Way (Pearl City) – Curved.
Aarona Pl. (Kailua) – Aaron.
'A'awa Dr. ('Ewa Beach) – Wrasse fishes.
'Ae'ae St./Pl. ('Ewa Beach) – A small native shrub that grows near salt marshes among rocks near the sea.
'Aekai Pl. ('Ewa Beach) – Place where sea and land meet; water's edge.
'Aelike St./Pl. (Mililani) – Agreement, contract.
A'eloa St. (Kāne'ohe) – Trade wind name.

A'ahu

'Aelike

Aeʻo Pl. (Pearl City) – The Hawaiian black-necked stilt bird, an endangered shorebird found where the receding tide exposes black mud, or near brackish or freshwater ponds.

ʻAe ʻoia St. (ʻEwa Beach) – To be well supplied with comforts and necessities.

ʻAha Way (ʻEwa Beach) – Needlefish.

ʻAha ʻAina Pl. (Honolulu) – Feast, banquet. Literally: meal gathering.

ʻAhaana Way (Honolulu) – Design resembling duck tracks, carved on tapa beaters.

ʻAhahui Pl./Way (Mililani) – Society, club, association, organization, company.

ʻAhahuina Pl. (Mililani) – Corporation, association.

ʻAhaiki St./Pl. (Pearl City) – Small gathering for private conversation.

ʻAhakapu St. (Pearl City) – A sacred assembly.

ʻAhakea St. (Honolulu) – Native trees in the Coffee family. Their wood was shaped into poi boards, paddles, and canoe rims.

ʻAhakū Pl. (Honolulu) – Cord used for measuring, as in laying out a garden or house.

ʻAhakuhina Pl. (Pearl City) – Cabinet; assembly of ministers.

ʻAhakūkā Pl. (Pearl City) – Council meeting; discussion meeting.

Aha Maka Way (Honolulu) – Should be ʻAha Maha: place or assembly for practice of athletic games. Literally: assembly for relaxation.

ʻAhamele Pl. (Honolulu) – Yellow-spotted needlefish, common on most reefs. Feared because they leap out of the water when startled, and may cut a fisherman while descending into water.

ʻAhamoa St. (Pearl City) – An assembly watching a lua contest called hakakā-a-moa, in which contestants fought with their feet, legs, shoulders and heads, but not their hands.

ʻAhana St. (Honolulu) – Origin not known.

ʻAha Niu Pl. (Honolulu) – A native sedge (plant) used for dry bouquets. Literally: coconut sennit (because its leaves, like sennits, were used for tying).

ʻAhaʻōlelo Rd. (Kāneʻohe) – Legislature, assembly, council meeting.

ʻAhapiʻi Pl. (Honolulu) – A kind of tapa dyed with kukui bark and decorated with fine lines, for chiefs.

ʻAhapule St. (Pearl City) – Congregation, prayer assembly.

ʻAhaʻula St. (Mililani) – Council of chiefs. Literally: regal meeting.

Ahe St./Pl. (Honolulu) – Breeze, breezy.

ʻAhea St./Pl. (Mililani) – A native shrub.

Aheahe Ave./St./Pl. (Wahiawā, ʻAiea) – Light breeze.

Ahekai St. (Waiʻanae) – Ocean breeze.

Ahi Pl. (Honolulu) – Fire.

Ahiahi St./Pl. (Honolulu) – Evening.

Ahi

'Āhihi St. (Honolulu) – Any plant with long runners; any creeping vine.

Ahikao St. (Mililani) – Fireworks.

Ahiki St. (Waimānalo) – Definition not known.
An O'ahu mountain peak (the least pointed of
3 Olomana peaks, 1,643 feet). Named for an
O'ahu land section.

Ahikao

Ahikoe St. (Kapolei) – Match. Literally: scratch-
ing fire.

'Ahiku St. (Mililani) – Seven.

Ahilama Pl./Rd. (Kāne'ohe) – Torch flame.

'Āhina St./Pl. (Honolulu) – Gray.

'Āhinahina Pl. (Honolulu) – The silversword, a rare native plant found only
on Haleakalā, Maui and on high mountains of Hawai'i Island. Takes up to
20 years to mature, then dies. It has a tall stalk with a rounded, rose-
shaped arrangement of 100 purple flowers (that blossom once), growing
atop a round 6-foot base with long silver leaves.

'Āhinalū Pl. (Hau'ula) – Scattered gray.

Ahipu'u St. (Honolulu) – Hill fire. Named for an O'ahu hill.

'Āhiu Pl. (Mililani) – Wild, untamed, as animals or plants.

'Āhiwa St. (Kapolei) – Dark, dusky.

'Ahohui St. (Mililani) – Thatch purlin (roof support).

'Ahokā St./Pl. (Mililani) – Small lashing on the main purlin (roof support).

'Ahokele St. (Mililani) – Horizontal thatch purlin (roof support).

Āhole Pl. ('Ewa Beach) – An endemic fish found in fresh and salt water.

Āholehole St. (Honolulu) – Young stage of the āhole, Hawaiian flagtail, a
fish resembling white perch or sea bass.

Ahona St. ('Ewa Beach) – Better, well, fortunate, improved.

Ahonui St. (Honolulu) – Patient, enduring, long suffering.

Ahu Ln. (Honolulu) – Heap, pile, collection.

Āhua St. (Honolulu) – Heap. Perhaps should be 'Āhua: an aku, kawakawa,
or moano fish in the second stage of growth. Named for an O'ahu land
section and a former fishpond.

Ahuahu Pl. (Honolulu) – Healthy, vigorous; strength and vigor, as an
animal or plant; to grow rapidly, thrive.

Āhualani Pl. (Honolulu) – Heavenly hillock (little hill).

'Ahu'awa Lp./Pl. (Honolulu) – A sedge (plant). Fiber stripped from the
stem was used to strain 'ava or was spun into rope.

'Āhui St. (Honolulu) – Bunch, cluster.

'Āhuimanu Lp./Pl./Rd. (Kāne'ohe) – Bird cluster. Named for an O'ahu
land section, which is the same as Āhuimanu.

'Āhui Nani Pl. (Kāne'ohe) – Lovely cluster.

Ahukini St./Pl. (Honolulu) – Altar (for) many (blessings). Named for a Kaua'i land section.

'Āhuli Pl. (Honolulu) – To look for, seek.

'Ahulili St. (Mililani) – A peak on Maui. Literally: glowing, dazzling.

'Āhulimanu Pl./Way (Kāne'ohe) – Birds looking (for water). Named for an O'ahu land section. Same as 'Āhuimanu.

'Ahunāli'i Pl. (Mililani) – To collect, as leaves in a stream.

'Ahuua St. ('Ewa Beach) – Old type of raincoat made of dried tī leaves.

'Ahu'ula St. (Honolulu) – Feather cloak or cape, usually red or yellow trimmed with black or green.

Ahuwale St./Pl. (Honolulu) – Conspicuous, exposed, in plain view.

A'ia'i Pl. (Kāne'ohe) – Bright, fair, white, clear.

'Aiali'i St./Pl. (Kāne'ohe) – To enjoy the ease, honor and dignity of a chief.

'Ai'ami Pl. ('Ewa Beach) – Type of hula with little foot movement, but with the hip revolving throughout the dance.

'Aiau Ln. (Hale'iwa) – A family name. Probably Hawaiianized Chinese.

'Aiea Access Rd./Gulch Access Rd./Hts. Dr. ('Aiea) – Four species of endemic shrubs and trees in the Tomato family. Named for an O'ahu land division.

'Aiea Kai Pl./Way ('Aiea) – Lower 'Aiea. Named for the subdivision.

Aiea Loa Pl. ('Aiea) – Lower 'Aiea. Named for the subdivision.

'Aiea Nui Pl. ('Aiea) – Tall 'aiea tree. See 'Aiea.

'Aiea Uka St./Pl. ('Aiea) – Large 'aiea tree. See 'Aiea.

'Aiealani Pl. ('Aiea) – Upland 'Aiea. See 'Aiea.

'Aikahi Lp./Pl. (Kailua) – Eat scrape (as the sides of a poi bowl; to eat all). Named for an O'ahu land section.

'Aikanaka Pl./Rd. ('Ewa Beach) – Man-eating; to eat human flesh.

Aikāne St./Pl. (Kailua) – Friend; to become a friend.

'Aikapa St./Pl. (Kailua) – A privileged friend who shares the profits of a friend's land.

Aikaula St. (Waialua) – Definition not known. Named for original grantee.

'Aiko'o Pl. (Pearl City) – A wind at Nu'alolo Valley, Kaua'i.

'Aila St. (Honolulu) – Oil.

'Ailaiki St. ('Ewa Beach) – Rice-eating; to eat rice.

'Ailaiki

'Ailana Pl. (Wahiawā) – Island.

'Ailolo Pl. (Pearl City) – Ceremony marking the end of training. The student ate ('ai) a portion of the head, and especially the brains (lolo) of a fish, dog, or hog offered to the gods.

Ailona St. (Mililani) – Sign, symbol, emblem.

Ailuna St. (Honolulu) – Up there.

ʻAimāmā Pl. (Pearl City) – Light meal, snack. Literally: fast food.

ʻAimīkana St. (Kailua) – Linnet, California house finch, or papaya bird. Literally: papaya eater.

ʻAimoku St. (Honolulu) – Ruler of a moku (district or island); to rule a moku.

ʻĀinahou St. (Honolulu) – New land. Possibly named for a Hawaiʻi Island land section.

ʻAinakea Way (Honolulu) – A variety of sugar cane, used medicinally.

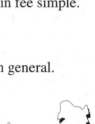

ʻAimāmā

ʻĀinakoa Ave. (Honolulu) – Land of soldiers.

ʻĀinakūʻai Pl. (Mililani) – Land purchased or for sale; land in fee simple.

ʻĀina Lani Pl./Way (Honolulu) – Royal land.

ʻĀinamakua Dr. (Mililani) – Fatherland.

ʻĀina Mōʻī Pl. (Kāneʻohe) – King's land.

ʻĀinana Pl./Way (Mililani) – Commoner, populace, people in general.

ʻĀinanani Pl. (Honolulu) – Beautiful land.

ʻĀinanui Lp. (ʻAiea) – Great power, great land, mainland.

ʻĀinapō St./Pl. (Honolulu) – Darkened land. Named for a Hawaiʻi Island land section.

ʻĀinapua St. (Honolulu) – Poetic name for China. Literally: flower land.

ʻAinoni St. (Kailua) – Eat noni fruit. Named for an Oʻahu land section.

ʻĀinapua

ʻAiʻokoʻa St. (Kailua) – Cooked unpounded taro. Literally: whole taro.

ʻAipaʻakō St. (Honolulu) – Ruler of a dry area. Named for an Oʻahu land section, called Kūʻaipaʻakō during Great Mahele era.

ʻAipō St./Pl. (Honolulu) – Eating (by) dark. Named for a Kauaʻi swamp.

ʻAipoʻolā St./Pl. (ʻEwa Beach) – Feast to celebrate the completion of a hard task or project.

ʻAipuni St. (Honolulu) – To encircle, make a circuit.

Aka Pl. (Kāneʻohe) – To laugh, laughter.

Akaaka St. (ʻAiea) – Transparent, clear, luminous.

Akaʻakaʻawa St. (Kailua) – A rare, endemic begonia (a tropical herb) with small pink and white flowers, found in damp ravines.

ʻĀkaʻakoʻa St./Pl. (Kailua) – An unidentified variety of seaweed.

Akaʻawa St./Pl. (Kapolei) – A tall endemic climber (vine), used for tying rafters.

Akahai St. (Kailua) – To be tender of heart, gentle.

Akahele Pl. (Kailua) – Slow or moderate, cautious, careful.

ʻAkahi St. (Honolulu) – One.

Akaholo St. (ʻEwa Beach) – To sail or run cautiously.

Aka

'Āka'ika'i Lp. (Pearl City) – Plump.

'Akaiki St. (Kailua) – Sly laughter; to laugh a little, giggle, chuckle.

Akāka Pl. (Honolulu) – Clearness. Named for an O'ahu hill.

'Akaka Ln. (Honolulu) – Named for 'Akaka Lee Tsiark (?-1918), a Chinese immigrant who lived here, owned a stable here, and subdivided the land. Grandfather of the Rev. Abraham Akaka, pastor emeritus of Kawaiaha'o Church.

'Akakē Pl./Way (Kailua) – Spry, quick, nimble, especially about getting into people's way or into trouble.

'Akaki Way (Kailua) – Agate.

Akakoa Pl. (Kāne'ohe) – Brave reflection.

Akakū St./Pl. (Mililani) – Vision, trance.

'Ākala Ln. (Honolulu) – Two native raspberries and the thimbleberry. Literally: pink (color of the berry's juice).

Akamainui

'Ākalakala St. (Pearl City) – Raspberry. See 'Ākala.

Akalani Lp./Pl. (Kailua) – Afterglow.

Akalei Pl. (Kailua) – String of multi-colored glass beads.

Akaluli St. (Mililani) – To move slowly, carefully.

Akamai St./Pl. (Kailua) – Clever, smart, expert; smartness, skill.

Akamainui St. (Wahiawā) – High technology.

'Akamu Pl. (Honolulu) – Adams. Named for Annie K. Adams (1886-1951), wife of Andrew Adams, subdivision owner and Kahuku sugar plantation manager. Descendant of Maui chiefs.

Akana Pl. (Honolulu) – Origin not known.

Akanahe Pl. (Kailua) – Careful, gentle in behavior or speech.

Akanoho Pl. (Hale'iwa) – To sit quietly.

'Akapane Pl. (Kāne'ohe) – See 'Apapane.

'Ākau Ln./St. (Honolulu, Wahiawā) – North.

Aka'ula St./Pl. (Kapolei) – Red sunset.

'Ākea Pl. (Kailua) – Starboard or outer hull of a double canoe.

Akeakamai St. (Honolulu) – A seeker after knowledge, lover of wisdom.

Akeakamai

Akeake St. (Mililani) – Ready, as to do a kindly deed; helpful.

'Ākeke Pl. (Kailua) – Cindery or pebbly soil; cinder.

'Ākeke'e Pl. ('Ewa Beach) – A honey creeper bird.

'Akekeke Pl. (Kailua) – Ruddy turnstone, a winter migratory bird.

'Akele St. (Kailua) – Acre.

'Ākepa St. (Honolulu) – A group of small scarlet or yellow-green Hawaiian honeycreepers (birds).

'Akepo Ln. (Honolulu) – A family name. A hackman of this name lived here in 1890.

'Akeu Pl. (Waipahu) – Pleasant, sociable.

'Ākeukeu St. (Pearl City) − Pleasant, sociable.

'Ākia Pl. (Mililani) − Endemic shrubs and trees whose bark, roots, and leaves yield a narcotic used to poison fish.

Akiahala St./Pl. (Kailua) − Small endemic trees. Their dark-red to black berries were believed to help with fertility.

'Aki'aki Pl. (Honolulu) − Seashore rush grass, sometimes used for beach home lawns.

'Akialoa Pl./Way (Kailua) − A group of Hawaiian honeycreepers (birds).

'Akihiloa St. (Waipahu) − A group of Hawaiian honeycreepers (birds).

'Āki'iki'i Pl. (Kailua) − Dip net, used in fishing for uhu (parrotfishes).

'Akiki Pl. (Pearl City) − Dwarfed.

'Akilolo St. (Honolulu) − A green fish with blue underbody. Literally: brain biting.

'Akimala St./Pl. (Kāne'ohe) − Admiral. Usually: 'akimalala.

'Akimona St. (Kailua) − Kukui nut relish. Commonly called: 'inamona.

'Akina St. (Honolulu) − A family name. Possibly named for Joseph 'Apukai 'Akina (1856-1920) of Kaua'i, Speaker of the first Territorial House of Representatives (1901).

'Akiohala St./Pl. (Kailua) − A native hibiscus with pink flowers, found in marshy land. Also called hau hele.

'Akipohe St./Pl. (Kailua) − Round, compact, concise. Name of a wind at Waihe'e, Maui.

Akipola St. (Kailua) − Definition not known.

'Akiu Pl. (Kailua) − To search, seek, spy.

'Akoa Pl. (Mililani) − An unidentified small tree said to resemble koa. Dye made from its bark was used to color tapa.

'Akiu

'Ākoakoa St./Pl. (Kailua) − To assemble, heap.

'Akoki St. (Waipahu) − A variety of sugar cane, deep-red and green when young, changing to purple and brown-yellow.

'Akoko St. (Honolulu) − Endemic shrubs and trees of the dry forest. Its wood was used for firewood.

'Ākōlea Dr. (Wahiawā) − A large endemic fern.

'Akolo St./Pl. (Kapolei) − To put out small roots, as potatoes.

'Ākone Pl. (Honolulu) − Should be 'Akoni: Antone.

Akowai Rd. (Wai'anae) − Origin not known.

Akua St. ('Ewa Beach) − God, spirit, image, idol.

Akualele Pl. (Mililani) − Meteor. Literally: flying god.

Akuila Pl. (Kailua) − A red seaweed.

Akule St. (Waialua) − Full grown big-eyed or goggle-eyed scad (fish).

Akua

ʻĀkuleana Pl. (Kailua) – To give property or a right to it; to delegate responsibility.

ʻĀkulikuli Ter. (Honolulu) – General name for succulent plants.

ʻAkumu St./Pl. (Kailua) – Broken or cut off, as a pencil point; stumpy.

ʻAkupa St./Pl. (Kailua) – An abundant freshwater fish, the largest of the ʻoʻopu.

ʻAlaʻa St. (Kapolei) – A large endemic native tree.

Ala ʻĀkau St. (Waiʻanae) – North road.

Ala ʻĀkulikuli (Honolulu) – ʻĀkulikuli road. See ʻĀkulikuli.

ʻĀlaʻalaʻa Lp. (Mililani) – An unidentified star, said to be one of three stars in the Piscis Austrinus.

ʻAkumu

Ala Aliʻi St./Pl. (ʻAiea) – Chief's road.

Ala Aloalo Pl. (Honolulu) – Hibiscus road.

Ala ʻAmoʻamo Lp./Pl. (Honolulu) – Sparkling road. Named for an Oʻahu land section.

Ala Aolani Pl. (Honolulu) – Heavenly cloud road.

Ala Aoloa Lp./Pl. (Honolulu) – Long cloud road.

Ala Aupaka Pl. (Honolulu) – Aupaka road. See Aupaka.

Ala ʻAwapuhi Pl. (Honolulu) – Wild ginger road.

ʻAlae St. (Honolulu) – Mudhen (bird).

ʻAlaeloa St./Pl. (Honolulu) – Distant mudhen (bird). Named for a Maui land division.

Ala Hāhānui (Honolulu) – Hāhānui road. See Hāhānui.

Alahaka St./Pl. (Waialua) – Plank bridge, trestle, ladder. Literally: platform path.

Alahaki St. (Kailua) – Mountain ladder or steps cut into a cliff.

Alahao Pl. (Honolulu) – Railroad track. Literally: iron road.

Ala Hāpuʻu Pl. (Honolulu) – Tree fern road.

Ala Haukulu Pl. (Honolulu) – Dripping hau road. See Hau.

Alaheʻe St. (Honolulu) – A large native shrub or small tree. Its hard wood was shaped into digging sticks and adze blades to cut soft wood. Its leaves yield black dye.

Ala Hekili Pl. (Honolulu) – Thunder road.

Alahele St. (Waiʻanae) – Pathway, route, road.

Ala Hema St. (Waiʻanae) – South road.

Ala Hīnalo (Honolulu) – Male pandanus flower road.

Ala Hīnano Pl. (Honolulu) – Male pandanus flower road.

Alahao

Alahoʻi (Kapolei) – Return road.

Ala Hōkū Pl. (Honolulu) – Star road.

Ala Holo Lp. (Waiʻanae) – Road (for) traveling.

Ala Hou (Honolulu) – New road.

Alahula Way (Wahiawā) – A frequented and well-known path.

'Ala'i Pl. (Wahiawā) – Gentle, as a breeze.

'Ala'ihi St. (Waimānalo) – Various species of squirrelfishes, bright or rose red with white stripes.

Ala 'Ike (Pearl City) – Road (to) knowledge. Leeward Community College is located here.

Alāiki St. ('Ewa Beach) – Appropriation of property by force as practiced by some chiefs on their travels.

Ala 'Ilima Pl. (Honolulu) – 'Ilima road. See 'Ilima.

Ala 'Iolani Pl. (Honolulu) – Royal hawk road.

Alakai St. (Kāne'ohe) – Road (by the) sea.

Alaka'ina St. (Mililani) – Leadership, guidance.

Ala Kamaile (Honolulu) – The maile road. See Maile.

Ala Kapua (Honolulu) – The flower road.

Ala Kapuna (Honolulu) – The spring road.

'Alakē

Alakawa St. (Honolulu) – Road to the leaping place, as a precipice from which a swimmer leaps into a pool.

'Alakē St./Pl. (Mililani) – To jump, hurry from place to place.

Alakea St. (Honolulu) – White road. Alakea originally passed over a stretch of white coral rocks. The street name derives from that rock formation.

Ala Kī'ao Pl. (Honolulu) – Cloud pillar road. Kī'ao: name of a Moanalua land section.

Ala Kīkā Pl. (Honolulu) – Cigar flower road.

Ala Kimo Dr./Pl. (Honolulu) – James road. Named for British Navy Captain Samuel James Dowsett (1794-1834?). Founded the Dowsett family in Hawai'i. Lost at sea. See Kimopelekane.

Ala Kipa (Honolulu) – Visitor's path.

Ala Koa (Waimānalo) – 1) Soldier's road. 2) Koa (tree) road.

Alakoa St. (Honolulu) – Soldier's road.

Alakoko St. (Honolulu) – Definition not known. Named for a Kaua'i place.

Ala Kolopua (Honolulu) – Fragrant road.

Ala Kōpiko (Honolulu) – Kōpiko road. Kōpiko: about 13 species of trees belonging to a native class in the Coffee family. The wood of at least one species was shaped into tapa anvils.

Ala Kula Pl. (Honolulu) – Field road.

Alala Pl./Rd. (Kailua) – Awakening. Named for an O'ahu promontory.

Ala Lani (Honolulu) – Heavenly road.

Ala Laulani (Honolulu) – Heavenly leaf road.

Ala Lehua (Honolulu) – Lehua road. See Lehua.

Ala Le'ie (Honolulu) – Le'ie road. Le'ie: a native tree in the Lily family. Its soft wood was carved into images. Its branches were among the five standard plants placed on the hula altar built for Laka (goddess of the hula). The other plants are: halapepe (same as ala le'ie), 'ie'ie, 'ilima, maile, and palai (same as palapalai).

Ala Leleu (Honolulu) – Leleu road. Leleu: an unidentified fruit tree.
Ala Līlia (Honolulu) – Lily road.
Ala Liliko'i Pl. (Honolulu) – Passion fruit road. See Liliko'i.
Ala Loa ('Ewa Beach) – Long road.
Alaloa St./Pl. (Kāne'ohe) – Main road.
Ala Loke St. (Honolulu) – Rose road.
Ala Lonomea (Honolulu) – Lonomea road.
Lonomea: a tall native tree. Its wood was
used for spears and building houses.
Ala Mahamoe Pl. (Honolulu) – Attractive road.
Ala Mahikū St. (Wai'anae) – Plantation clearing
road.

Ala Mahina Pl. (Honolulu) – Moon road.   Alamuku
Ala Maile Pl. (Honolulu) – Maile road. See Maile.
Ala Mākāhala Pl. (Honolulu) – Mākāhala road. Mākāhala: the orange
cestrum, a climbing shrub. Its orange flowers are used for leis.
Ala Makani Pl./Way (Honolulu) – Windy (breezy) road.
'Alamea Pl. (Mililani) – Hard volcanic stone, used for adzes.
Ala Melia Pl. (Honolulu) – Plumeria road. See Melia.
'Alamihi St./Pl. (Wai'anae) – A common crab found at muddy flat reefs and
river mouths.
Ala Moana Blvd./Pk. Dr. (Honolulu) – Ocean road.
Alamuku St. (Honolulu) – Cut-off or unfinished road, dead-end road.
Alana St. ('Ewa Beach) – Awakening, rising.
Ala Na'auao Pl. (Wai'anae) – Path (of) enlightenment.
Ala Nānālā (Honolulu) – Sunflower road. See Puanānālā.
Ala Nānū (Honolulu) – Gardenia road. See Nānū.
Ala Napuaa Pl. (Honolulu) – Should be Ala Nāpua: road (of) the flowers.
Ala Napunani (Honolulu) – Should be Ala Nāpuanani: road (of) the
beautiful flowers.
Ala Naupaka (Honolulu) – Naupaka road. See Naupaka.
'Alaneo St. (Honolulu) – Clear, serene, unclouded.
Alani Dr. (Honolulu) – Definition not known.
'Alani St. (Honolulu) – Any kind of orange, both fruit and tree.
Alania St. ('Aiea) – Smooth, even, not rough.
Ala Nīoi Pl. (Honolulu) – Nīoi road. See Nīoi.
Ala Noe Pl./Way (Honolulu) – Misty road.
Ala Nolunolu (Honolulu) – Boggy road.
Ala Noni Pl. (Honolulu) – Noni road. Noni: Indian mulberry, a small
evergreen tree or shrub. Its bark yields a red dye; its root yields a yellow
dye; its leaves, fruit, and bark yield a medicine.
Ala Nui Mauka ('Ewa Beach) – Inland highway.
Ala'oki St./Pl. (Mililani) – Short cut.
Ala 'Oli (Honolulu) – Happy path.

Ala 'Ōliko Pl. (Honolulu) – 'Ōliko road. 'Ōliko: an uncommon shrub or small tree.

Ala 'Oloa Pl. (Honolulu) – 'Oloa road. 'Oloa: a short native shrub, with strong bark used for making tapa.

Ala 'Opeha Pl. (Honolulu) – 'Opeha road. See 'Opeha.

'Alapa Lp. (Wahiawā) – Athletic, active; athlete.

'Ālapa Pl. (Kahuku) – Name of a former Kahuku Plantation employee.

'Alapa

Alapa'i St. (Honolulu) – Definition not known. Named for High Chiefess Alapa'i (1814-1849), wife of John Young II (see Keoniana). House of Nobles (1845-49), and Privy Council.

'Alapaki St. (Wai'anae) – Albert.

Alapali Pl. (Honolulu) – Cliff road.

Alapi'i St. (Hale'iwa) – Stairs, steps, ladder, ascent. Named for an O'ahu land section.

Ala Pili Lp./Pl. (Honolulu) – Pili road. See Pili.

Alapine St. (Honolulu) – Quick.

Alapi'o Pl./Rd. (Hale'iwa) – Curved road.

Alapō'ai St./Pl. (Mililani) – Orbit of the stars. Literally: circular road.

Ala Pohā Pl. (Honolulu) – Pohā road. See Pohā.

Ala Poko (Wai'anae) – Short street.

Alapi'i

Ala Pua'ala Pl./Way (Honolulu) – Road (of) fragrant flowers.

Ala Pū'awa Pl. (Honolulu) – Young white pandanus leaf road.

Ala Pu'e Pl. (Honolulu) – Pu'e road. Pu'e: a Kaua'i mountain lobelia (a plant). Its large flowers are white, streaked with purple.

Ala Pūnēnē Pl. (Honolulu) – Pūnēnē road. Pūnēnē: a native plant with black berry-like fruits.

Ala Puumalu Pl. (Honolulu) – Should be Ala Pu'umāla: garden hill road.

Alau St. (Waipahu) – Dividing, branching, as of winds and lineages.

Ala Uahi Pl. (Honolulu) – Smoky road.

Alaula Way (Honolulu) – Light of early dawn, sunset glow.

Alaulau St. (Pearl City) – Clothes, tapa, mats.

Ala Ulike Pl. (Honolulu) – Should be Ala Ulihi: ulihi road. Ulihi: a small endemic shrub in the Mint family.

Ala'ume St./Pl. (Mililani) – To draw, pull, attract, as a magnet.

Ala Uwila Pl. (Honolulu) – Lightning road.

'Alawa Pl. (Wai'anae) – To glance, look quickly.

Ala Wai Blvd. (Honolulu) – Canal. Literally: water path.

Ala Waina (Wahiawā) – Wine road.

Ala Wai'ōpua (Honolulu) – Wai'ōpua road. Wai'ōpua: a pleasant breeze at Wailua, Kaua'i.

Ala Walua St. (Wai'anae) – Middle or interior road.

Alaweo St./Pl. (Honolulu) – A native shrub. Young plants, leaves, and plant tips were eaten as green vegetables.

Alawiki St. (Kāne'ohe) – To hurry; quick.

Alea Lp. (Wahiawā) – Definition not known. May be a misspelling.

'Aleka Pl. (Kailua) – Large tree of the pine family, cedar, fir.

'Alekoki Pl. (Honolulu) – Short ripples. Named for an O'ahu pool.

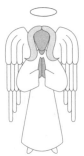

Ali'i'ānela

Alelo St. (Waipahu) – Tongue, language.

Alena Lp./Pl. (Waialua) – A lowland weed. Its swollen roots were used medicinally as a diuretic (to increase the flow of urine).

Alenale Pl. (Mililani) – Clear.

'Ale'o Pl. (Honolulu) – Watchtower.

'Alepa St. (Kapolei) – Alpha (something that is first; beginning).

'Ālewa Dr./Pl. (Honolulu) – Suspended (on a height). Named for an O'ahu land section.

Ālia Pl. ('Aiea) – Salt bed, salt-crusted area. Named for an O'ahu land section.

Āliali Pl. (Honolulu) – Crystal clear, white; clarity.

Āliamanu Dr./St./Pl. (Honolulu) – Bird salt-pond. (Many vegetarian birds eat salt). Named for an O'ahu crater.

Ali'ikoa

Aliana St. (Mililani) – Let me see.

'Alihi Pl. (Kailua) – Cords or fine ropes used to attach floats and sinkers to the edges of fish nets.

'Alihilani Pl. (Honolulu) – Horizon.

Ali'i Rd. (Honolulu) – Chief, chiefess, king, queen, noble.

Ali'i'ānela Pl. (Kāne'ohe) – Archangel.

Ali'ikāne Pl. (Kāne'ohe) – Male chief, king.

Ali'ikoa St. (Honolulu) – Military officer, army or navy officer.

Ali'inui Dr. (Kapolei) – High chief.

Ali'ipapa Pl. (Kāne'ohe) – Offspring of a high chiefess and a commoner (or lesser chief) father.

Ali'ipoe Dr. ('Aiea) – The ornamental cannas, large herbs with red or red and yellow flowers. Its round black seeds are worn in leis or placed in la'amia fruit shells for hula rattles. See La'amia.

'Alika Ave. (Honolulu) – Alex. Named for Alexander Cartwright Dowsett (1868-1937). Song "Alika" was written for him. He was named for his father's friend, Alexander Cartwright (many say he created the game of baseball in 1845). See Kimopelekane.

ʻAlina Pl. (Kāneʻohe) – Ah Lin, a Chinese family. Y Ah Lin opened a store and restaurant here in the early 1900s.

Alo Pl. (Mililani) – An unidentified star, possibly one of three stars in the Piscis Austrinus.

Aloala St./Pl./Way (Wahiawā) – Should be Aloalo: hibiscus.

Aloaliʻi St. (ʻAiea) – In the presence of chiefs; royal court.

Aloalo Ct./St./Pl. (Wahiawā, Honolulu) – All kinds of hibiscus, including the native hibiscus. Hibiscus is the state flower of Hawaiʻi.

Aloalo

Aloha Ave./Dr./Tower Dr. (Pearl City, Honolulu) – Love, affection, compassion, mercy.

Aloha ʻĀina Pl. (Honolulu) – Love of the land; love of one's country, patriotism.

Aloha ʻOe Dr. (Kailua) – "Farewell to Thee." Title of famous Hawaiian song composed in 1877 by then-Princess Liliʻuokalani.

Alohea Ave. (Honolulu) – Definition not known.

ʻAlohi Way (Honolulu) – To shine.

ʻAlohikeu St. (Kapolei) – The morning light of the sun.

Alohiki St. (Waiʻanae) – Families united by marriage, in-laws.

ʻAlohilani St. (Mililani) – Brightness of heaven.

ʻĀloʻiloʻi St. (Waimānalo) – Demoiselle fish, a popular and tasty fish.

Alokahi St./Pl. (Kāneʻohe) – Single weft in weaving; mat of single thickness, with only one shiny side.

Alokele St. (Honolulu) – Attractive, of fine appearance.

Alolua St. (ʻAiea) – Two-sided.

ʻAlu St./Pl. (Honolulu) – Descent, as of a trail or road.

ʻĀluka Lp. (Pearl City) – Mixed, crowded, heaped.

Ālula Pl. (Mililani) – An endemic lobelia (plant) which bears long, white, fragrant flowers. Found only on Kauaʻi and Molokaʻi.

Ama Rd. (Honolulu) – Definition not known. May be a misspelling.

ʻAmaʻama St. (ʻEwa Beach) – Mullet fish.

ʻAmana St. (Honolulu) – Definition not known. Possibly a Hawaiianization of Armand.

ʻAmaʻu St. (Honolulu) – All species of an endemic genus of ferns.

ʻAmaʻumaʻu Pl. (Haleʻiwa) – Many ʻamaʻu ferns. See ʻAmaʻu.

ʻĀmikamika Pl. (Pearl City) – A relish, morsel, or bit of food.

ʻAmikūkū Pl. (Pearl City) – A hula step.

Āmio St. (ʻEwa Beach) – Narrow channel, as to a sea pool.

ʻĀmokemoke St./Pl. (Pearl City) – Irregular, uneven.

ʻAmokiʻi St. (Waipahu) – Stem of fruits or (underground) tubers.

ʻĀmoʻomoʻo St. (Pearl City) – Small strip of tapa or matting which may be used as a sample.

Ana Ln. (Waipahu) – 1) A model, pattern. 2) Cave, cavern.

Anaʻāina Pl. (Honolulu) – Land surveying; to survey.

ʻAnae Pl. (ʻEwa Beach) – Full-sized ʻamaʻama mullet fish.

Anahola St. (Honolulu) – Definition not known. Named for a Kauaʻi land division.

Anahulu Pl. (Haleʻiwa) – Period of ten days. Named for an Oʻahu land section.

Anakahi Pl. (Waipahu) – Unit of measurement.

Anakole Pl. (Pearl City) – Definition not known. Possibly a Hawaiianization of Anatole or Andre.

Anakua St. (Honolulu) – God cave. Named for a Kauaʻi place.

ʻAnaliʻi St./Pl. (Honolulu) – Hawaiian fern that thrives on mountain sides, in caves, and other damp places.

Analio Pl. (ʻAiea) – Great distance, remoteness.

Analipo St./Pl. (Waiʻanae) – Distant, faraway space, beyond the horizon.

ʻAnalū St. (Honolulu) – Andrews. Named for Judge Lorrin Andrews (1795-1868). Arrived in Hawaii with the 3rd Missionary Company (1828), but resigned (1842) when the missionary society accepted money from America's southern slave states. Founded Lahainaluna Seminary (1831), and published the first Hawaiian newspaper there (1834). Authored Hawaiian dictionary, grammar, and other translation books. First non-Hawaiian appointed Supreme Court judge. Served Kamehameha III and IV.

Anania Cir./Ct./Dr./Pl. (Mililani) – Star, perhaps the North Star.

ʻAnapa St. (Honolulu) – To shine, gleam, glitter, sparkle.

Anapālau St./Pl. (Honolulu) – War club cave. Named for a Kauaʻi promontory. Also called: Lae o Keanapalau.

ʻĀnapanapa St. (Pearl City) – A smooth shrub with twining stems. Used as a soap because its leaves form a lather in water.

ʻAnapau Pl. (Waipahu) – To leap, frisk, frolic.

Anapuni St. (Honolulu) – Circumference, perimeter. Named for an Oʻahu land area.

ʻĀnaunau St. (ʻEwa Beach) – A type of shellfish.

ʻAneko Pl. (Kāneʻohe) – Anise, an herb in the Parsley family.

ʻĀnela Pl. (Honolulu) – Angel.

ʻAnemoku St. (Lāʻie) – Peninsula. Literally: almost island.

Ani St. (Honolulu) – To blow softly, as a breeze.

Ania Pl. (Kapolei) – Breezy.

Aniani Pl. (Waipahu) – Cool, refreshing, agreeable.

Anianikū St. (Honolulu) – Standing mirror.

ʻĀnihinihi St. (Pearl City) – Small taro tubers.

ʻAnini Pl./Way (Pearl City) – Dwarfish, tiny.

Anipeʻahi St./Pl. (Kapolei) – To wave or beckon, with the hand or a fan.

Anipeʻahi

ʻĀniʻuniʻu St. (Pearl City) – Root connecting the sweet potato to the vine.
ʻAno Ln. (Honolulu) – Resemblance, image.
ʻAnoʻai Pl. (Honolulu) – Greeting, news; to greet.
ʻAnoʻi Pl./Rd. (Kāneʻohe) – Desire, longing, love; desired one, lover.
ʻAnoiki St. (Waipahu) – Humble.
ʻAnoʻilei Pl. (Hauʻula) – Cherished sweetheart.
ʻAnolani St. (Honolulu) – Of heavenly or royal character.
ʻAnolike St./Pl. (Honolulu) – Resembling; resemblance.
ʻĀnoni St. (Wahiawā) – To mix; interweave.
ʻAnonia St. (Honolulu) – Mixed.
ʻAnonui St. (Waipahu) – Important, vital, main.
ʻAnopili St. (Mililani) – Property, as of a number; fraction.
Anounou St./Pl. (ʻAiea) – Should be Kūnounou: a cigar wrasse fish, olive-green to rusty red.
Anu Lp./Pl. (Kāneʻohe, Wahiawā) – Cool, cold.
Anuanu St./Pl. (Mililani) – Cold; chilly.
Ānuenue St. (Honolulu) – Rainbow.
Anuhea St./Pl. (Honolulu) – Cool, soft fragrance, as of upland forests.
ʻAnuʻu Pl. (Honolulu) – Stairs, jogs, steps, terrace, dais, ledge.
Ao Pl. (Mililani) – 1) Light, day. 2) World, earth.
Aoakua St. (Mililani) – Godly cloud. Figuratively: rainbow.
ʻAoʻao St./Pl. (Honolulu) – Side.
Aohōkū Pl. (Mililani) – A star, possibly Jupiter. Literally: star light.
Aokea Pl. (Honolulu) – White cloud.
Aokū St. (Waipahu) – Rain cloud; mist.
Aolani Pl. (Honolulu) – Heavenly cloud.
Aolele St. (Honolulu) – Flying cloud.
Aolewa Pl. (Honolulu) – Floating cloud.
Aoloa St./Pl. (Kailua) – Distant cloud. Figuratively: a distinguished person.

ʻĀnuenue

Aʻoloko St./Pl. (Kapolei) – Innermost teaching, inspiration.
ʻĀone Pl. (Waiʻanae) – Sandy soil.
Aopoko Pl. (Honolulu) – Short cloud.
Aouli Pl. (Mililani) – Firmament, sky, blue vault of heaven.
Aowena Pl./Way (Honolulu) – Rosy cloud.
ʻĀpaʻa St. (ʻEwa Beach) – Arid, dry.
ʻĀpaʻakuma St./Pl. (Pearl City) – Native of a place and descendant from its earliest line of chiefs.
ʻApai Pl. (ʻEwa Beach) – A fishtrap.
ʻApakeʻe St. (Waiʻanae) – Deceitful, inaccurate.
Apaki St. (Honolulu) – Origin not known.
ʻĀpala Lp. (ʻAiea) – Apple.
ʻĀpana Rd. (Waiʻanae) – Portion, part.

ʻĀpala

ʻĀpapa St. (Pearl City) – Flat, especially a coral flat.

ʻApapane St./Pl. (Kāneʻohe) – The most common of the surviving species of Hawaiian honeycreepers (birds).

Apau Lp./Pl. (Kāneʻohe) – All, entirely.

ʻApeʻape Pl. (Honolulu) – Huge-leafed, perennial forest herbs.

ʻĀpela St. (ʻAiea) – Old, aged.

ʻĀpele St./Pl. (Mililani) – Volcanic lava of any kind.

ʻApelekoka St. (ʻAiea) – Apricot.

ʻĀpiʻi St. (Waipahu) – A variety of taro. Literally: curly (because it is crinkled under the leaf).

ʻĀpiki St. (Kāneʻohe) – Crafty, mischievous.

ʻApio Ln. (Honolulu) – Named for John ʻApio, a care-taker of Oʻahu Cemetery who lived here from 1880s.

Apo Dr. (Honolulu) – Circle.

Apoālewa Pl. (Kāneʻohe) – Highest heavens or space.

Apo

ʻApoʻepoʻe St./Pl. (Pearl City) – To assemble.

Apohele Pl. (Mililani) – Orbit, as of stars and planets.

ʻApoke Pl. (ʻEwa Beach) – A short piece; cut, broken off.

Apokula St./Pl. (Kailua) – Gold bracelet.

ʻApole Pl. (ʻEwa Beach) – Smooth.

ʻĀpona St. (Honolulu) – Embracing, grasping.

ʻApowale St. (Waipahu) – A native variety of wet-land taro grown primarily for poi.

ʻĀpua Pl. (Honolulu) – Fish basket. Named for Hawaiʻi Island land divisions.

Apuahi St. (Kāneʻohe) – Definition not known.

ʻĀpuakea St./Pl. (Kāneʻohe) – White fish basket. Named for an Oʻahu land section.

ʻApuʻapu St. (Kāneʻohe) – Cup-shaped.

Apuhihi St. (Waialua) – A shellfish resembling the hīhīwai, found in brackish water.

ʻApuki St. (Mililani) – Short.

ʻApuʻu St./Pl./Way (ʻEwa Beach) – An endemic native fern.

ʻĀpuʻupuʻu Rd. (Waiʻanae) – Rough, lumpy, bumpy.

ʻApuwai Pl. (Honolulu) – A variety of taro. Its tender leaves make excellent lūʻau.

Aʻu St. (Waialua) – Swordfish, sailfish, marlin, spearfish. Large deepwater gamefishes.

ʻAua Pl. (Mililani) – Betelgeuse, the second brightest star in the constellation Orion.

Auahi St. (Honolulu) – An unspecified distant relationship.

Aualiʻi St. (Waipahu) – Royal, chiefly.

Aʻu

'Auamo St. ('Aiea) – Pole or stick used for carrying burdens across the shoulders.

'Au'aukī St. (Kailua) – 1) A young eel. 2) An unidentified fish, said to resemble weke (goatfish).

Auhaele Lp./Pl. (Mililani) – A star, companion to Hōkū'ula and Pai-kauhale. Perhaps the three stars are Antares, Sigma and Tau Scorpii.

Auhaku Pl. (Mililani) – An unidentified star.

'Auhau Pl. ('Aiea) – Tax, assessment, levy, charge, price.

Auhea Pl. (Honolulu) – Poetic name of Kekāuluohi. See Kekāuluohi.

Auhili Pl. (Wahiawā) – To turn off the course, wander, deviate.

'Auhola St./Pl. ('Ewa Beach) – A type of shrub.

'Auhuhu St./Pl. (Pearl City) – A slender, shrubby legume (a flowering plant with pods that split open when dry). Hawaiians caught fish by poisoning them with pounded pods of this plant.

'Auiki St. (Honolulu) – Small handle.

'Auina St./Pl. (Mililani) – Bending, sloping.

Aukahi St./Pl. (Kapolei) – Even, smooth, clear; united, flowing together.

'Aukai Ln. (Hale'iwa) – Seafaring.

'Aukai Ave. (Honolulu) – Seafaring. Possibly named for Edward 'Aukai (1876-1947), property caretaker of the Judd family.

'Auhau

Āukauka Pl./Rd. (Hale'iwa) – Inland.

'Aukele St. (Kailua) – 1) Audrey. 2) Traveling by sailcraft.

'Auku'u Ln. (Honolulu) – Black-crowned night heron (bird).

'Aulena Pl. (Honolulu) – A variety of native banana.

A'ulepe St. (Kailua) – Sailfish. Literally: cockscomb swordfish.

'Auli'i St. (Honolulu) – Neat, nice, perfect.

Aulike St. (Kailua) – Even, smooth.

'Aulima Lp. (Kailua) – Bone of arm below the elbow.

Auloa Rd. (Kailua) – Definition not known. Named for Hō'auloa, an O'ahu land section.

'Aumaka Pl. (Waipahu) – A carrying pole.

'Aumakiki Lp./Pl. ('Aiea) – A variety of sweet potato.

'Aumakua St. (Pearl City) – Family or personal gods.

Aumea Lp./Pl. (Mililani) – Aldebaran, the star.

Aumoa'e St. (Honolulu) – Time of the tradewind.

'Aumoana Pl./Way (Kāne'ohe) – Seafarer.

Aumoe Rd. (Kailua) – Late at night, about midnight. Literally: time to sleep.

'Aumoku St. (Kāne'ohe) – Fleet of ships.

'Āuna St./Pl. (Kāne'ohe) – Large group, flock.

'Āunauna St. (Kailua) – A common shellfish.

Aupaka St. (Pearl City) – Small endemic shrubs in the Violet family, bearing greenish-white or red flowers.

Aʻupapaʻohe St. (Kailua) – A variety of aʻu (fish). Literally: bamboo-board aʻu.

Aupula Pl. (Kailua) – Fishing with a pula stick or pulale (a leafy branch) to drive fish into a net.

Aupuni St. (Honolulu) – Government.

Aupuni

Aupunimōʻī Pl. (ʻAiea) – Monarchy.

Aupūpū St./Pl. (Kailua) – A shellfish.

Auwaea St. (Kapolei) – Distant, remote.

ʻAuwaha St. (ʻEwa Beach) – Ditch, furrow, trench, channel.

ʻAuwai Dr./St. (Kailua, Wahiawā) – Ditch.

Auwaiku St. (Kailua) – Should be Awaikū: good spirits, as the messengers of Kāne.

ʻAuwaiolimu St. (Honolulu) – Ditch of moss. Named for an Oʻahu land section.

ʻAuwina St./Pl. (Kailua) – Bending.

ʻAuwinalā Rd. (Kailua) – Afternoon. Literally: declining sun.

Awa St. (Honolulu) – Harbor.

Awaawaʻānoa Pl. (Honolulu) – Dry valley.

Awaawahea Pl./Way (Kapolei) – Cloudy valley.

ʻAwaʻawaloa St. (Honolulu) – Too salty. Named for a former Oʻahu fishpond.

ʻAwahiwa St. (Pearl City) – A variety of kava, used by chiefs for the gods, and on ceremonial occasions. Literally: black kava.

ʻAwai Ln. (Haleʻiwa) – A family name.

Awaiʻa St. (Waipahu) – Fish landing.

Awaiki St./Pl. (Waipahu) – Small landing place for canoes.

Awakea Rd. (Kailua) – Noon, midday.

Awakūmoku St. (Kailua) – Ship harbor or anchorage, port.

Awalaʻi St./Pl. (Waipahu) – Calm landing.

Awalau St. (Waipahu) – Channel or harbor of many inlets.

ʻAwaliʻi St. (Pearl City) – Type of hard stone from which adzes were made.

Awalua St./Pl. (Waipahu) – Site on northern Lānaʻi overlooking Kalohi Channel.

ʻAwamōʻī St./Pl. (Waipahu) – A variety of kava, used by chiefs for the gods, and on ceremonial occasions. Used in sacrificial ceremonies for Pele. Literally: royal kava.

Awakea

Awamoku St./Pl. (Waipahu) – Landing for a steamship.

Awanani St./Pl. (Waipahu) – Beautiful landing.

Awanei St. (Waipahu) – Definition not known.

ʻAwanēnē Pl./Way (Kāneʻohe) – A variety of kava.

Awanui St. (Waipahu) – Large landing.

ʻAwapapa Pl. (Kāneʻohe) – A variety of kava used by chiefs for the gods, and on ceremonial occasions. Especially offered to female gods. Literally: flat kava.

ʻAwapuhi St./Pl. (Honolulu, Wahiawā) – Wild ginger.

Awāwa St./Pl. (Kapolei) – Valley, gulch, ravine.

Awāwamalu St. (Honolulu) – Shady valley. Possibly named for nearby Wāwāmalu, the old name for the area mauka of Sandy Beach.

ʻAwapuhi

Awāwelēʻī Pl. (ʻEwa Beach) – Sister of Laniloa who traveled with her eel companion Papaphui.

ʻĀwela St. (Kapolei) – A flowerless variety of sugar cane, named for the fish.

ʻĀwele Pl. (Kāneʻohe) – Goal, mark, line, goal post.

ʻĀweoweo St. (Waialua) – Various species of small red fishes, sometimes called "bigeye." Many years ago, a great school of ʻaweoweo seen inshore or in harbors was regarded with awe and sorrow, foretelling the death of a high chief.

ʻĀweuweu Pl. (Kapolei) – A native variety of taro, often growing wild.

ʻĀwiki St./Pl. (Mililani) – To hurry, be quick.

ʻĀwele

ʻĀwikiwiki St./Pl. (Pearl City) – A vine native to Hawaiʻi, used for making small, temporary fish traps.

ʻĀwini Pl./Way (Honolulu) – Sharp, bold, forward. Named for a Hawaiʻi Island land division where Kamehameha was reared.

ʻĀwiwi Pl./Way (Mililani) – A small native herb with white or pale pink flowers.

Beretania St. (Honolulu) – Britain, Britannia. (The British Consul Office was located here in 1800s).

Eaea Pl. (Honolulu) – Air, breath, air current.

East Mānoa Rd. (Honolulu) – Vast. Named for an Oʻahu valley.

ʻEʻeka Pl. (Mililani) – A wind at Kona, Hawaiʻi Island.

ʻEhā Way (ʻEwa Beach) – Four.

ʻEhakō Pl. (Honolulu) – The Chinese lace- or ring-necked dove, a grayish brown bird with rosy breast.

Ehehene Way (Kāneʻohe) – To laugh merrily, giggle in glee.

ʻĒheu St. (Honolulu) – Wing, as of bird, kite, or airplane.

Beretania

'Ehiku Way ('Ewa Beach) – Seven.

'Eho'eho Ave. (Wahiawā) – Stone pile.

'Ehu St. (Wai'anae) – Reddish tinge in hair, of Polynesians and not of Caucasians.

'Ehukai St. (Waimānalo) – Sea spray, foam.

'Ehupua St./Pl. (Honolulu) – Flower pollen.

'Ehu Wai Pl. (Honolulu) – Spray from water.

'Ēkaha Ave./Cir. (Honolulu, Wahiawā) – The bird's-nest fern. It has large, sword-shaped fronds. The black midrib is used for decorating small mats, and woven lauhala objects.

'Ekahi Way ('Ewa Beach) – One.

'Eke Pl. ('Aiea) – Pocket, sack, bag, basket.

'Ekekela Pl. (Honolulu) – Esther.

'Ekela Ave. (Honolulu) – Ethel or Ezra.

'Ekemau'u St. ('Ewa Beach) – Gunny sack, burlap.

'Ekepu'u Pl. (Kāne'ohe) – An unidentified bird.

Ēkoa Pl. (Honolulu) – False koa tree, a common shrub or small tree. Its seeds are strung for leis, purses, and table mats. Also called koa haole.

'Ēlau

'Ekolu Pl./Way (Wahiawā, 'Ewa Beach, Honolulu) – Three.

'Ēlau Pl. (Mililani) – Tip, point, end.

'Ele'ele Pl. (Honolulu) – Black. Named for a Kaua'i land section.

'Elehe'i Pl. (Mililani) – Short.

'Elekū Kuilima Pl. (Kahuku) – North Kuilima. Should be Kuilima 'Elekū, or even better: Kuilima 'Ākau.

'Elele St./Pl. (Kapolei) – Messenger, delegate, ambassador, envoy, any diplomatic representative.

'Elelupe Pl./Rd. (Honolulu) – Definition not known.

'Elemakule Pl. ('Ewa Beach) – Old man.

'Elemika Pl. (Kapolei) – Hermit.

'Elena St. (Honolulu) – Ellen.

'Elepaio St. (Honolulu) – A species of fly-catcher, a forest bird. Goddess of canoe-makers.

'Eleu St./Pl. (Waipahu) – Active, alert, energetic, lively, nimble, quick, agile, spry, prompt.

'Elemakule

'Elima Way ('Ewa Beach) – Five.

'Elua St./Wy (Honolulu, 'Ewa Beach) – Two, twice.

'Eluwene St. (Honolulu) – Edwin.

'Ema Pl. (Honolulu) – Should be 'Eme: Amy. (note: 'Ema means: Emma).

'Emekona Pl. (Honolulu) – Emerson. Named for Nathaniel B. Emerson (1839-1915). A Hawaiian language scholar and author who lived here. President, Board of Health. Member of secret Hawaiian League, established in 1887 to oppose King Kalākaua. Son of missionary, the Rev. John Emerson.

'Emepela Pl. (Kāne'ohe) – Emperor.

'Emoloa Pl. (Mililani) – A native grass.

'Ena Rd. (Honolulu) – Named for John 'Ena II (1849-1912), part-Hawaiian son of John 'Ena and High Chiefess Kaikilaniopuna. Privy Councilor to Queen Lili'uokalani, member of House of Representatives, and president of Inter-Island Steamship Company (1899-1902).

'Eono Way ('Ewa Beach) – Six.

'Epukane St. (Honolulu) – Spouse.

'Eu Ln. (Honolulu) – Rascal.

Ēulu St./Pl. (Mililani) – Top of tree or plant.

'Ewa Beach Rd. ('Ewa Beach) – Crooked, out-of-shape, imperfect. Figuratively: unjust. Named for an O'ahu town and district.

'Ewalu Way ('Ewa Beach) – Eight.

Ēwelani St. ('Aiea) – Chiefs of divine descent.

Gilipake St. (Wai'anae) – Gilbert. Usually: Kilipaki. Probably named for Leopold Gilbert Blackman. See Palakamana.

Haa'a St. (Waipahu) – To send greetings or love; joyous hospitality; joy at greeting a loved one.

Ha'aha'a St. (Ka'a'awa) – Low, humble, meek, unpretentious, modest.

Ha'aheo Pl. ('Aiea) – Proud.

Ha'akei St. ('Ewa Beach) – Proud, haughty, vain; to scorn, scoff.

Ha'ako'a Pl. (Waipahu) – Short, as a bantam.

Ha'akualiki St./Pl. (Mililani) – An officer who preceded a chief and his train.

Ha'alau St. (Waipahu) – To produce leaves.

Ha'alelea Pl. (Honolulu) – Chief Levi Ha'alelea (1822-1864), the last Hawaiian ali'i to own the ahupua'a of Kalawahine. Member, king's Privy Council (1852-1855) and House of Nobles (1853-1862).

Ha'aliki St. (Honolulu) – To boast, brag.

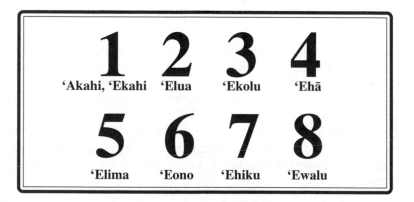

1	2	3	4
'Akahi, 'Ekahi	'Elua	'Ekolu	'Ehā

5	6	7	8
'Elima	'Eono	'Ehiku	'Ewalu

Ha'alilo St./Pl. (Mililani) – Far off, distant.

Ha'alohi St. (Mililani) – Sparkling.

Hā'ama Pl. (Wai'anae) – To begin to turn yellow, as a ripening mango or papaya.

Ha'āmaile St./Pl. (Kāne'ohe) – Medium-sized hardwood trees.

Ha'anopu Way (Kāne'ohe) – To swell, surge, as the sea.

Ha'awale Pl. (Honolulu) – A flatfish.

Hā'awi Way (Pearl City) – To give, grant; to offer.

Ha'awina St./Pl. (Kapolei) – Lesson, assignment, task, gift, appropriation, allowance, grant or contribution, honorarium, allotment, award, as of money.

Ha'alohi

Hā'ea Pl. (Waipahu) – Clouds.

Ha'eha'e Pl. ('Ewa Beach) – Strong affection and desire.

Haele Pl. (Kāne'ohe) – To go, come.

Hā'ena Dr. (Honolulu) – Red-hot, burning, red. Named for a Kaua'i land division.

Haha'ione St./Pl. (Honolulu) – Sand broken. Named for an O'ahu Valley.

Hahana St./Way/Pl. (Waipahu) – Heat, warmth.

Hahani St. (Kailua) – To touch.

Hāhānui St. ('Ewa Beach) – A native shrubby lobelia (plant) from Maui, with thorny branches and rough, lobed leaves.

Haiamū St./Pl. ('Ewa Beach) – To gather, crowd, flock.

Ha'i'ano Pl. ('Ewa Beach) – To describe, tell the nature of.

Hai'e'a Pl. ('Ewa Beach) – A variety of fish.

Hā'ike Pl. (Mililani) – To show, exhibit.

Hāiki Pl. (Honolulu) – Narrow.

Ha'ikū Rd./Plantations Dr./Pl. (Kāne'ohe) – Haughty, conceited. Named for an O'ahu valley.

Haili Rd. (Honolulu) – 1) Sudden remembrance. 2) Spirit, ghost.

Hailimanu Pl. ('Aiea) – Definition not known.

Hailimoa Pl. ('Ewa Beach) – A type of shellfish.

Hailipo St. ('Ewa Beach) – A sting ray.

Ha'ilono Pl. (Mililani) – An unidentified star.

Hainoa Pl. ('Ewa Beach) – Definition not known.

Ha'inole

Ha'inole Pl. (Mililani) – To incite, encourage, stimulate.

Hāipu Pl. ('Ewa Beach) – Stem of a gourd leaf, used medicinally.

Haiwā Pl. ('Ewa Beach) – To plant far apart, as taro or coconuts.

Ha'iwale Lp./Pl. (Mililani) – Slender, soft-wooded forest shrubs with white tube-shaped flowers.

Haka Dr. (Honolulu) – Literally: shelf, perch. An ancient O'ahu chief who lived 13 generations before Kamehameha. Overthrown by his cousin Ma'ilikukahi because he was cruel. Grandson of Lakona, and uncle of Kalonaiki.

Haka Dr. (Honolulu) – Crested feather helmet.

Hākai Lp. (Waipahu) – Stem, stalk

Hakakā St./Pl. (Honolulu) – To fight, quarrel.

Hakaka

Hākala St. (Mililani) – End of a house, gable.

Hakalau Pl. (Honolulu) – Many perches. Named for Hawai'i Island land divisions.

Hakalau'ai Pl. (Mililani) – 1) A star, associated with Hanakauluna, signifying pestilence or calamity. 2) Name of a legendary place.

Hakalina Rd. (Wai'anae) – Showy, pompous, vain.

Hakamoa St. (Mililani) – A constellation important to astrologers, perhaps the Southern Cross. Literally: chicken roost.

Hakanū St. (Honolulu) – Silent, sullen.

Hākea St./Pl. (Waipahu) – A variety of banana.

Hākeakea St. (Wai'anae) – Pale, white, faded.

Hakimo Pl./Rd. (Wai'anae) – Definition not known.

Hakina St. ('Aiea) – Fragment, broken piece.

Hako Lp./St. (Wahiawā, Kāne'ohe) – Definition not known.

Haku St./Pl. (Honolulu) – Lord, master, overseer, employer, owner.

Haku'āina Pl. (Honolulu) – Landowner; landlord.

Hakuhaku St. (Honolulu) – Lumpy, as poi.

Hakuhale St. (Kāne'ohe) – Landlord, house owner.

Hakumele Pl. (Honolulu) – Poet, composer.

Hakuola Rd. (Hale'iwa) – Living lord. Named for an O'ahu gulch.

Hakuone St./Pl. (Wahiawā) – Small land division, as cultivated for a chief.

Hakupapa St. (Honolulu) – To sew feathers to a band, for a hat.

Hakupōkano Lp. (Mililani) – An unidentified star. Literally: lord (of the) dark night.

Hala Dr. (Honolulu) – Pandanus tree. Known for its slanting aerial roots and pineapple-shaped fruits. Its tough, pliable hala leaves (lau hala) are woven into floor and sleeping mats, baskets, fans, sandals and pillows. The fleshy ends of unripe fruits are strung in leis.

Halahīnano St. (Kapolei) – A male pandanus having the hīnano blossom.

Halahua St. (Kapolei) – A female pandanus having fruit.

Hāla'i St./Pl. (Hau'ula) – Calm.

Halakahiki Pl. (Wahiawā) – Pineapple. Literally: foreign hala.

Halakau St./Pl. (Honolulu) – To perch high, as a bird.

Halakea St. ('Aiea) – A variety of pineapple, reputedly native to Hawai'i.

Halaki St. (Honolulu) – Charlotte.

Halakahiki

Halalani Pl. ('Ewa Beach) – Royal hala.

Halāliʻi St. ('Ewa Beach) – A vigorous and large variety of sugar cane. Perhaps named for Hālaliʻi, Niʻihau, where sugar cane growing in sand dunes was used in ceremonies to forgive sins.

Hālawa

Hālana St./Pl. (Kapolei) – Quiet, calm, tranquility.

Halapepe St. (Honolulu) – A native tree in the Lily family. Its soft wood was carved into images. See Ala Leʻie.

Halapia Pl. (Honolulu) – A small, native, yellow pandanus prized for leis.

Halapoe Pl. (Waiʻanae) – Round pandanus. Named for the place where the legendary eel, Puhinalo, lived at Pōkaʻī Bay, Waiʻanae.

Halaʻula Pl. (Honolulu) – Pandanus with orange-red fruit sections. Named for a Kauaʻi land division.

Hālaulani St. (Kāneʻohe) – An unidentified star.

Hālawa Valley St./Dr./View Loop ('Aiea, Honolulu) – Curve, as a road or along the beach. Named for an Oʻahu land division.

Hālawa Heights Rd. ('Aiea) – Curve, as a road or along the beach. Named for an Oʻahu land division.

Haleʻaha Rd. (Hauʻula) – Meeting house. Named for an Oʻahu land division.

Haleahi Rd. (Waiʻanae) – Fire house.

Haleʻaina St. (Waipahu) – In ancient times, the eating house for women.

Haleakalā Ave. (Waiʻanae) – House (used) by the sun. Probably should be Heleakalā: snare of the sun, a nearby mountain.

Healeialiʻi Rd. (Honolulu) – Chief's house, royal residence, palace.

Hale ʻEkahi Dr. (Waiʻanae) – First house.

Hale ʻElua St. (Waiʻanae) – Second house.

Halehaka St. (Honolulu) – Hollyhock, an herb, grown for its large flowers.

Halehaku Pl. (Mililani) – A bay, gulch, land section and point on Maui. Literally: master house.

Halehala Ln. (Honolulu) – Pandanus house. Queen Kalama received this land section in the 1848 Great Mahele.

Halehau St./Pl. (Waipahu) – House built with posts and thatch sticks of hau wood and thatch tied with hau cord.

Halehoʻōla Pl. (Honolulu) – Convalescent home.

Haleiki Pl. (Waimānalo) – Little house. Should be Halekiʻi: image house, a heiau at Wailuku, Maui.

Haleʻiwa Lp./Pl./Rd. (Haleʻiwa) – House (of) frigate bird. Named for an Oʻahu town.

Halekamani St. (Honolulu) – Kamani-wood house.

Halekāpiʻo St. (Waipahu) – Lean-to shelter.

Halekauwila St. (Honolulu) – Kauwila-wood house. Named for the first government building, built with kauwila wood brought to Honolulu in 1830 by Kaʻahumanu, from a royal mausoleum at Hōnaunau, Hawaiʻi Island. Used by Kamehameha III as a palace. In modern Hawaiian, uwila: lightning, electricity.

Halekī St. (Waialua) – Tī-plant house. Named for original grantee.

Halekia St. (Mililani) – Portico; veranda with pillars; porch of pillars.

Halekipa Pl. (Honolulu) – Lodging house.

Halekoa Dr./Pl. (Honolulu) – Soldiers' home, armory, barracks.

Halekou Rd./Pl. (Kāneʻohe) – An Oʻahu fishpond. Literally: kou wood house.

Halekua St./Pl. (Mililani) – House where tapa was made.

Halekula Way (Honolulu) – Schoolhouse.

Halelā St. (Kailua) – Sunny house.

Hale Laʻa Blvd. (Lāʻie) – Temple. Literally: sacred house.

Halekula

Halelāʻau Pl. (Honolulu) – Wooden or frame building.

Halelani Dr. (Honolulu) – Chief's house.

Haleleʻa Pl. (Honolulu) – Joyful house.

Halekuʻai Pl. (Waipahu) – Store, shop.

Halelau Pl. (Mililani) – House thatched with leaves rather than with pili grass.

Halelehua St. (Waipahu) – Lehua blossom house. Name of a sea goddess. Named for an Oʻahu land section.

Haleleka Pl. (Mililani) – Post Office.

Halelena Pl. (Honolulu) – Yellow house. Named for an Oʻahu land section.

Hālelo Pl. (Kāneʻohe) – 1) Jagged, rocky. 2) Coral sea cavern. 3) Yellowish.

Haleloa Pl. (Honolulu) – Long house.

Haleloke Pl. (Kāneʻohe) – A lavender or purplish-red chrysanthemum.

Hale Mākaʻi St. (Honolulu) – Police Station.

Halemaluhia Pl. (Waiʻanae) – Peaceful house.

Halemano St. (ʻEwa Beach) – Many houses.

Halemanu St. (Kāneʻohe) – Aviary, birdhouse.

Halemalu St. (Mililani) – Shaded house, shed.

Halemaʻumaʻu St./Pl. (Honolulu) – Fern house. Probably named for the fire pit (3,646 feet) inside the active Kilauea Volcano crater (4,093 feet), on Hawaiʻi Island.

Halemanu

Halemoe Pl. (Waipahu) – Sleeping house, dormitory.

Hale Momi Pl. (ʻAiea) – Pearl house. Probably refers to Pearl Harbor.

Halemuku St./Pl./Way (Kāneʻohe) – A measurement (from fingertips of one hand to elbow of the other arm when both arms are extended to the side) for houses. Named for an Oʻahu land section.

Halenani Pl. (Kāneʻohe) – Beautiful house.

Halenoho Pl. (Honolulu) – Residence, dwelling house.

Haleola St./Pl. (Honolulu) – Home (of) life. Named for Haleola Hart Jr.

Halepā Pl. (Honolulu) – Cupboard, safe. Literally: dish house.

Halepāhu St. (Mililani) – Drum house, especially in a heiau where prayers were uttered; a place of refuge in time of war.

Halepakuʻi St. (Mililani) – Tower, fortified house; addition to a house, annex.

Halepili St. (Waipahu) – House thatched with pili grass.

Halepiʻo Pl. (Mililani) – Type of ancient house.

Halepule Pl. (Mililani) – Church, chapel.

Halepuna St. (Waipahu) – House built of limestone or coral.

Haleʻumi Pl. (Honolulu) – 1) Tenth house. 2) Choke house (possibly refers to the place where servants were choked to death for violating the ancient kapu).

Halepili

Halewili St. (Waipahu) – Mill.

Halewilikō St./Pl. (ʻAiea) – Sugar mill.

Haliʻa St. (Kailua) – Sudden remembrance, especially of a loved one; fond recollection; premonition; to recall, recollect fondly.

Hālike Pl. (Waiʻanae) – Alike, similar.

Halilo St. (Waialua) – Definition not known. Named for original grantee.

Hālina St. (Honolulu) – Appearance, bearing.

Hāloa Dr. (Honolulu) – 1) Long breath. 2) Long life.

Hāloko Pl. (ʻEwa Beach) – Pool, pond.

Haloku St./Pl. (Mililani) – To ripple.

Hālolani St. (ʻEwa Beach) – To move quietly, as a soaring bird.

Hālona Rd. (Waiʻanae) – Peering; place to peer from.

Hālona St./Pl. (Honolulu) – Peering; place to peer from. Named for an Oʻahu land section.

Halepule

Halualani Pl. (Kāneʻohe) – Definition not known. Probably named for an original awardee.

Hālula Pl. (Kailua) – A sea urchin with long spines.

Halulu Way (Honolulu) – To roar, thunder.

Hālupa St. (Honolulu) – Flourishing, of luxuriant growth.

Hāmākua Dr./Pl. (Kailua) – Definition not known. Probably named for a Hawaiʻi Island district.

Hāmana St. ('Ewa Beach) – Branching, forked.

Hāmau St. (Honolulu) – Silent; silence; hush.

Hame St./Pl. (Kapolei) – Two native species of trees.

Hāmiha Pl. ('Ewa Beach) – Calm, quiet.

Hāmoa Pl. ('Ewa Beach) – Samoa.

Hamoʻula St. ('Ewa Beach) – Ribbed tapa.

Hamumu St./Pl. (Mililani) – To whisper, murmur, hum.

Hāna St. (Waiʻanae) – Alert. Named for a Maui district.

Hanahanai Pl. (Honolulu) – Edge of a precipice or slope.

Hānai Lp. (Honolulu) – Foster child, adopted child.

Hānaimoa St. (Hauʻula) – Feeding chickens.
Named for an Oʻahu land section.

Hanakahi St. ('Ewa Beach) – Single task. Name
of an ancient Hilo chief, used poetically to
designate the Hilo district.

Hanakāpīʻai St. (Honolulu) – Bay sprinkling
food. Named for a Kauaʻi land division.

Hanakealoha Pl. (Honolulu) – Love-making.

Hānaimoa

Hanakoa St./Pl. (Honolulu) – 1) Bay (of) koa
trees. 2) Bay (of) warriors. Named for a Kauaʻi land section.

Hanalē Pl. (Kailua) – Henry.

Hanalei St. (Waiʻanae) – Crescent bay. Named for a Kauaʻi district or land
division.

Hanalima Pl. (Honolulu) – Handmade, manual.

Hanaloa St./Pl. ('Ewa Beach) – Long bay. Named for an Oʻahu land section.

Hanalulu Pl. (Waimānalo) – Protected bay.

Hanamaʻulu St. (Honolulu) – Tired bay. Named for a Kauaʻi land division.

Hānana Pl. (Honolulu) – To overflow, flood.

Hanapaʻa St. (Kapolei) – To make secure, fasten, shut up.

Hanapēpē Lp./Pl. (Honolulu) – Crushed bay. Named for a Kauaʻi land
division.

Hanapouli Cir. ('Ewa Beach) – A place in 'Ewa named in
honor of the young chief's clever spear-handling skills.
Literally: making a darkness.

Hanapule St. (Waialua) – Prayer work. Named for original grantee.

Hānau St. (Wahiawā) – To give birth.

Hanauma Bay Rd. (Honolulu) – 1) Curved bay.
2) Hand-wrestling bay. Named for an Oʻahu bay.

Hanauna St. (Waipahu) – Generation; relative whose
relationship was established several generations previously;
ancestry, birth.

Hānau

Hanawai Cir. (Waipahu) – Irrigation; to irrigate.

Hani Ln. (Honolulu) – To step or move lightly or softly.

Hanile St. (Mililani) – To prepare for or receive company.

Hanina St. (Waipahu) – To step or move lightly or softly.

Haniu Pl. (Waipahu) – Heavy end of a coconut frond.

Hanohano Pl./Way (Honolulu) – Glorious, magnificent, noble.

Hanole Pl. (Honolulu) – Origin not known.

Hanopu St. (Kahuku) – Origin not known.

Hanu Ln. (Honolulu) – To breathe; breath.

Hānuʻa St. (Kapolei) – Thick. Possibly should be Honua: land.

Hanupaoa Pl. (Waipahu) – Two native shrubs or small trees in the daisy family. Literally: fragrant breath.

Hao St./Pl./Way (Honolulu) – To gather up. Named for the Hind property on Hawaiʻi Island. See Hind Iuka.

Haokea Dr. (Kailua) – A variety of taro.

Haona St. (Waialua) – Handful. Named for original grantee.

Hapalua

Hāpaikō St. (ʻEwa Beach) – To carry sugar cane bundles on the back, as formerly done by plantation workers.

Hapaki St. (ʻAiea) – Herbert. Named for Herbert Horita, a prominent real estate developer. Established Herbert Horita Realty, Inc. (1959). Subdivided this Newtown Estates area (1970). First developer of the Kō ʻOlina ("fulfillment of joy") community.

Hapalima Pl. (Waipahu) – Fifth; one fifth.

Hapalua St. (ʻEwa Beach) – Half; in two portions.

Hapanui Pl. (Waipahu) – Majority, most; largest portion.

Hāpapa St./Pl. (Waipahu, Wahiawā) – Rock layer covered with thin earth. Named for an Oʻahu mountain peak.

Hapawalu Pl. (Waipahu) – One eighth; eighth part.

Hapo St. (Waialua) – Definition not known. Named for original grantee.

Hāpua St. (ʻEwa Beach) – Flowering season.

Hāpue Lp. (ʻAiea) – An unidentified medicinal plant.

Hāpuku St. (ʻAiea) – To collect, gather together in haste or indiscriminately.

Hāpuna Pl. (Honolulu) – Spring. Named for Hawaiʻi Island bays.

Hāpuʻu Ct./Lp./St. (Wahiawā, ʻAiea) – An endemic tree fern.

Hau St. (Honolulu) – A native lowland tree in the Hibiscus family. Its inner bark fiber was shaped into ropes, net bags, and tapa.

Hāpuʻu

Hauhele Rd. (Kaʻaʻawa) – An endemic, small pink-flowered hibiscus shrub. Literally: traveling hau.

Hauiki St. (Honolulu) – Small hau tree. Named for an Oʻahu land division, usually called Kahauiki.

Haukaʻekaʻe Pl. (Kāneʻohe) – A kind of hau tree.

Haukapila Rd. (ʻAiea) – Hospital.

Haukoi Pl. (Hauʻula) – Floater, as on a fish net.

Haukulu Rd. (Honolulu) – 1) Dripping dew.
2) Dripping hibiscus. Named for an Oʻahu land section.

Hāʻulelau

Hāʻula St. (Waipahu) – Reddish.

Haulani St. (Waipahu) – To surge, as the sea.

Hāʻulelau St./Pl. (Mililani) – Fall, autumn. Literally: Leaf falling.

Haumalu Pl. (Wahiawā) – Quiet.

Haumana Pl. (Honolulu) – Student, apprentice, recruit.

Haumea St. (Kapolei) – Name of mother of Kapo; great source of female fertility. Kapo: a sister of Pele.

Haunani Pl. (Kāneʻohe) – Beautiful hau tree.

Hāunapō Ln. (Honolulu) – Night striking. Named for an Oʻahu land section.

Haunaukoi St. (Waimānalo) – Blow that grinds adzes. Should be Hauhaukoʻi: swelling of the groin. Named for an Oʻahu land section.

Haunone Pl. (Mililani) – Name of a cold wind.

Haunuʻu St. (Waipahu) – Plant goddess. Daughter of Hina (moon goddess), sister of Kamapuaʻa (pig demigod). Literally: elevated ruler.

Hauʻoli

Hauola Ave. (Wahiawā) – Dew (of) life.

Hauʻoli St. (Honolulu, Kailua) – Happy, joyful; happiness.

Hauʻoliʻoli St. (ʻEwa Beach) – Happy, glad, gay, joyful.

Hauone St. /Pl. (Kapolei) – Soft limestone.

Haupoa St. (Kāneʻohe) – To soften the earth, as for planting.

Hāʻupu Pl. (Honolulu) – To recollect, recall, remember. Named for original awardee.

Hauʻula St./Lp. (Wahiawā) – Red hau tree.

Hauʻula Homestead Rd./Pk. Pl. (Wahiawā, Hauʻula) – Red hau tree. Named for an Oʻahu land division.

Hawaiʻi St. (Honolulu, Wahiawā) – Definition not known. Named for Hawaiʻi Island. A similar name is found in Polynesia: Havaiki (New Zealand, North Marquesas), ʻAvaiki (Cook Islands), and Savaiʻi (Samoa).

Hawaiʻi Kai Dr. (Honolulu) – Sea Hawaiʻi. Kai is short for Kaiser. Named for Henry J. Kaiser (1882-1967). One of world's richest men. He built Hawaiʻi

Hawaiʻi

Kai community and Hilton Hawaiian Village. Established steel, cement, aluminum, and health plan companies.

Hawai'i Loa St. (Honolulu) – 1) Distant Hawai'i. 2) Long Hawai'i. Named for an O'ahu mountain ridge.

Hāwane Pl. (Honolulu) – Edible nut of the loulu palm.

Hāwea St. (Kapolei) – Name of one of two drums that announced the birth of Kākuhihewa.

Hāwena St. (Kailua) – White lime, used for dressing hair and turning the hair brown.

Hāweo Pl. (Honolulu) – Glowing. Perhaps should be Hawea: named for original awardee.

Heahea St./Pl. (Waipahu) – To call frequently and hospitably; to welcome; friendly.

Heainoa Pl. (Waipahu) – To give a name; to chant a name chant.

Heau Pl. (Waialua) – Native shrubs and small trees in the Sandalwood family.

He'eia St. (Kāne'ohe) – Definition not known. Named for an O'ahu land division.

Hehina St. (Mililani) – Foot rest, any place on which to step or tread.

Hē'ī Pl. ('Ewa Beach) – Papaya; found in backyards of 'Ewa Villages.

Hekaha St. ('Aiea) – A mark.

Hekau St. ('Aiea) – Anchor.

Hekili St. (Kailua) – Thunder.

Hekiliiki Pl. (Waimānalo) – Lesser Hekili (thunder).

Hekilinui Pl. (Waimānalo) – Greater Hekili (thunder).

Hele St. (Kailua) – To go, come, walk.

Helekula Way/Pl. (Wai'anae) – Go to school.

Helelua St./Pl. (Wai'anae) – To travel together, of two.

Helemano St. (Honolulu) – Herman.

Helemano Rd. (Waialua) – 1) Many snared. 2) Many going. Named for an O'ahu land section.

Hekau

Hele Mauna Pl. ('Aiea) – Mountain climber.

Helena St. (Kapolei) – Helen.

Helepū St. (Mililani) – To go with company.

Heleuma St. (Wai'anae) – Stone anchor.

Helo Pl. (Honolulu) – Red, as 'ōhelo berries.

Helu Pl. (Wahiawā) – To count, list.

Helumoa Rd. (Honolulu) – Chicken scratch. Named for an O'ahu land section.

Hema Pl. (Honolulu) – 1) Left, left side. 2) South.

Hemolele Pl. (Honolulu) – Perfect, holy.

Hene St. (Waipahu) – Slope, as of a hill.

Heno Pl. (Kāne'ohe) – To cherish, love.

Henoheno St./Pl. (Kāne'ohe) – Lovable, sweet.

Hele Mauna

Henokea St./Pl. (Waipahu) – Lovely or graceful.

Hepa St. (Waipahu) – Imbecile, idiot, moron.

Hepaki Pl. (Kailua) – Herbert. Usually: Hapaki.

Hēpia Pl. (Waipahu) – Pale yellow, of the domesticated ʻilima flower.

Heulu St. (Honolulu) – A breadfruit. Probably named for a chief living at time of Kamehameha I.

Heumiki Pl. (Kāneʻohe) – Beautiful, attractive.

Heulu

Heʻupueo Pl. (Kāneʻohe) – A reedlike grass.

Hiaʻai Pl. (Waipahu) – Pleased with, delighted with; delightful, pleasing.

Hiahia Lp./Pl. (Waipahu) – Faded, gray, hazy.

Hīaku Pl. (Waipahu) – To cast (baited fishing line) for bonito fish.

Hiʻali Pl. (Waipahu) – 1) Food offering to the gods. 2) To stir, as a fire; to signal with the hands.

Hiʻaloa St. (Honolulu) – Same as ʻuha-loa: a small weed with clustered yellow flowers. Its bitter leaves and inner root bark were used for tea, or chewed to relieve sore throat. One of the plant forms of the pig demigod Kamapuaʻa.

Hiana Pl. (Waipahu) – Depression or hole, as under water.

Hiʻanakiʻu St. (Waipahu) – Stems by which plant tubers are attached to vines.

Hiapaʻiʻole Lp./Pl. (Waipahu) – Foremost, expert.

Hiapo St./Pl. (Waipahu) – First-born child; first born, oldest.

Hie Pl. (Waipahu) – Attractive, distinguished, noble, becoming.

Hiehie St. (Honolulu) – Attractive, distinguished, noble, becoming; superb.

Hiena Pl. (Waipahu) – Kind of soft, porous stone used to smooth and polish utensils; harder than the ʻana stone, used on wood.

Hihialou Pl. (Kapolei) – A plant with small yellow flowers.

Hīhīmanu St. (Waimānalo) – Various sting rays and eagle rays, only occasionally eaten by Hawaiians.

Hihiʻo Pl. (Honolulu) – A dream or vision, as while dozing.

Hīhīwai St. (Honolulu) – Endemic grainy snail found in both fresh and brackish water.

Hiʻiaka Rd. (Kaʻaʻawa) – Twelve younger sisters of Pele.

Hiʻialo St. (Mililani) – Carried in the arms, as a beloved child.

Hiʻikala Pl. (Honolulu) – Hook used for kala (a fish) and baited with kala (a seaweed).

Hiʻikua Pl. (Mililani) – An unidentified star that rises and sets at the same times as Hiʻilei. Literally: to carry (on the) back (as a child).

Hiʻilani St. (Honolulu) – Praise, exaltation.

Hiʻialo

Hiʻilawe St. (Honolulu) – To lift, carry. Named for original awardee.

Hiʻilei Pl. (Mililani) – An unidentified star that rises on the night of Hoaka and sets on the night of Muku in the month of Welehu. Hiʻikua is its companion.

Hiʻipoi St. (Kāneʻohe) – To tend, feed, cherish, as a child.

Hīkā St. (Waialua) – To stagger, reel. Named for original grantee.

Hiʻilawe

Hiki St. (Honolulu) – 1) Can, to be able. 2) To appear, come.

Hikianalia Pl. (Mililani) – A star, perhaps Spica, medium-bright and near the equator. It guided mariners and fishermen.

Hikikaulia St. (Miliani) – Name of a star, perhaps it is Sirius.

Hikiku Pl. (Mililani) – Portion of the sky immediately above the horizon.

Hikimoe St./Pl. (Waipahu) – West. Literally: come to rest.

Hikina Ln. (Honolulu) – East.

Hikino St. (Honolulu) – All right, O.K., certainly, it can be done.

Hikiwale St./Pl. (Kāneʻohe) – Easy.

Hila St./Pl. (Waiʻanae, Pearl City) – Hill.

Hilala St. (Honolulu) – To lean or tilt sideways.

Hilihua Pl./Way (Waipahu) – To grope here and there.

Hilinaʻi St. (Kāneʻohe) – Trust, confidence; to lean on, rely on.

Hilinamā St. (Kāneʻohe) – Ancient Hawaiian lunar month.

Hilinehu Pl. (Mililani) – 1) An unidentified star. 2) An ancient Hawaiian month.

Hiliu Pl. (ʻAiea) – Sound or call of a wind instrument, as the conch shell.

Hilo Pl. (Honolulu) – To twist, braid. Named for the Matson steamship, Hilonian (purchased 1905).

Hilo Holly Pl. (Honolulu) – A short-branched evergreen shrub sometimes grown for hedges.

Hilu St. (Waimānalo) – Several kinds of colorful reef fishes, with prominent horizontal stripes.

Hiliu

Hiluhilu St./Pl. (Kapolei) – Elegant, beautiful.

Hima Rd. (Wahiawā) – Should be Hema: south.

Hīmeni Pl. (Waipahu) – Hymn, any song not used for hulas.

Hina St. (Waipahu) – Name of moon goddess. Literally: prostrate.

Hinaʻea St. (Waipahu) – Goddess of sunrise and sunset.

Hinahina St. (Honolulu) – The silversword. See ʻĀhinahina.

Hinalani St./Pl. (Kāneʻohe) – An unidentified star.

Hīnālea St. (Waimānalo) – Several kinds of deep green or blue wrasses (fishes), found abundantly on coral reefs.

Hinaliʻi St./Pl. (Mililani) – An unidentified star, the companion of Polowehilani.

Hīnalo Pl. (Honolulu) – Male pandanus blossom.

Hinamoe Lp./Pl. (Kāneʻohe) – To lie down to sleep.

Hīnano St./Way (Honolulu, Kailua) – Male pandanus blossom.

Hinapū St. (Kāneʻohe) – A rare variety of upland taro.

Hind Iuka Dr. (Honolulu) – Inland Hind. Named for Robert Hind (1863-1938). Part-Hawaiian rancher and dairy farmer on Hawaiʻi Island, and Territorial Senator (1917-1938). Son of a sugar planter. The Hind-Clarke Dairy was located nearby. Āina Haina is named for Robert Hind.

Hinu Pl. (Pearl City) – Smooth and polished, lustrous, slick.

Hinuhinu Way (Waipahu) – Bright, shining, lustrous, glittering, of polished stones or shells.

Hiō Pl. (Kāneʻohe) – To fall sideways, lean, slant, oblique, diagonal.

Hiʻolani Pl. (Honolulu) – To lie at ease, lounge, relax, slumber.

Hipawai Pl. (Honolulu) – Water foolishness. Named for an Oʻahu land section.

Hiu St. (Honolulu) – Hugh.

Hiwahiwa St./Pl./Way (Kaʻaʻawa, Waipahu) – Precious, beloved, esteemed; favorite.

Hiwalani Pl. (Kāneʻohe) – Esteemed chief; beloved child or favorite.

Hiwi Pl. (Wahiawā) – Skinny, bony, angular.

Hoa St. (Honolulu) – Companion, friend, associate.

Hōʻāahi Pl. (Kāneʻohe) – To kindle fire.

Hoaʻāina St./Pl. (Honolulu) – Tenant, caretaker.

Hōʻaeʻae St./Pl. (Waipahu) – To make soft or fine. Named for an Oʻahu land division.

Hinamoe
Hiʻolani

Hōʻaha St./Pl. (Waiʻanae) – To braid.

Hoahana Pl. (Honolulu) – Fellow worker, colleague, partner.

Hoahele Pl. (Mililani) – Traveling companion, fellow traveler.

Hōʻahiahi Pl. (Mililani) – Evening.

Hoahui St. (Mililani) – Associate.

Hōʻailona St./Pl. (Mililani) – Sign, symbol, insignia, emblem.

Hoaka Pl. (Mililani) – Second day of ancient Hawaiian lunar month. Literally: crescent.

Hoakakeʻa Pl. (Mililani) – Arch over a door.

Hōʻākea Pl. (Mililani) – To widen, broaden, extend, enlarge, make public.

Hoakoa Pl. (Honolulu) – Buddy. Literally: soldier friend.

Hoakua St./Pl. (Mililani) – Companion of a god, godly companion.

Hōʻailona

Hoakula St. (Mililani) – Schoolmate.

Hōʻāla St. (ʻAiea) – To waken, rise up.

Hoalauna St./Pl. (ʻEwa Beach) – Neighbor, close associate or friend.

Hōʻālīa St. (Mililani) – To wait.

52

Hoali'i St./Pl. (Kapolei) – Companion of a chief.
Hoalike Rd. (Hale'iwa) – Companion of equal status.
Hoaloha Pl. (Honolulu) – Friend. Literally: beloved companion.
Hō'alu Pl. (Honolulu) – Depression; slack.
Hoalua St. (Hale'iwa) – Two friends.
Hoaluhi Pl. (Mililani) – Fellow worker, especially one helping to rear a child.

Hoalua

Hoalumi St. (Mililani) – Roommate.
Hō'ama St. (Mililani) – To begin to ripen.
Hoana Pl. (Honolulu) – Porcupine fish. Its body is covered with spines capable of inflicting a painful wound. Some Hawaiians regard this fish as poisonous. Literally: grindstone.
Hoanāulu Pl. (Kapolei) – Companion of the Naulu sea breeze.
Ho'āni Pl. (Mililani) – To beckon.
Ho'āno St./Pl. ('Ewa Beach) – Awe.
Hoanoho Pl. (Honolulu) – Neighbor, roommate.
Ho'ā'o Pl. (Mililani) – To try, taste.
Hoapili Ln. (Honolulu) – Close friend. Possibly named for David Hoapili Sr., formerly employed at Theo H. Davies.

Ho'ā'o

Ho'āpono Pl. ('Aiea) – To approve.
Ho'āuna St./Pl. (Kāne'ohe) – To flock together, collect.
Hō'awa St./Ln. (Honolulu) – Native species of trees. Its pounded fruit valve was placed on body sores.
Hoe St./Way (Honolulu, Wahiawā) – Paddle.
Hoea St. (Kapolei) – Let's get started.
Hoehoe Pl. (Honolulu) – A long, melancholy sound, as of the nose flute.
Hoene Pl. (Kāne'ohe) – To sound softly, rustle.
Hoenui St. (Honolulu) – Big paddle. Named for original awardee.
Hoewa'a Pl. (Kapolei) – Oarsman, paddler. To paddle a canoe.
Hō'eu Pl. (Mililani) – An unidentified star. Literally: to stir up.
Hohiu Pl. (Honolulu) – A native fern with finely divided fronds.
Hohola St. (Waipahu) – To spread out, unfold, unfurl, as tapa, mats, clouds, wings.
Hō'ihi Pl. (Honolulu) – To make sacred, holy.
Ho'iho'i Ave. (Wahiawā) – To return, send back, restore.
Hō'ikaika Pl. (Waipahu) – Strong.
Hō'ike Pl./Way (Kapolei) – To show, exhibit.
Hō'imi Pl. (Honolulu) – To look for.

Hoewa'a

Hoʻina St. (Kapolei) – Returning, coming back; farewell gift, as to a parting guest after a feast.

Hōʻiʻo Cir./St./Pl. (Wahiawā, ʻAiea) – A large, native, edible fern.

Hokea St. (ʻAiea) – Hosea.

Hōkeo St. (Kapolei) – To cherish secretly, as love.

Hōkio Pl. (ʻAiea) – Small gourd whistle.

Hōkiokio Pl. (Honolulu) – Gourd whistle; pipe; to whistle.

Hōkū

Hōkū Ave. (Honolulu) – Star.

Hōkūʻaeʻa Pl. (Waiʻanae) – Planet. Literally: wandering star.

Hōkūahiahi St. (Mililani) – Evening star.

Hōkūʻaiʻāina Pl. (Waiʻanae) – An unidentified navigation star. Literally: star ruling land.

Hōkūala St./Pl. (Mililani) – Planet. Literally: rising star.

Hōkūaliʻi St./Ct. (Mililani) – The planet Venus. Literally: royal star.

Hōkūao Pl. (Mililani) – The planet Venus, when seen in the morning. Literally: day star.

Hōkūʻaukai Way/Pl. (Kapolei) – Seafaring star.

Hōkūhele Pl. (Mililani) – Planet. Literally: traveling star.

Hokuili St./Pl. (Mililani) – Full moon that sets after daylight. Literally: stranded Hoku.

Hōkūʻimo St./Pl. (Kapolei) – Twinkling star.

Hōkūʻiwa St. (Mililani) – A Hawaiian constellation, perhaps Boötes. Literally: frigate bird star.

Hōkūkeʻa Ct./Pl. (Mililani, Waiʻanae) – Southern Cross. Literally: cross star.

Hōkūlani St. (Honolulu) – Heavenly star.

Hōkūleʻa Pl. (Mililani) – Arcturus, the star that guided ancient Polynesians to Hawaiʻi. Literally: star (of) joy.

Hōkūlele Pl. (Mililani) – Shooting star, meteor, any moving star.

Hōkūlewa Lp./Pl. (Mililani) – Moving star, planet.

Hōkūliʻiliʻi St./Pl. (Mililani) – Asteroid, small star.

Hōkūloa Lp. (Mililani) – The planet Venus when seen in the morning. Literally: distant star.

Hōkūlele

Hōkūnui St. (Kapolei) – Large star.

Hōkūpa St. (Kapolei) – Name of a constellation, perhaps Leo or the head of Cetus. Litererally: fence star.

Hōkūpaʻa St. (Waiʻanae) – Polaris, the North Star. Literally: fixed star.

Hokupalemo St./Pl. (Mililani) – Full moon that sets before daylight. Literally: drowned Hoku.

Hōkūukali St./Pl. (Waiʻanae) – Satellite star. Literally: following star.

Hōkūʻula Lp./Pl. (Mililani) – A star, possibly Antares. Literally: red star.

Hōkūulani St. (Honolulu) – Satellite star.

Hōkūwekiu St. (Kapolei) – Highest star.

Hōkūwelowelo Pl. (Mililani) – Shooting star, comet. Literally: streaming star.

Hōlani St. (Mililani) – Name of a mythical place.

Hōlaniali‘i St./Pl. (Mililani) – An unidentified star, said to be observed by priests.

Hōlanikū St./Pl. (Mililani) – An unidentified star, said to be observed by priests.

Hōlapa St. (Honolulu) – Ridge; to form a ridge.

Hōlawa St./Pl. (Hale‘iwa) – Perhaps short for Ho‘olawa: to supply, apportion sufficiently, equip.

Holi

Hōlei St. (Honolulu) – A small, rare native tree. Its bark and roots yield a yellow dye for tapa.

Holelua Pl. (Honolulu) – Wavering. Named for original awardee.

Holi St. (Kapolei) – To sprout.

Hōlio Pl. (Kāne‘ohe) – Two species of small, rare, endemic trees in the laurel family, found only on Kaua‘i and O‘ahu.

Holo Pl. (‘Aiea) – To run, sail, ride, go.

Holo‘ai St. (‘Aiea) – Food bundles, especially tī-leaf bundle of hard poi.

Holo‘anai Way (Kāne‘ohe) – To gallop.

Holoholo St. (Kailua) – To go for a walk, ride, or sail.

Holoimua St./Pl. (Kapolei) – To progress, advance, surpass, go ahead.

Holoka‘a St./Pl. (Kāne‘ohe) – To ride in a car or carriage.

Holokahana Ln. (Honolulu) – Success.

Holokai Pl. (Honolulu) – To sail on the sea; seaman, seafarer.

Holokia Pl. (Mililani) – To dart, as a bird.

Holokū Pl. (Wahiawā) – A loose, seamed dress with a yoke and usually a train, patterned after the "Mother Hubbard" dresses worn by missionary wives. The word holokū is said to originate when the seamstress said "holo" ("run") when turning the sewing machine wheel, and "kū" when stopping the machine and moving the cloth.

Holokūkū Pl. (Kāne‘ohe) – To trot, as a horse.

Hololani St. (Mililani) – Mission.

Holole‘a St. (Mililani) – To succeed, fare well, successful.

Hololio St./Pl. (Kāne‘ohe) – To ride horseback; horseman.

Holomakani St./Pl. (Kāne‘ohe) – Breezy, airy. Literally: wind running.

Holomālia St./Pl. (Wai‘anae) – To drive slowly.

Holomoana St. (Honolulu) – Seaman, seafarer; to sail on the sea; sea voyage or cruise.

Hololio

Holomoku St. (Kapolei) – Sailor, passenger, anyone who sails; to make a sail or ocean trip. (formerly Holomoana St.)

Holomua Pl. (Honolulu) – Improvement, progress.

Hōlona Pl. (Honolulu) – Unskilled, far from expert; novice.

Holonui Pl. (Kāneʻohe) – To gallop, run fast.

Holopapa St. (ʻEwa Beach) – To spread, overrun, prevail, overcome, control, defeat.

Holopeki St./Pl. (Kāneʻohe) – To trot. Literally: pace run.

Holopono St./Pl. (Waiʻanae) – To drive correctly.

Holopū Pl. (Kāneʻohe) – To run together.

Holopuni St. (ʻAiea) – To sail or travel around, circumnavigate; everywhere.

Holouka Pl. (Kāneʻohe) – Draft, air current, as in the mountains.

Holowai St./Pl. (Kāneʻohe) – Water ditch or course.

Holu Pl. (Mililani) – An unidentified star.

Hōlua Pl./Way (Honolulu, Wahiawā) – Sled, especially the ancient sled used on grassy slopes; the sled course.

Holunape St. (Kapolei) – To sway, wave, swaying.

Homelani Pl. (Honolulu) – Heavenly home.

Homohana Rd. (Wahiawā) – Should be Komohana: west.

Hone Ln. (Honolulu) – Sweet and soft, as music.

Honehone St. (Wahiawā) – Sweet and soft, as music.

Honekoa St. (Kāneʻohe) – Bold pranks, mischief; sassy, impudent.

Honohina St./Pl. (ʻAiea) – Wild spiderflower, a lowland weed. Its small, odd, spider-like flowers are white with a purple tinge.

Honohono St. (ʻAiea) – The wandering Jew or dayflower, a creeping weed with small, irregular-shaped, bright-blue flowers lasting just one day. Used as a cattle feed in dairies.

Honokahua St./Pl. (Honolulu) – Sites bay. Named for a Maui land division.

Honokawela Dr. (Kahuku) – Kawela bay. Literally: bay (of) the heat.

Honokoa Pl. (Honolulu) – Abounding (in) soldiers.

Honomanū St. (ʻAiea) – Definition not known. Named for a Maui land division.

Honomū St./Pl. (Hauʻula) – Silent bay.

Honono St. (Honolulu) – Definition not known. Named for a Kauaʻi promontory.

Honopū Pl. (Honolulu) – Conch bay. Named for a Kauaʻi land division.

Honu

Honowai St./Pl. (Waipahu) – Definition not known.

Honu St. (ʻAiea) – General name for turtle and tortoise. Ancient Hawaiians knew of only two large sea turtles. Honu referred to the edible, green turtle.

Honua St. (Honolulu) – Land, earth.

Hoʻohaʻaheo Pl. (Pearl City) – To act haughty.

Hoʻohaʻi St./Pl. (Pearl City) – To flirt.

Hoʻohakanū Pl. (Pearl City) – To cause silence; silent.

Hoʻohaku St./Pl. (Pearl City) – To act as master, overseer, employer or owner; to rule others, sometimes without authority.

Hoʻohālāwai Pl. (ʻAiea) – To arrange a meeting.

Hoʻohale St. (Pearl City) – To lodge in a house; to receive in a house.

Hoʻohaliʻa St. (Pearl City) – To evoke reminiscence or recollection; remembrance.

Hoʻohālike St. (Pearl City) – To compare, make alike, resemble, copy.

Hoʻohamo Pl. (Pearl City) – To anoint, rub, as with oil; to fondle, caress.

Hoʻohana Pl. (Pearl City) – To use, employ, carry out, administer; use, employment, administration.

Hoʻohani Pl. (Waipahu) – To touch.

Hoʻōheke St. (Pearl City) – To cause shyness, to be modest.

Hoʻohele St./Pl. (Waipahu) – To cause to move, set in motion.

Hoʻoheno St./Pl. (Pearl City) – To cherish, love, caress.

Hoʻohiamoe St. (Pearl City) – To put to sleep, lull to sleep; to pretend to sleep.

Hoʻohie Pl. (Pearl City) – To make or cause to appear distinguished; distinguished, stately, regal; delightful.

Hoʻohiki St./Pl. (Pearl City) – To vow, swear, take an oath, promise.

Hoʻohilu St. (ʻEwa Beach) – To decorate, beautify.

Hoʻohoa Pl. (Pearl City) – To make friends.

Hoʻohoihoi St./Pl. (Pearl City) – To entertain, charm, delight, encourage, please.

Hoʻohonua St. (Pearl City) – Firmly established.

Hoʻohuali Pl. (Pearl City) – To polish.

Hoʻohui St. (Pearl City) – To join; to add on, annex; to introduce one person to another.

Hoʻohulili St. (Pearl City) – To blaze, dazzle, vibrate, swell.

Hoʻohulu St./Pl. (Pearl City) – To esteem, prize.

Hōʻoia St. (Pearl City) – To confirm, audit, verify.

Hoʻoikaika Pl. (Pearl City) – To make a great effort, encourage, animate, strengthen, try, strive.

Hoʻoiki St. (Pearl City) – To lessen, diminish, make small.

Hoʻoilo Pl. (ʻEwa Beach) – Winter seas or the season of germination designated by the setting sun moving south of Puʻuokapolei.

Hoʻokaʻahea St./Pl. (ʻEwa Beach) – To smoothe.

Hoʻokāʻau St. (Mililani) – Witty, clever, funny, entertaining.

Hoʻokahe St./Pl. (ʻEwa Beach) – To water or irrigate.

Hoʻokahi St./Way (Pearl City, Honolulu) – One, alone, one only.

Hoʻokahua St. (Pearl City) – To lay a foundation, establish, found; to settle down and develop a place, as homesteaders.

Hoʻokala St. (Pearl City) – To sharpen, grind.

Hoʻokahe

Ho'okanahē St. (Mililani) – To drive or urge forward, accelerate, hurry, quicken.

Ho'okani St. (Pearl City) – To play a musical instrument, to cause to sound.

Ho'okanikē St. (Pearl City) – To toll, strike, as bells.

Ho'okano St. (Pearl City) – Haughty, proud, conceited, rude, disdainful of others.

Ho'okaulana Pl. ('Ewa Beach) – Resting place, place to put things, placement; restful; quiet.

Ho'okaulike Pl. ('Ewa Beach) – To equalize, balance.

Ho'okeha St./Pl. (Kapolei) – To cause height; to cause pride, boasting.

Ho'okani

Ho'okela Pl. (Honolulu) – Excel.

Ho'okele St./Pl. (Wai'anae) – Steersman, helmsman; to drive, as a car.

Ho'okelewa'a St. (Mililani) – Sirius, a star of the mariner. Literally: causing the canoe to sail.

Ho'okena St. (Pearl City) – To satisfy thirst. Possibly named for a Hawai'i Island land division.

Ho'oki'eki'e St. (Pearl City) – To elevate, promote; proud, lording it over others; disrespectful or disobedient to seniors.

Ho'okele

Ho'okili Pl. (Kapolei) – To rain gently.

Ho'okipa Way (Honolulu) – Hospitality; to entertain, treat hospitably.

Ho'okō Pl. (Kapolei) – To fulfill; to carry out, as a contract.

Ho'okoe St. (Pearl City) – To save, reserve for later use.

Ho'okomo St. (Kapolei) – To insert, put in, sink into, deposit, admit, let in.

Ho'okōwā St./Pl. (Mililani) – Name of a star.

Ho'oku'i St. (Honolulu) – To join, connect; to dovetail, fit, splice.

Ho'oku'ikahi St. (Wai'anae) – To unite, reconcile, agree; to make peace.

Ho'okumu Pl. (Pearl City) – To originate, establish, found, start.

Ho'okupa St. (Pearl City) – To naturalize, make a citizen.

Ho'okupu St. (Mililani) – Sprout, growth.

Ho'ōla Pl. (Pearl City) – To save, heal, cure, spare; salvation; healer, savior.

Ho'ola'a Pl./Way (Pearl City) – To consecrate, dedicate, hallow.

Ho'ola'i St. (Honolulu, Kailua) – To cause to be still; to quiet, as a mob; to cease talking; calm; peaceful, quiet.

Ho'olako Pl. (Honolulu) – To supply.

Ho'olana St./Pl. (Pearl City) – To cause to float, launch; to right a canoe. Possibly an ancient Hawai'i Island surfing area, perhaps Holana Bay.

Ho'olaua'e St. (Pearl City) – To cherish, as a beloved memory.

Ho'olaule'a St. (Pearl City) – Celebration, gathering for a celebration, large party; to reconcile, restore peace or friendship, appease.

Hoʻolauna St. (Pearl City) – To introduce one person to another; to be friendly.

Hoʻolawa Pl. (Pearl City) – To supply, apportion sufficiently, equip.

Hoʻoleʻa Pl. (Kailua) – To cause pleasure, joy; to praise, please, delight.

Hoʻolehua St./Pl. (Pearl City) – Swift, strong.

Hoʻolele St. (Pearl City) – To fly, as a kite; to disembark; to embark, as on a project.

Hōʻoli Cir./Pl. (Pearl City) – To give joy, make happy.

Hoʻolōkahi St. (Waiʻanae) – To bring about unity; to make peace and unity.

Hōʻolu St. (ʻEwa Beach) – To make pleasant, cool, comfortable, soft; please, satisfy.

Hoʻolele

Hoʻolulu Rd. (Wahiawā) – To lie quietly in calm water, as a ship in port.

Hoʻolulu St. (Honolulu) – To lie quietly in calm water, as a ship in port. Named for High Chief Hoʻolulu. He helped his older half-brother Hoapili hide Kamehameha I's bones when the king died. (Ancient Hawaiians hid the bones of honored chiefs so the bones would not be found and violated).

Hōʻoluʻolu Pl. (ʻEwa Beach) – To satisfy.

Hoʻoluʻu St. (Pearl City) – To dip, immerse.

Hoʻomaʻalili St./Pl. (ʻEwa Beach) – To cause to cool; appease, soothe, quiet, pacify.

Hoʻomaʻemaʻe St. (Pearl City) – To clean, cleanse.

Hoʻomaha St./Way (Waimānalo, Honolulu) – Vacation; to take a rest or vacation; to retire, stop work; to obtain relief.

Hoʻomāhie Lp. (Pearl City) – Delightful, charming; to cast shy glances, as of a coy child.

Hoʻomahilu St. (Pearl City) – To beautify, adorn, bedeck.

Hoʻomaikaʻi St. (Honolulu) – To thank, bless, render thanks, congratulate; gratified, thankful; to improve, perfect.

Hoʻomāʻike St. (Pearl City) – To show.

Hoʻomailani St. (Pearl City) – To cause or pretend to extol, praise, treat as a chief or great favorite.

Hoʻomaka St. (ʻEwa Beach) – To begin.

Hoʻomakoa St. (Waipahu) – To act bravely.

Hoʻomālie St. (ʻEwa Beach) – To make calm, hush, smooth.

Hoʻomalimali St. (Pearl City) – To flatter; to mollify with soft words or a gift; to soothe, quiet.

Hoʻomaliu St. (Kapolei) – Name of a star.

Hoʻomalolo St. (Pearl City) – To cease work for a time, recess; adjourn temporarily.

Hoʻomalu St. (Pearl City) – To protect; to keep quiet, still as during kapu; to restrict, confine, quarantine; to make peace between warring parties.

Ho'omaluhia St. (Wai'anae) – To cause or give peace, protect.
Ho'omalule Pl. ('Ewa Beach) – To make lax, limp, weak, to relax.
Ho'omana Pl. (Waialua) – To place in authority, empower, authorize.
Ho'omana'o St. ('Ewa Beach) – To remember, recall, commemorate.
Ho'omele Pl. (Waipahu) – To cause to sing or chant.
Ho'omoana St./Pl./Way (Pearl City) – To camp.
Ho'omoe St./Pl. (Pearl City) – To put to sleep, to lay down.
Ho'omohalu Pl. ('Ewa Beach) – To slacken; to cause relaxation; to ease.
Ho'omua St. (Mililani) – To push forward, to do something first.
Ho'onā St./Pl. (Pearl City) – To relieve pain, soothe,
   comfort, quiet, appease; to settle a claim.
Ho'onanea St. (Honolulu) – To pass the time in ease,
   peace and pleasure; to relax; absorbed, contented.
Ho'onani Pl. (Kāne'ohe) – To beautify, adorn, decorate;
   to glorify, honor, exalt.
Ho'one'e Pl. (Honolulu) – To cause to move, hitch along,
   push ahead.
Hō'oni Pl. (Mililani) – To move.

Ho'onanea

Ho'onipo St. (Pearl City) – 1) To make love, court, yearn
   for. 2) To cause sleepiness, make drowsy.
Hō'ono St. (Pearl City) – To tempt the appetite; to make tasty.
Ho'onu'a Pl. ('Ewa Beach) – To give generously and continuously.
Ho'onui Pl. (Mililani) – To enlarge, expand.
Ho'opa'a Pl. ('Ewa Beach) – To make fast, firm, hard, tight, solid.
Ho'opai St./Pl. (Pearl City) – To encourage, cause to rouse, stir up, excite.
Ho'opala St. (Kāne'ohe) – To ripen, turn yellow.
Ho'opiha Pl. (Wahiawā) – Full.
Ho'opi'i Pl. (Honolulu) – To cause to rise, mount, come up.
Ho'opili St. ('Ewa Beach) – To bring together, stick.
Ho'opi'o St./Pl. ('Ewa Beach) – To arch, bend, curve.
Ho'opohu Pl. ('Ewa Beach) – To calm, quiet; to bring into calm, as a ship.
Ho'opuhi St. (Wai'anae) – To cause to blow; blow.
Ho'opulapula St. (Waimānalo) – To rehabilitate.
Ho'ōpūloa Pl. (Pearl City) – Put in together (for a) long (time). Named for
   a Hawai'i Island village and land division.
Ho'opuni Dr. (Kailua) – 1) To surround, get control of. 2) To deceive.
Ho'ou'i Pl. (Pearl City) – To beautify, make beautiful.
Ho'oulu St. (Kailua) – To grow, sprout, cause to increase, as the surf; to
   inspire.
Ho'owae St. (Pearl City) – To choose, pretend to choose; finicky.
Ho'owalea St./Way/Pl. ('Ewa Beach) – To pass the time in ease, peace and
   pleasure; to relax.
Ho'owali St. (Pearl City) – To make soft, smooth, as soil; to mix, as poi or
   dough; to digest.

Hoʻowehi Pl. (ʻEwa Beach) – To beautify, decorate, adorn.

Hopaka St. (Honolulu) – Hobert.

Hope St./Ln. (Honolulu, Kunia) – After, behind; last, back, rear.

Hopeloa Pl. (Honolulu) – Youngest, very last, final.

Hopemanu St. (Waialua) – Ornamental canoe stern endpiece. Named for original grantee.

Hopena Way (Honolulu) – Result, conclusion, ending.

Hōpoe Pl. (Waipahu) – Fully developed, as a lehua flower.

Hou Pl. (Wahiawā) – Definition not known.

Hua Pl. (Kāneʻohe) – Egg.

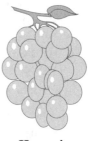

Hua

Huaʻala Pl. (Mililani) – Nutmeg. Literally: fragrant fruit.

Huaka Cir. (Wahiawā) – Clear as crystal, bright, dazzling, white, shining, flashing.

Huʻakai St. (Waipahu) – Any of the various sponges found in Hawaiian waters. Not used as food or medicine. Literally: foam (of the) sea.

Huakanu St./Pl. (ʻAiea) – Seed, as of mango; bulb.

Huakē Pl. (Honolulu) – Full and plump, as a healthy person; well-proportioned, as a properly built canoe.

Hualani St./Pl. (Kailua) – Offspring of a chief.

Hualau Pl. (Pearl City) – A variety of banana. Literally: many fruits.

Huali St. (Honolulu) – Bright, polished, clean, pure, white, glittering; morally pure.

Hualūkini Pl. (Kāneʻohe) – Musk, used in making perfume.

Huamalani St. (Kaʻaʻawa) – A star in the heaven. Hua is the name of a specific star.

Huamoa St. (Waiʻanae) – A variety of sweet potato.

Huanu St. (Honolulu) – Juan. Named for original awardee.

Huanui St./Pl. (Honolulu) – A variety of banana. Literally: big fruit.

Huaʻono Pl. (Pearl City) – A variety of sweet potato.

Huapala St. (Honolulu) – Orange trumpet or sweetheart vine, an ornamental vine bearing many orange flowers.

Huawai Pl. (Waipahu) – Drop of water, spray, mist.

Huawaina Pl. (Kāneʻohe) – Grape. Literally: wine fruit.

Hue St. (Honolulu) – Gourd, water calabash, any narrow-necked container for holding water.

Huʻea Pl. (Honolulu) – Removed, lifted off, exposed; washed out, of flood waters.

Huehu St./Pl. (Kahuku) – A strong northwesterly wind of the winter months.

Huelani Dr./Pl. (Honolulu) – Royal gourd.

Huelo St. (Haleʻiwa) – Tail, of a dog, cat, or pig.

Huene St. (Honolulu) – A wheezing sound, as of asthmatic persons; a prolonged shrill cry.

Huawaina

Huewai Pl. (Waipahu) – Gourd water container, water bottle.

Hui St. (Kailua) – Club, association, corporation, union; to meet, associate.

Hui ʻAeko St./Pl./Way (Kāneʻohe) – Group (of) eagles.

Hui ʻĀkepa Pl. (Kāneʻohe) – Group (of) ʻākepa. See ʻĀkepa.

Huewai

Hui ʻAkikiki Pl. (Kāneʻohe) – Group (of) ʻakikiki. ʻAkikiki: the Kauaʻi honeycreeper, a forest bird common in the Alakaʻi swamp.

Hui ʻAlaiaha Pl. (Kāneʻohe) – Group (of) ʻalaiaha. ʻAlaiaha: an unidentified upland bird (not reported seen since 1863).

Hui ʻAlalā St. (Kāneʻohe) – Group (of) ʻalalā. ʻAlalā: Hawaiian crow, a rare upland bird found only on Hawaiʻi Island.

Huialoha St. (Honolulu) – Meeting (of) compassion. Named for a Kaupō, Maui church.

Hui ʻAukuʻu Pl. (Kāneʻohe) – Group (of) ʻaukuʻu. See ʻAukuʻu.

Huihui Pl. (Mililani) – The Pleiades, a constellation. Literally: group, cluster.

Hui ʻIo St./Pl. (Kāneʻohe) – Group (of) ʻio. See ʻIo.

Hui ʻIwa St./Pl. (Kāneʻohe) – Group (of) ʻiwa. ʻIwa: great frigate bird, primarily black.

Huikahi St. (Pearl City) – United in one; in accord and agreement.

Huikala Pl. (Waiʻanae) – To absolve entirely, forgive all faults; ceremonial cleansing.

Hui Kēlū St./Pl. (Kāneʻohe) – Group (of) kēlū. Kēlū: California valley quail.

Hui Koloa Pl. (Kāneʻohe) – Group (of) koloa (ducks). See Koloa.

Huina St. (Honolulu) – Angle; corner, of a house or street; crossroads, intersection.

Huinawai Pl. (Kāneʻohe) – Pool, meeting place of two or more streams.

Hui Nēnē St. (Kāneʻohe) – Group (of) nēnē (geese). See Nēnē.

Hui ʻŌʻō Pl./Way (Kāneʻohe) – Group (of) ʻōʻō. See ʻŌʻō.

Hui Palila Pl. (Kāneʻohe) – Group (of) palila. Palila: a large-billed, large-headed honeycreeper, a forest bird found only on Hawaiʻi Island.

Huipū Dr. (Waiʻanae) – To mix, unite, blend, assemble, combine.

Hui ʻŪlili St. (Kāneʻohe) – Group (of) ʻūlili. See ʻŪlili.

Hūkaʻa St. (ʻAiea) – Pitch, resin, gum from a tree; resinous timber drifting to Hawaiʻi from the northwest coast of America.

Huki Pl. (Waipahu) – To pull, as on a rope.

Hukilau Lp. (Waialua) – Seine (a fish net with sinkers on bottom and floaters on top); to fish with a seine. Literally: pull ropes.

Hula St. (Waipahu) – The hula, a hula dancer; to dance the hula.

Hulahē St. (Waipahu) – To jump for joy, cavort with happiness.

Hulahula Pl. (Hauʻula) – Ballroom dancing with partners, American dancing; ball; massed hula dancing; to dance.

Hulakai Pl. (Kāneʻohe) – Sea hula. Named for cruiser of Herbert Melville Dowsett (1890-1969). An avid yachtsman with Pearl Harbor Yacht Club. See Kimopelekane.

Hula

Hulakuʻi Dr. (Honolulu) – Any interpretive hula. Literally: joined hula (ancient and new hula steps are joined together).

Hulali Pl. (Honolulu) – Shining, glittering; to shine, glitter, reflect light.

Huleʻia Pl. (ʻEwa Beach) – A kind of soft pumice stone.

Huli St. (Honolulu, Waimānalo, Kunia) – To turn; to change.

Huliau St. (ʻEwa Beach) – Turning point, time of change.

Hulihana Pl. (ʻEwa Beach) – Diligent in work.

Hulikoʻa Pl. (ʻEwa Beach) – To seek into the depths of a matter, to describe fully.

Hulili St. (ʻEwa Beach) – Dazzling light, vibration, undulation; to blaze, dazzle, vibrate, swell.

Hulinuʻu Pl. (Kāneʻohe) – Highest rank or grade.

Hulu Pl. (Honolulu) – Feather, quill.

Huluhulu St. (ʻEwa Beach) – Kinds of seaweeds and mosses.

Hulukoa Pl. (Kapolei) – Bird crest.

Hulumanu St. (ʻAiea) – Bird feathers.

Hulu

Hulumoa Pl. (Mililani) – The Hawaiian mistletoe.

Hulupala Pl./Way (Kāneʻohe) – Light brown, bay, as a horse.

Humu St./Pl. (Kāneʻohe) – Altair, a star in the constellation Aquila.

Humukā Lp. (Waimānalo) – Cross-stitching; to do cross-stitching.

Humuna Pl. (Waimānalo) – Sewing, seam.

Humuniki St./Pl. (Waimānalo) – A geometric pattern in weaving.

Humupaʻa St./Pl. (Waimānalo) – Lock stitch, a stitch that does not loosen easily; to sew thus.

Humuʻula St./Pl. (Kailua) – Red jasper stone, used for adzes.

Humuwili Pl. (Kailua) – Overcasting stitch; to hem.

Huna St. (Honolulu) – Hidden secret; hidden.

Hunaahi St. (Kāneʻohe) – Fire spark, live cinder.

Hunakai St. (Honolulu) – Sanderling (bird), a small winter migrant to Hawaiʻi. While feeding on the beach, it races after a receding wave, then runs back, just ahead of the next wave. Literally: sea foam.

Hunalepo St. (Kāneʻohe) – Dust particle.

Hunalewa St. (Honolulu) – Van of an army, front ranks.

Hunapa'a St. (Honolulu) – Rear guard of an army.
Hunekai St./Pl. (Kapolei) – Sea spray, sea foam.
Huo Pl. (Mililani) – An unidentified star.
Hupua Lp. (Honolulu) – To draw together.
I'a Pl. (Mililani) – Milky Way. Literally: fish.
'Iako Pl. (Honolulu) – Sail boom (a horizontal pole) of an outrigger canoe.

Ihe

'Iakopo Pl. (Kāne'ohe) – James.
I'aleleiaka Pl. (Mililani) – Milky Way. Literally: fish jumping in (the) shadows.
Iana St./Pl. (Kailua) – Ostrich, owl. Iana is a Biblical word. The Hawaiian short-eared owl is called Pueo.
'Iao Ln. (Honolulu) – Silversides, a large-scaled, small bluish-white fish, used primarily as bait for aku and other fishes.
I'aukea St. (Honolulu) – Definition not known. Named for Curtis Pi'ehu I'aukea (1855-1940), a descendant of Hawaiian chiefs. Diplomatic envoy to many nations for monarchy and territorial governments. His immigration policy studies resulted in Japanese laborers coming to Hawai'i. Chamberlain and royal court official, O'ahu County Sheriff (1907-1909), Territorial Senator (1912-1914), Secretary of Territory and often Acting Governor (1911 1921), and chairman of Hawaiian Homes Commission (1935-1936).
'Ie'ie Pl. ('Aiea) – An endemic woody, branching climber (vine). Its long, narrow roots were shaped into baskets and calabashes. See Ala Le'ie.
Ihe St. (Honolulu) – Spear, javelin, dart.
Īhe'e Pl. (Kapolei) – To spread out, prevail, as of calm, peace.
Iheihe Pl. ('Ewa Beach) – One of several half-beak fishes.
'Ihi'ihi Ave./Pl. (Wahiawā) – Sacred, majestic, dignified; created with reverence or respect.
'Ihilani St. (Kāne'ohe) – Heavenly splendor; sacredness of a chief; reverence due a chief.
Ihiloa Lp./Pl. (Honolulu) – Small, long-necked gourd, used for holding water.
'Ihipehu St. ('Ewa Beach) – Pink wood-sorrel (tree), with pink-lavender flowers. Its root was used medicinally.
Iho Pl. ('Aiea) – To go down, descend.
Ihoiho Pl. (Wahiawā) – Candle, torch.
Iholena St./Pl. (Honolulu) – A common native variety of banana.
Ihuanu Pl./Way (Mililani) – Name of a wind blowing down from the uplands of Kawela, O'ahu. Literally: cold nose.

Ihoiho

Ihukū St./Pl. (Honolulu, Waiʻanae) – A star. Probably a general term for any guiding star standing (kū) above the bow (ihu) of a canoe.

Ihumoe Pl. (Mililani) – An unidentified star.

Ihupani Pl. (ʻEwa Beach) – Expert, wise person. Literally: closed nose.

ʻĪʻī Pl. (Waipahu) – Sour, rancid, mouldy, musty. Probably named for John Papa ʻĪʻī (1800?-1870), a descendant of high chiefs. The name ʻĪʻī was coined by Liholiho when they were boyhood friends. Guardian of Liholiho. An early Christian convert, he helped missionaries translate texts into Hawaiian. Served Kamehameha III-V. Helped draft the 1852 constitution. Member of House of Nobles, Privy Council, Board of Commission to Quiet Titles, and Supreme Court Justice. His home, Mililani, stood at the present site of the State Judiciary Building. See Mililani. Awarded Waipiʻo, Oʻahu in 1848 Great Mahele.

ʻIʻimi Pl. (ʻEwa Beach) – To seek again and again; one seeking everywhere, as for knowledge.

ʻIʻini Way (ʻAiea) – To desire, crave, yearn for; desire, liking.

ʻIʻiwi St. (Honolulu) – A brilliant orange-red honeycreeper (bird) with prominently curved beak. Its feathers were used extensively in Hawaiian featherwork.

Ikaika Pl. (Mililani) – The planet Jupiter. Literally: strong.

Ikaloa St./Pl. (Mililani) – Section of the Milky Way. Literally: very strong.

Ikawelani Pl. (Mililani) – Should be Ikawaolani: an unidentified star. Literally: in the mountain area (occupied by) gods or high chiefs.

ʻIke Pl. (ʻEwa Beach) – Knowledge, awareness, understanding, recognition, comprehension and hence learning.

Ikea Lp. (Hauʻula) – Definition not known.

Ikeanani Dr. (Kāneʻohe) – Beautiful view.

ʻIkeloa St. (Waipahu) – To know very well, knowledgeable, versed, wise.

ʻIkemaka Pl. (Kailua) – Eyewitness; visible; to see or witness personally.

ʻIkena Pl./Cir. (Honolulu) – View.

ʻIkepono St./Pl. (Waipahu) – To see clearly; to know definitely; certain knowledge.

Iki Pl. (Honolulu) – Small, little.

Ikiiki St. (Kāneʻohe) – Ancient Hawaiian lunar month. Literally: stifling heat and humidity.

Ikūlani St. (ʻEwa Beach) – Highest officer, head, president.

Ikūone Pl. (Waiʻanae) – Treasurer.

Ikuwai Pl./Way (Haleʻiwa) – Visiting place in a grass house, between the sleeping place and the door.

Ilalo St. (Honolulu) – Below, underneath.

Ilaniwai St. (Honolulu) – Definition not known.

ʻIlauhole St. (Waimānalo) – Name of the chief who married Kauholokahiki in the legend of Muliwaiʻōlena. He fetched water from that stream for her to bathe in.

'Iliahi St. (Honolulu) – All kinds of Hawaiian sandalwood, shrubs and trees with fragrant wood, exported to China (1790-1830).

'Ili'āina St./Pl. (Kailua) – A land section smaller than an ahupua'a (land division).

'Ilie'e St./Pl./Way ('Aiea) – Wild plumbago, a native shrub. Its leaves were used medicinally; its sap was used to blacken tattoo marks.

'Ilihau St. (Kailua) – Bark of the hau tree, used for rope and for modern grass skirts.

'Ili'ili Rd. (Wai'anae) – Pebble, small stone, used in dances or kōnane (an ancient Hawaiian game resembling checkers).

'Ilika'a Pl. (Kailua) – Harness.

'Ilikai St. (Kailua) – Surface of the sea.

'Ilikala Pl. (Kailua) – Skin of kala (fish), sometimes stretched over a coconut shell to form the top of the pūniu (knee drum). See Kala.

'Ilikea Pl. (Kailua) – Fair skin, of Hawaiians.

'Ilikūpono St. (Kailua) – A nearly independent 'ili (land section) within an ahupua'a (land division), paying tribute to the king and not to the chief of the ahupua'a. See 'Ili'āina.

Ililani St. (Kailua) – Unexpected rain, from a sunny sky; to rain thus.

'Ilima Dr./Ln./St. (Honolulu, Wahiawā) – Native shrubs with yellow, orange, green, or red flowers. Used for leis. The yellow 'ilima is the flower of O'ahu. See Ala Le'ie.

Ilimalia Lp./Pl. (Kailua) – Should be 'Ilimā'ila: fair skin, of Hawaiians.

'Ilimanō St./Pl. (Kailua) – Skin of shark, used in making heads for temple or hula drums.

'Ilimapapa Pl. (Wai'anae) – A wild form of 'ilima (plant).

Iliohe St. (Kapolei) – Name reported for a green, fresh-water moss.

'Ili'ohu Pl./Way (Hale'iwa) – Wild spiderflower, a lowland weed. Its small, odd, spider-like flowers are white with a purple tinge. Literally: mist skin.

'Ilipilo St. (Kailua) – Smelly skin, said approvingly of industrious farmers.

'Ili'ula Pl. (Mililani) – An unidentified star. Literally: red surface.

'Iliwahī Lp. (Kailua) – A case for a sword or dagger blade; sheath, scabbard.

'Iliwai Dr. (Wahiawā) – Surface, of water; level, flat.

Iluna Pl. (Honolulu) – Upward; above, over, upper.

'Īmaka Pl. (Wahiawā) – Watchtower; lookout, observation point.

'Imiloa St. (Kāne'ohe) – To seek far; distant traveler. Figuratively: one with great knowledge.

'Imina Pl. (Mililani) – Looking, seeking.

'Imipono St./Pl. (Wai'anae) – To seek or strive for righteousness; endeavor.

Imua Pl. (Hau'ula) – Forward; first, foremost.

'Īnana St./Pl. (Mililani) – To come to life or activity; to show liveliness; animated.

'Īnea Pl. ('Aiea) – Hardship, suffering, distress.

'Īnia Pl. (Pearl City) – The pride of India, a shade tree, with small, fragrant, lilac flowers. Its wood was shaped into musical instruments.

'Iniki Pl. (Wai'anae) – To pinch, nip; sharp and piercing, as wind or pangs of love.

Inoa St. (Waimānalo) – Name.

Inoa'ole St. (Waimānalo) – Nameless, without a name.

Inuwai Pl./Way (Honolulu) – Name of a sea breeze. Literally: water drinking.

'Io Ln. (Honolulu) – Hawaiian hawk, said to be a symbol of royalty because it flies to great heights. Found only in Hawai'i Island forests, where it is considered an 'aumakua (family god).

'Ioko'o Pl. (Waipahu) – Young pandanus leaves, white at the base and light green at the apex, as used in fine mats.

'Iolana Pl. (Honolulu) – To soar, poise, as a hawk.

'Iolani Ave. (Honolulu) – Royal hawk. A name of Kamehameha II and IV.

'Iole St./Pl. (Kāne'ohe) – Hawaiian rat; introduced rat, mouse.

'Iomea Pl. (Wahiawā) – A variety of 'io hawk with dark markings. See 'Io.

Ipu

'I'opono Lp. (Kailua) – Blood relative.

'Iosepa St. (Lā'ie) – Joseph. Named for Joseph F. Smith, (1838-1918). He served as a missionary in Hawai'i (1854-1858). President of the Mormon Church (1901-1918). Nephew of Mormon Church founder, Joseph Smith.

'Iouli Pl. (Kāne'ohe) – Dark 'io hawk. See 'Io.

Ipo Pl. (Honolulu) – Sweetheart, lover.

Ipolani St. (Kapolei) – Heavenly sweet heart.

Ipu Pl. ('Aiea) – Watermelon.

Ipu'ai St. (Honolulu) – An edible melon. Literally: edible gourd.

Ipu'ala Lp./Pl. ('Aiea) – Cantaloupe melon. Literally: fragrant gourd.

Ipuhao Pl. (Wahiawā) – Iron pot; kettle or saucepan of any sort, whether glass, aluminum, or enamel. Literally: iron container.

'Īpuka St./Pl. (Kāne'ohe) – Door, entrance, exit, gate.

Ipukula St./Pl. (Honolulu) – The cup of gold, a large climbing shrub.

Ipulei Pl./Way (Honolulu) – Container for leis.

Ipu Lepo Way (Kāne'ohe) – Earthenware pot, clay pot, chamber pot. Literally: dirt container.

Ipupa'i Pl. (Waipahu) – Gourd drum.

Ipupa'i

'Iu'iu St. (Kāne'ohe) – Majestic, lofty, very high; distant, far away; a distant realm of the gods.

Iuka Pl. (Honolulu) – Inland, upland, towards the mountain.

Iupika Pl. (Mililani) – The planet Jupiter.

'Iwa Cir. (Wahiawā) – A native fern with narrow, feather-shaped fronds. Its stems were shaped into hats.

Iwaena St. (Honolulu) – Between, among.

Iwaho Pl. (Honolulu) – Outside, beyond.

'Iwa'iwa St./Pl./Way ('Aiea) – All maiden-hair ferns, popularly grown as ornamental pot plants.

'Iwalani Pl. (Honolulu) – Heavenly frigate bird. A common female name.

Iwi Way (Honolulu) – Bone.

Iwiā Pl. (Hale'iwa) – Jawbone.

Iwilei Rd. (Honolulu) – Collarbone. Named for an O'ahu land section.

Ka'aahi St./Pl. (Honolulu) – Train, locomotive engine. Literally: fire wagon.

Ka'aahi

Ka'a'awa Pk. Ln./Pl./Valley Rd. (Ka'a'awa) – The 'a'awa. 'A'awa: certain wrasse fishes, common on coral reefs. Named for an O'ahu land division.

Ka'a'ei Pl. (Mililani) – An unidentified star.

Kā'aha St. (Honolulu) – Stick or rod with leaves and tapa at one end, held by the priest while sacrificing in the temple. Named for John Ka'aha (1879-1947), a Mo'ili'ili resident, and principal of Kalihi Kai School (1914-1933).

Ka'ahele St./Pl. ('Aiea) – To make a tour, travel about.

Ka'aholo St./Pl. (Waipahu) – To speed ahead, run.

Ka'ahue St. (Honolulu) – To pass by quickly. Named for a Hawai'i Island land area.

Ka'ahumanu St. (Pearl City, 'Aiea) – The bird (feather) cloak. Named for High Chiefess Ka'ahumanu (1768?-1832). Favorite wife of Kamehameha I, and first Kuhina Nui of Hawaiian Kingdom (1819-1832). Led Kamehameha II in breaking religious kapu that separated men and women from eating together, and ordered destruction of heiau and images (1819). Married Kaua'i King Kaumuali'i to improve alliance with Kaua'i (1821). Baptized (1825) after an illness. Banished French Catholic missionaries, and forbade Hawaiians from attending Catholic religious services. Banned public hula dancing (1830). Proclaimed a code of civil laws based on missionary teachings. Held firm reigns of power.

Ka'ahupahau St. ('Ewa Beach) – The shark goddess of 'Ewa.

Kā'ai St. (Honolulu) – Belt, girdle of any kind. Named for original awardee.

Ka'ai'ai St. (Waimānalo) – The dependent.

Ka'aimalū Pl. ('Ewa Beach) – Secret eating place of 'Ewa legend where, a little girl broke a kapu by secretly sharing a fish with her young brother.

Ka'aipū Ave. (Honolulu) – The eating together. Named for an O'ahu land section. One legend says a stone god, Ka'aipū, had two mouths, one in front and one in back of his head. An artifact was dug up in this area. Another legend mentions Queen Kaʻahumanu, who owned a summer home near here. She helped to break the kapu on men and women eating together (1819).

Kaʻaka St./Pl. (Waipahu) – Fellow, chap, person.

Kaʻakaʻaniu St. (Honolulu) – Rolling coconut. Named for a Kauaʻi land division.

Kaʻākau Pl. (ʻAiea) – The north.

Kaʻakina St./Pl. (ʻEwa Beach) – Grandmother of Pukilaka, the tame eel of ʻEwa legend.

Kaʻala Ave./St./Pl./Way (Wahiawā, Honolulu) – Definition not known. The highest Oʻahu mountain (4,040 feet), located in the Waiʻanae range.

Kaʻalaea Lp./Rd. (Haleʻiwa, Kāneʻohe) – The ocherous earth (red-colored mineral soil). Named for an Oʻahu land division.

Kaʻalākei St. (Honolulu) – The proud water-worn stone. Named for an Oʻahu valley.

Kaʻalalo Pl. (Wahiawā) – To sail to leeward. Figuratively: full of lies, underhanded, deceitful.

Kaʻalani Pl. (Honolulu) – Members of the royal court.

Kaʻalawa St. (Haleʻiwa) – The glance. Named for original awardee.

Kaʻalāwai Pl. (Honolulu) – The water basalt (a rock). Named for an Oʻahu land section.

Kaʻaleʻo Pl. (Honolulu) – The tower. Named for an Oʻahu land section.

Kāʻalo St. (ʻAiea) – To pass by, go by.

Kaʻaloa St. (Honolulu) – Much traveled. Named for original awardee, possibly Samuel K. Kaʻaloa (1879-1945), a law office clerk.

Kaʻalolo Pl. (Mililani) – An unidentified star, said to be the guardian star of Niʻihau, probably Hamal.

Kaʻalula Pl. (Honolulu) – Definition not known. Named for a Kauaʻi stream.

Kaʻaluna Pl. (Kāneʻohe) – To sail or turn against the wind. Figuratively: to dominate; overbearing.

Kaʻamāhu Pl. (Honolulu) – Steam-propelled vehicle.

Kaamalio Dr. (Honolulu) – Should be Kāmaʻalio: horseshoe.

Kaʻamea St. (Waipahu) – To change, as the wind or an idea.

Kaʻamilo St./Pl. (ʻAiea) – Definition not known.

Kaʻamoʻoloa Rd. (Waialua) – The long strip of tapa.

Kaʻana St./Pl. (Kapolei) – To divide, share, apportion.

Kaʻanuʻa Pl. (Kailua) – An elevated place; sleep-ing place in a grass house.

Kaʻao Pl. (Waipahu) – Legend, tale, usually fanci-ful; fiction; to tell a fanciful tale.

Kāʻaoʻao Pl. (Kapolei) – Garden patch.

Kaʻaʻōhua Way (Kāneʻohe) – Vehicle carrying passengers for hire, as bus, taxi, stagecoach.

Kaʻaʻōhua

Ka'aoki Pl. (Waipahu) – To finish or complete; to put on the last touches.

Ka'aona Pl. (Mililani) – 1) An unidentified star. 2) An ancient Hawaiian lunar month.

Ka'apeha St. (Mililani) – Large mass of clouds.

Ka'apuna Pl. (Waipahu) – Definition not known.

Ka'apuni Dr. (Kailua) – To make a tour, go around, travel.

Ka'apuni

Ka'au St. (Honolulu) – Forty. Named for an O'ahu crater.

Ka'auiki Pl. (Waimānalo) – Probably should be Keauiki: the small current.

Ka'aumana Pl. (Waimānalo) – Probably should be Keaumana: the powerful current.

Ka'aumoana Pl. (Waimānalo) – Probably should be Keaumoana: the ocean current.

Ka'auwai Pl. (Honolulu) – The ditch. Named for original awardee.

Ka Awakea Pl./Rd. (Kailua) – Should be Ke Awakea: the midday.

Ka'āwela Pl. (Mililani) – A planet, variously identified as Venus, Jupiter, or Mercury. Literally: the hot fire.

Kā'e'e Lp. ('Aiea) – A sea bean, a high-growing vine. Its powdered seeds were used for strong laxative effect, or strung as leis.

Ka'e'ele St./Pl. (Waipahu) – A wind.

Kaekae St. (Mililani) – An unidentified star.

Kā'eke'eke Way (Honolulu) – Bamboo pipes, a musical instrument.

Kaela Pl. (Mililani) – Beam, bar, rail, shelf, railing.

Ka'elekū St. (Honolulu) – The basaltic rock. Named for a Maui land division.

Kā'eleloi Pl. (Honolulu) – Roll, ruffle, of a drum.

Ka'elepulu Dr. (Kailua) – The moist blackness. Named for an O'ahu land section.

Kā'elo Pl. (Mililani) – 1) A star, probably Betelgeuse. 2) An ancient Hawaiian lunar month.

Kaena Ln. (Honolulu) – To boast, brag.

Ka'ena Lp. (Wahiawā) – The heat.

Ka'eolau Way/Pl. (Mililani) – A variety of taro.

Kā'eleloi

Ka'eonui Pl. (Mililani) – A variety of taro.

Kaha St./Pl. (Kailua) – Place.

Kahae Rd. (Hale'iwa) – The flag.

Kaha'ea Pl. ('Aiea) – Cumulus clouds, often colored, considered a sign of rain.

Kāhāhā St. (Honolulu) – To wonder, be surprised, astonished, puzzled. Name of a Great Mahele awardee who received an O'ahu land section in Kalihi.

Kāhai St. (Honolulu) – Belt, girdle of any kind.

Kahae

Kahaikaha'i Pl. (Mililani) – An unidentified star. Literally: going to Kaha'i (an unidentified place, or the name of an ancient navigator).

Kahakai Dr. (Honolulu) – Beach, seashore. Named for an O'ahu land section.

Kahakea St. (Waipahu) – High, inaccessible, as a cliff.

Kahakiki St. (Mililani) – Roaring sound, as of a wind or rushing waters.

Kahakō St./Pl. ('Ewa Beach) – Steep, sheer.

Kahakui St. (Mililani) – Reference mark in writing or printing, to direct attention, as an asterisk.

Kahakuloa Pl. (Honolulu) – The tall lord. Named for a Maui land division.

Kahala Ave. (Honolulu) – The pandanus. See Hala. Named for an O'ahu land section.

Kahalewai

Kahalakua St. (Honolulu) – In back of Kahala.

Kahalewai Pl. (Hale'iwa) – The prison, the jail.

Kahaloa Dr./Pl. (Honolulu) – A kind of fine tapa, used in religious ceremonies, as for divining with pebbles. Named for an O'ahu land section.

Kahana St. (Kahuku) – Name of a former Kahuku Plantation employee.

Kahana St. (Wahiawā) – Definition not known.

Ka-Hanahou Cir./Pl. (Kāne'ohe) – The remaking. Abbreviation of Kalokohanahou: the repaired pond. A former Kāne'ohe fishpond.

Kahanu St. (Honolulu) – The breath. Possibly named for William Kahanu, a blacksmith employed at the Wright Carriage Company.

Kahanui St. (Mililani) – A Moloka'i land section. Literally: large place.

Kahaone Lp./Pl. (Waialua) – Sandy beach.

Kahapili St. ('Aiea) – Tangent of a circle. Literally: line that touches.

Kahau St. (Wai'anae) – The hau (tree). See Hau.

Kahauiki St./Pl. (Honolulu) – The small hau (tree). Named for an O'ahu land division.

Kahauloa Pl. (Honolulu) – The tall hau (tree). Named for Hawai'i Island land divisions.

Kahauola St. (Hale'iwa) – 1) The dew (of) life. 2) The life sacrifice.

Kahawai St. (Honolulu) – Stream, river; wet or dry ravine.

Kahawalu Dr. (Honolulu) – Eight marks. Named for Mrs. Phoebe Kahawalu Dowsett Raymond. See Kimopelekane.

Kāhea St. (Kapolei) – To call, cry out, invoke, greet, name.

Kaheaka Rd. (Waialua) – Definition not known. Named for an O'ahu land section.

Kāheka St. (Honolulu) – Pool, especially a rock basin where the sea washes in through an opening, and salt forms.

Kahekili Hwy. (Kāne'ohe) – The thunder. Named for Chief Kahekili (1737?-1794), ruler of Maui and O'ahu. One entire

Kāhea

side of his body was tattooed from head to toe. After conquering Oʻahu (1780s), he killed most of the Oʻahu chiefs. He fought Kamehameha in an historic but indecisive sea battle near Waipiʻo, Hawaiʻi Island (1791). It was the first time two opposing forces used cannon in Hawaiian canoes.

Kāhela St./Pl. (Mililani) – An unidentified star.

Kahelu

Kāhele St./Pl. (Mililani) – Decoration for a journey, as with a lei.

Kahelu Ave. (Wahiawā) – Computer, computing.

Kahema Pl. (ʻAiea) – The south.

Kahena St./Pl. (Honolulu) – Flowing, trickling.

Kahewai Pl. (Honolulu) – Flowing (of) water.

Kahiau Lp. (Honolulu) – To give generously or lavishly with the heart, and not with the expectation of return.

Kahiki Pl. (Waipahu) – Tahiti; any foreign country.

Kahikinui Ct./Pl. (Mililani) – An unidentified star, reputedly named for one of the eight rowers of Hawaiʻi Loa, discoverer of Hawaiʻi. Literally: great Tahiti.

Kahiau

Kahiko St. (Kāneʻohe) – Old, ancient.

Kahikole Pl. (Hauʻula) – To have lost the red glow of dawn.

Kahikolu Pl./Way (Honolulu) – Trinity, three in one.

Kahiku Pl. (Mililani) – An unidentified star.

Kāhili St./Pl. (Kailua) – Feather standard, symbolic of royalty.

Kahilinaʻi Pl. (ʻAiea) – The trust, the confidence.

Kahimoe St./Pl. (Waipahu) – Place to sleep, bed, cot.

Kahinani Pl./Way (Kāneʻohe) – The beautiful place.

Kāhinu St. (Honolulu) – To anoint; to rub with oil, grease, vaseline.

Kahiʻukā St. (ʻEwa Beach) – A shark god whose duty was to warn the people of ʻEwa of the presence of strange and unfriendly sharks.

Kāhili

Kāhiwa Pl. (Honolulu) – Dark pupil, of the eye. Named for original grantee.

Kahiwelolā St. (Waiʻanae) – Where the sun sets.

Kahoa Dr. (Kailua) – The companion.

Kahoaloha Ln. (Honolulu) – The friend.

Kahoʻea St. (Mililani) – An unidentified star.

Kaholi Pl. (ʻAiea) – The sprout. Named for an Oʻahu land section.

Kāholo St./Pl. (Mililani) – An unidentified star.

Kāhonua St. (Mililani) – Globe of the earth.

Kāhonua

Kahoʻolawe St. (Wahiawā) – The carrying away (by currents). Named for the island.

Kahowaʻa Pl. (Kāneʻohe) – Definition not known. Named for an Oʻahu land section.

Kahu St. (Waipahu) – Honored attendant, guardian, nurse, keeper, administrator; pastor of a church.

Kahua Pl. (ʻAiea) – The fruit.

Kahuahale St. (Waipahu) – House foundation or site.

Kahuahele St. (Waipahu) – Moving platform.

Kahuailani St. (Waipahu) – Site in heaven.

Kahuʻāina St. (Waipahu) – Headman of a land section.

Kahualeʻa St. (Mililani) – Playground.

Kahualei Pl. (Waipahu) – Lei foundation.

Kahualena St./Pl. (Waipahu) – 1) Yellow foundation. 2) The yellow fruit.

Kahualiʻi St. (Waipahu) – Royal guardian in the family of a high chief.

Kahualoa St./Pl. (Waipahu) – Long foundation.

Kahuamo St./Pl. (Waipahu) – Definition not known.

Kahuamoku St./Pl. (Waipahu) – Island foundation.

Kahuanani St./Pl. (Waipahu) – Beautiful site.

Kahuanui St. (Waipahu) – Large foundation.

Kahuapaʻa St./Pl. (Waipahu) – Solid earth. Figuratively: security.

Kahuapāʻani St. (ʻAiea) – Stadium; playground of any kind. Literally: site (for) play. (Aloha Stadium is located here).

Kahuapili St. (Waipahu) – Pili foundation. Pili: lining of a quilt under the layer of cotton or wool.

Kahuawai St. (Waipahu) – The water gourd. Named for an Oʻahu land section.

Kahue Pl. (Waipahu) – The gourd.

Kahuhipa St. (Kāneʻohe) – Shepherd; to tend sheep.

Kahui St. (Waialua) – The club, the society. Named for original grantee.

Kahuku Airport Rd. (Kahuku) – The projection. Named for an Oʻahu land division.

Kāhuli St. (Waipahu) – Land shells.

Kahuliali'i St. (Mililani) – An unidentified star. Literally: to overthrow royalty.

Kahulio Pl. (Waipahu) – Coachman, groom. Literally: horse tender.

Kahului St. (Honolulu) – The winning. Named for a Maui town.

Kahuna Ln. (Honolulu) – Priest, minister, sorcerer, expert in any profession.

Kahuwai Pl. (Honolulu) – Water tender. Named for a Hawaiʻi Island bay or land division.

Kaiʻa St. (Honolulu) – The fish. Named for original awardee.

Kahuawai

Kahuhipa

Ka'iahea St. (Mililani) – To resound from a distance.

Kaiaka St. (Hale'iwa) – Shadowed sea. Named for an O'ahu bay.

Kaiakua St. ('Ewa Beach) – Raging sea so dangerous that man can't survive. Literally: supernatural sea.

Kaiali'i Pl. (Honolulu) – Hard type of rock, used for adzes.

Kai'ali'u St. (Honolulu) – The salted fish.

Kai'ama Pl. (Honolulu) – Mullet sea. Named for an O'ahu land section.

Kaiāmū St. (Waipahu) – To sit in silence, as at a meeting.

Kai 'Anae St. ('Ewa Beach) – Ocean area where the 'anae fish is found.

Kaiao St./Pl. (Waipahu) – Dawn.

Kaiapo St. ('Ewa Beach) – Rising or high tide. Literally: encircling sea.

Kaiau Ave. (Kapolei) – Sea where a moving current is visible.

Kaiāulu St./Pl. (Kapolei) – A pleasant, gentle tradewind breeze, at Wai'anae, O'ahu, famous in song.

Ka'īawe St. (Mililani) – To move slowly along.

Kaiea Pl. (Waialua) – Rising tide; sea washing higher on land than usual. Literally: rising sea.

Kaie'e St. ('Ewa Beach) – Tidal wave. Literally: mounting sea.

Kāī'ele'ele St./Pl. ('Ewa Beach) – One of three types of kāī taro for which 'Ewa was well known, this one being the black kāī taro.

Kaiemi St. (Kailua) – Ebbing sea. Literally: decreasing sea.

Kaiewa St. (Waipahu) – To take life philosophically as it comes, sometimes in poverty, sometimes in wealth.

Kaihānupa St. ('Ewa Beach) – Choppy sea.

Kaihāwanawana St. ('Ewa Beach) – Whispering sea.

Kaihe'e St. (Honolulu) – Receding sea or wave.

Kaihe'enalu St. ('Ewa Beach) – Sea for surfing.

Kaihī St. ('Ewa Beach) – Flowing sea, especially one that goes through a channel gate into fish ponds.

Ka'ihikapu St. (Honolulu) – The kapu sacredness. Named for the former Moanalua fishpond.

Kaihe'enalu

Kaihohonu St. ('Ewa Beach) – Deep sea, high tide.

Kaiho'i St. ('Ewa Beach) – Ebbing sea. Literally: returning sea.

Kaiholena Pl. (Waipahu) – Hill behind Pākua on Hawai'i Island. The local rain god Kūmauna had a field of ihohena bananas here.

Kaiholo St. (Kailua) – Rim among sea or current.

Kaiholu St./Pl. (Kailua) – Rippling sea.

Kaihone Way (Kailua) – Softly sounding sea.

Kaiho'olulu St. (Wai'anae) – Calm, quiet sea.

Kaihuopala'ai St. ('Ewa Beach) – Hawaiian name for the West Loch of Pearl Harbor.

Kai'ikuwā St. ('Ewa Beach) – Roaring sea.

Kaikā Pl. (Haleʻiwa) – Cultivated patch; bank of taro patch.

Kaikaina St. (Kailua) – Younger sibling or cousin of the same sex.

Kaikala St. (ʻEwa Beach) – Ocean where the kala fish is found.

Kaikāne St. (ʻEwa Beach) – Strong sea. Literally: male sea.

Kaikauhaʻa St. (ʻEwa Beach) – Dancing or undulating sea.

Kaikea Pl. (Kailua) – White sea foam, especially as washed up on a beach.

Kai Kekuma St. (Kapolei) – Ocean area where the kukuma crab is found.

Kaikī St. (Waipahu) – Tide beginning to flow in. Literally: shooting sea.

Kaikō St. (ʻEwa Beach) – Sea with a strong current.

Kaikoʻele St. (ʻEwa Beach) – Sea too shallow to float a canoe but good for seeking shellfish. Literally: thumping sea, because the canoe thumps the coral.

Kaikohola St. (ʻEwa Beach) – Shallow sea within the reef, lagoon. Literally: reef sea.

Kāīkoi Pl. (ʻEwa Beach) – One of three types of kāī taro for which ʻEwa was well known, this one being the most favored and delicious.

Kaikoʻo Pl. (Honolulu) – Rough, strong sea. Name of the former home of Helen Carter (1866-1945), wife of Territorial Governor George Carter (1903-1907). A convalescent home for World War II soldiers. The estate has been subdivided.

Kaikua Pl. (Waipahu) – Countryman.

Kaikuahine St. (Honolulu) – Sister or female cousin of a male.

Kaikunāne Lp. (Honolulu) – Brother or male cousin of a female.

Kaikūʻono Pl. (Honolulu) – Inlet, gulf, bay.

Kaila Pl. (Waipahu) – Style, stylish.

Kaileoleʻa Dr. (ʻEwa Beach) – Sweet-voiced or echoing sea.

Kaileonui St. (Kapolei) – Loud-voiced sea.

Kaʻilewa St. (Mililani) – To carry or go to and fro.

Kāʻili St. (Honolulu) – To snatch, grab, take by force. Named for Emma Kāʻili Metcalf Beckley Nakuina. Kāʻili is her Hawaiian name. See Nakuina.

Kaʻilike St./Pl. (ʻEwa Beach) – To march in step or proceed in unity, as soldiers.

Kaʻilianu St. (Waipahu) – The cold skin.

Kaʻilihao St. (Waipahu) – The iron skin.

Kaʻīlio St. (Waipahu) – The dog.

Kaʻīlio

Kailiʻu Pl. (Honolulu) – Salty sea. Named for a Kauaʻi promontory. Also called Lae o Kailiʻu.

Kaʻiliʻula Lp./Pl. (Mililani) – An unidentified star, the guardian star of Kaʻū, Hawaiʻi Island. Literally: the red surface.

Kaʻiliwai Pl. (Kāneʻohe) – The (carpenter's or surveyor's) level.

Kailoa St. (ʻEwa Beach) – Distant Sea.

Kailua Rd. (Kailua) – Two seas. An Oʻahu land division named for Kawainui and Kaʻelepulu, two fishponds that used to be lagoons open to the sea.

Kailuana Lp./Pl. (Kailua) – Sea (of) comfort and ease.

Kailulu Way (Kailua) – Calm sea.

Kaima Pl. (Waipahu) – Thyme, a small plant in the Mint family. It adds flavor to food.

Kaimakani St. (ʻAiea) – Windy sea.

Kaimake Lp. (Kailua) – Low tide.

Kaimālie St. (ʻEwa Beach) – Calm sea.

Kaimalino St./Pl. (Kailua) – Calm sea.

Kaimalolo Pl. (Kāneʻohe) – Quiet sea, as in a calm cove.

Kaimaloʻo St. (Kāneʻohe) – An extreme low tide with reef exposed. Literally: dry sea.

Kaimalu Pl./Way (Kāneʻohe) – Peaceful sea.

Kaimanahila St. (Honolulu) – Diamond Head. Literally: diamond hill. A crater (760 feet). Hawaiians called it Lēʻahi because its silhouette resembles the ʻahi (tuna) profile. 19th Century British sailors believed volcanic crystals found there were diamonds.

Kaimanawai Pl. (Honolulu) – Depressed sea.

Kaimanu Pl. (Waialua) – Salty sea.

Kaʻimi St. (Kailua) – The seeking. Named for an Oʻahu land section.

Kaʻimi Way (Honolulu) – A kind of Spanish clover.

Kaimoani Way (Kailua) – Fragrance of the sea borne on the breeze.

Kaimoku Pl./Way (Honolulu) – Turning of the tide when it begins to recede. Literally: cut sea.

Kaimū Lp. (ʻAiea) – Gathering (at the) sea. Named for a Hawaiʻi Island land division.

Kaimukī Ave./Pl. (Honolulu) – The tī oven. Named for an Oʻahu land section.

Kaimuohema Pl. (Honolulu) – Should be Kaimuohena: the oven of Hena. Named for an Oʻahu land section.

Kaina St. (Honolulu) – Definition not known. Possibly a family name or a Hawaiianization of the Biblical name, Cain.

Kainalu Dr. (Kailua) – Billowy sea, rolling sea. Named for original awardee.

Kai Nani Pl. (Kailua) – Beautiful sea.

Kainapau Pl. (Honolulu) – Definition not known. Named for original awardee.

Kainehe St. (Kailua) – Whispering sea.

Ka'iniki St. (Hale'iwa) – The pinch. Named for original awardee.

Kainoa Pl. (Honolulu) – The name.

Kainui Dr./Pl. (Kailua) – High tide, big sea.

Kaio'e Pl. (Waialua) – An unidentified plant, mentioned in poetry. Named for original grantee.

Kai'ōhe'e St. ('Ewa Beach) – Sea for octopus fishing.

Kai'ōlena Dr. (Kailua) – 1) Water of purification composed of sea water (kai). 2) Water with salt and 'ōlena (turmeric ginger plant) root; to purify thus.

Kai'ōlino Way (Kailua) – Sparkling sea.

Kaiolohia Pl./Way (Honolulu) – Tranquil sea. Figuratively: peace of mind. Named for a Lāna'i bay.

Kai'olu St. (Honolulu) – Cool ocean.

Kai One Pl. (Kailua) – Sandy sea.

Kaio'o Dr. (Honolulu) – Strong sea.

Kai'ōpua St. ('Ewa Beach) – Sea with clouds on the horizon.

Kaipalaoa St. (Kapolei) – Ocean where the sperm whale is found.

Kaipāpa'u St./Lp. (Hau'ula) – Shallow sea. Named for an O'ahu land division.

Kaipiha St. (Kailua) – High tide, high sea, full sea, spring tide.

Kaipi'i St. (Kailua) – High or rising tide.

Kaipū St. ('Ewa Beach) – Sea where currents meet.

Kaipuha'a Pl. (Honolulu) – The low calabash. Named for a Hawai'i Island land division.

Kaipuhinehu St. (Kapolei) – Sea that blows in nehu (anchovy) fish.

Ka'ipu'u St. (Honolulu) – Division, portion; to divide into portions or heaps.

Ka'iulani Ave. (Honolulu) – The royal sacred one. Named for Princess Ka'iulani (1875-1899). Part-Hawaiian daughter of Governor Archibald Cleghorn and Princess Miriam Likelike. When age 5 (1881), King Kalākaua, on a world tour, suggested to Japan's Emperor that she marry a Japanese prince for a royal alliance (possibly to discourage U.S. efforts to dominate Hawaii). Educated in England, she spoke several languages. Queen Lili'uokalani named her heir to throne (1891). Pleaded with U.S. President Grover Cleveland in Washington, D.C. for monarchy restoration. Her family estate, 'Āinahau, was located here.

Kai Wana St. (Kapolei) – Ocean area where the wana sea urchin is found.

Kaiwi Rd. (Honolulu) – The bone. Named for an O'ahu land section.

Kaiwiki Pl. (Honolulu) – Quick sea. Named for a Hawai'i Island land division.

Kaiwiʻula St. (Honolulu) – The red bone. Named for an
O'ahu land section.

Kākaʻe Pl. (Mililani) – An unidentified star.

Kakahi St. (Waipahu) – Solitary, unique, outstanding.

Kakahiaka St. (Kailua) – Morning.

Kakaiāpola St. (Waiʻanae) – Tail of a kite.

Kākāili Pl. (Mililani) – An unidentified star.

Kakaʻina St./Pl. (Waimānalo) – Sequence.

Kakaiāpola

Kakalena St. (Waiʻanae) – Catherine. Usually: Kakalina.

Kakapa Pl. (Honolulu) – Border. Named for a Hawai'i Island bay.

Kākea Lp. (Wahiawā) – Name of a stormy wind.

Kākela Dr./Pl. (Honolulu) – Castle. Named for
George Castle (1851-1932). Son of American
missionary, Samuel Castle (1808-1894) who
founded Castle and Cooke (1851), and lived
nearby. C&C president (1903-1916). Member
of Honolulu Rifles and Citizens Guard which
overthrew Hawai'i monarchy (1893).

Kākela

Kākela Iki Pl. (Honolulu) – Little Castle. See Kākela.

Kākipi Pl. (Kahuku) – Poi made with an inferior grade of soggy taro.

Kakiwa Pl. (Honolulu) – Should be Kākīwai: definition not known. Named
for a Hawai'i Island coastal area.

Kākoʻi St. (Honolulu) – To make adzes; adze maker.

Kākoʻo Pl. (Kapolei) – To uphold, support, assist.

Kākū St. (Kāneʻohe) – The barracuda, a deep sea fish.

Kākuhihewa St./Pl. (Kapolei) – Famous chief of Oʻahu.

Kala Pl. (Honolulu) – Surgeon fish, a horned brownish fish. Its tough
scaleless skin was used for making small coconut-shell knee drums.

Kālāʻau Pl. (Honolulu) – Stick dancing; to stick dance.

Kālaʻe St. (Waipahu) – Clear, calm, unclouded. Named for a Molokaʻi land
area.

Kālau Pl. (Waimānalo) – To thatch the inside of the house with leaves,
especially pandanus leaves. Literally: knot leaf.

Kalaeloa Blvd. (Kapolei) – The long point. Named for an Oʻahu promontory called Barber's Point.

Kalaepaʻa Dr. (Honolulu) – The solid promontory. Named for an Oʻahu
land section.

Kalaepōhaku St./Pl. (Honolulu) – The stone promontory. Named for an
Oʻahu land section and mountain ridge.

Kalāheo Ave. (Kailua) – The proud day. Named for an Oʻahu land section.

Kalāhū Pl. (Honolulu) – The overflowing sun. Named for a Kauaʻi
mountain peak.

Kālai Pl. (Pearl City) – To carve, cut, hew, engrave; to divide, as land.

Kalaiaha Pl. (Waipahu) – Name of a bird.

Kalaʻikū St. (Waipahu) – The great calm.

Kalaimoku St. (Honolulu) – Literally: the island chief. Short for Kalanimoku. Named for High Chief Kalanimoku (1769?-1827). Prime Minister to Kamehameha I and Premier to Kaʻahumanu. He adopted the nickname "Billy Pitt" after the famous British Prime Minister William Pitt. Proposed adopting the Ten Commandments as a written legal code for Hawaiʻi.

Kalainanea St. (Haleʻiwa) – Short for Kalaninanea: the reposing chief.

Kalaʻiʻōpua Pl. (Honolulu) – The peace (of the) horizon cloud. Pen name King Kalākaua used to sign his songs.

Kalaiwa Way (Honolulu) – Driver, chauffeur.

Kalaka Pl. (Kailua) – Clark.

Kalākaua Ave. (Honolulu) – The day (of) battle. Named for King Kalākaua (1836-1891). Last king of Hawaiʻi (1874-1891). Lost election in the legislature for king to Lunalilo (1872). Elected monarch (1874), defeating Queen Emma, widow of Kamehameha IV. His election resulted in a violent protest. Nicknamed "merry monarch." Signed Reciprocity Treaties with U.S., allowing unrefined sugar and rice into U.S. tax-free (1875), and ceding Pearl Harbor to U.S. (1887). First monarch to visit U.S. (1874) and to make a world tour (1881). Wrote words to song, "Hawaiʻi Ponoʻi" (1874). Tried to restore Hawaiian culture, music, and hula. Dreamed of leading a Polynesian confederation. Under threat of violence, he signed "Bayonet Constitution" (1887), removing much of monarch's political power. See Kaʻiulani.

Kalakua St. (Honolulu) – Long ago. Named for Chiefess Kalakua (1780-1842). Wife of Kamehameha I, and later, of Maui Governor Hoapili. Mother of Kīnaʻu and Kamāmalu, grandmother of Lunalilo, and sister of Kaʻahumanu. See Kekāuluohi.

Kalālā St. (Wahiawā) – The branch.

Kalālani Pl. (Mililani) – An unidentified star. Literally: the row.

Kalalau St./Pl. (Honolulu) – The straying. Named for a Kauaʻi land division.

Kalalea St./Pl. (Honolulu) – Prominent. Named for a Kauaʻi mountain peak.

Kalalī Pl./Lp./St. (Kāneʻohe, Honolulu) – To go quickly, briskly, without noticing anyone; to walk or talk in a brisk, haughty way; proud.

Kalaloa St. (ʻAiea) – A variety of ʻalaʻihi, bright-red squirrelfishes. Literally: long cartilage.

Kalama St. (Honolulu, Kailua) – The lama (tree). Named for Harriet Kahakaleleponi (1817-1870). The longest reigning Hawaiian queen (1837-1854) wife of Kamehameha III. Born to a lesser royalty rank, some aliʻi looked down at her. She managed a sugar plantation in Kāneʻohe, possessed shrewd business sense, and became wealthy. Received Kailua in the 1848 Great Mahele.

Kalamakū St. (Honolulu) – The upright torch. Possibly named for a family of early Hawaiian Homelands residents at Papakōlea.

Kalamālō Pl. (Kāneʻohe) – An unidentified grass.

Kalamana Ct. (Wahiawā) – Should be Kalamona: three shrubs, with greenish-yellow, orange-yellow, and yellow flowers.

Kalapu

Kalama Pāka Pl. (Honolulu) – Kalama Park.

Kalamoho Pl. (ʻAiea) – Cliffbrake, a short slender American fern.

Kalani St. (Honolulu) – The chief. Reputedly named for David Kalani, a pilot who helped guide steamships into the harbor.

Kalania Pl. (Honolulu) – Smooth, as the sea.

Kalanialiʻi St. (Honolulu) – The royal chief.

Kalanianaʻole Hwy. (Oʻahu) – The chief (of) incomparably (high rank). Named for Prince Jonah Kūhiō Kalanianaʻole (1871-1922). Named heir to throne by uncle, King Kalākaua. Jailed one year for role in 1895 counterrevolution to restore monarchy. Agreed to a political alliance with Republican businessmen to provide jobs and land for Hawaiians. Hawaiʻi's Congressional Delegate (1902-1922). Advocated creating county governments (1905) to break up central government rule. Authored first federal bill for Hawaiʻi statehood (1919), and U.S. law creating the Hawaiian Homes Commission (1921).

Kalau

Kalaniiki St./Pl. (Honolulu) – The minor chief.

Kalanikai Pl. (Honolulu) – Seaward Kalani.

Kalanipuʻu St./Pl. (Honolulu) – The royal hill. Named for a Kauaʻi hill.

Kalaniuka Cir./St./Pl./Way (Honolulu) – Inland Kalani.

Kalaniwai Pl. (Honolulu) – Freshwater Kalani.

Kalapakī St./Pl. (Honolulu) – The tī ridge. Named for a Kauaʻi beach.

Kalapu St. (ʻEwa Beach) – The ghost.

Kalau St./Pl (Waimānalo) – The leaf.

Kalāua Pl. (Kāneʻohe) – The rainy day.

Kalauipo St./Pl. (Pearl City) – An unidentified moss, found in water.

Kalaunu St. (Honolulu) – Crown.

Kalauokalani Way (Honolulu) – The multitude of the royal chief. Named for David Kalauokalani Jr. (1874-1936). Honolulu City Clerk (1905-1933).

Kalāwahine Pl. (Honolulu) – The day (of) women. Possibly the name of a god who protected the fresh-water springs. Named for an Oʻahu land section.

Kalaunu

Kalawai Pl. (Kailua) – To surround, go around

Kalawao St./Pl. (Honolulu) – Definition not known.

Kalawina Pl. ('Aiea) – Calvin; Calvinistic.
Kale Pl. (Honolulu) – Charles.
Kalehua St. (Honolulu) – The 'ōhi'a (tree) blossom. Named
for an O'ahu land section.

Kalehuna St. (Kapolei) – Son of Kākuhihewa.
Kalei Rd. (Honolulu) – The lei.
Kaleikini Way (Honolulu) – The many leis. Kaleikini or
Kalaikini was a demigod that many Hawaiian blowholes
are attributed to. This street name refers to Hālona
blowhole.
Kaleilani St./Pl. (Pearl City) – The heavenly lei, the royal lei.   **Kalei**
Kaleimamahū St. (Honolulu) – Short for Kalanimamahū: the
peaceful chief. See Kekāuluohi.
Kaleinani St. (Honolulu) – The beautiful lei.
Kaleiokalani St. (Honolulu) – The chief's lei.
Kaleiwohi St. (Wai'anae) – First name of Princess Kahanu's father,
Kaleiwohi Ka'auwai.
Kalele Rd. (Honolulu) – The altar.
Kalemakapi'i St. (Kapolei) – A variety of moss.
Kalena Dr. (Honolulu) – Glen.
Kalena St. (Wahiawā) – The lazy one. Named for an O'ahu land section.
Kalenakai Pl. (Kāne'ohe) – Seaward Kalena. Perhaps named for a song.
Kaleo Pl./Way (Kapolei) – The voice.
Kalepa St./Pl. (Honolulu) – 1) The flag. 2) Caleb.
Kalewa St. (Honolulu) – The sky.
Kalia Rd. (Honolulu) – A native Hawaiian tree found in O'ahu and Kaua'i
rain forests. Its bark was shaped into rope; its branches were used for
grass houses. Named for an O'ahu land section.
Kaliawa St. (Honolulu) – Definition not known. Named for an O'ahu land
section.
Kalie St./Pl. (Wahiawā) – Definition not known.
Kalihi St. (Honolulu) – The edge; the boundary. Named for an O'ahu land
division.
Kalihiwai Pl. (Honolulu) – Kalihi (with a) stream. Named
for a Kaua'i land division.
Kalike Pl. ('Aiea) – The similarity.
Kalikimaka St. (Honolulu) – Christmas.
Kaliko Dr. (Wahiawā) – The leaf bud; the newly opened leaf.

Kalili Pl. (Honolulu) – The jealousy. Probably a family name.
Kalimaloa St. (Kāne'ohe) – The long arm. Named for an
O'ahu land section.
Kālina Pl. (Honolulu) – Long vine, of a sweet potato.
Kaliponi Dr./St./Pl. (Honolulu, Wahiawā) – California.   **Kaliponi**
Usually: Kaleponi.

Kali'unā St. (Waialua) − Perhaps: the twilight. Named for original grantee.

Kalo Pl. (Honolulu) − Taro, a perennial herb. It grows in irrigated patches or on dry land. The staple food of Hawaiians from ancient times. The stem base is pounded into poi, and the leaves are cooked as lū'au.

Kalo

Kāloa Way (Honolulu) − Names of three nights in the ancient Hawaiian lunar month, sacred to the god Kanaloa.

Kalo'alo'a St. (Honolulu) − The pits. Named for a Hawai'i Island mountain peak.

Kalo'aluiki St./Pl. (Honolulu) − Taro (in a) small depression. Reputedly the name of a taro patch god. Probably should be Kolowaluiki: small Kolowalu. See Kolowalu. Named for an O'ahu land section.

Kāloapau St. (Mililani) − The 26th day of the ancient Hawaiian month. Literally: last Kaloa.

Kalohelani Pl. (Honolulu) − 1) The royal news. 2) Royal rascal. A poetic name of Victoria Kamāmalu (1838-1866). Sister of King Kamehameha IV and V. Daughter of Kīna'u. Granddaughter of Kamehameha I. Kuhina Nui (1855-1863). Founder of Ka'ahumanu Society to aid elderly and ill Hawaiians. Granted all of Maunalua (site of Hawai'i Kai) in 1848 Great Mahele.

Kalo'i St./Pl. ('Ewa Beach) − A spring in 'Ewa. Literally: the taro patch.

Kaloko Ln. (Honolulu) − The pond.

Kaloli Lp./Pl. (Waipahu) − Point on Hawai'i Island.

Kalolina St./Pl. (Kailua) − Caroline. Usually: Kalolaina.

Kalonaiki Walk (Haka Dr.) (Honolulu) − The small canoe supporting block. Named for an O'ahu chief who lived 12 generations before Kamehameha. See Haka.

Kalōpā St. (Honolulu) − The tenant farmer. Named for a Hawai'i Island land division.

Kalou St. (Waipahu) − The hook.

Kalua Rd./Pl. (Honolulu) − The pit. Named for original awardee.

Kalua'ā Pl. (Honolulu) − The fiery pit. Named for a Kaua'i stream.

Kaluamoi Dr./Pl. (Pearl City) − Definition not known. Named for an O'ahu land section.

Kaluamo'o St. (Kailua) − The lizard pit.

Kaluanui Rd./Pl./Way (Honolulu) − The big pit. Named for an O'ahu mountain ridge.

Kaluaopalena St. (Honolulu) − The pit of Palena. See Palena. Named for an O'ahu land section.

Kaluawa'a St. (Honolulu) − The furrow. Named for original awardee.

Kaluhea St. (Wahiawā) – Fragrant.

Kaluhia Pl. (Haleʻiwa) – The luhia (shark). Named for original awardee.

Kaluhia

Kaluhikai Ln. (Honolulu) – The sea fatigue.

Kalukalu St. (Waipahu) – An unidentified fern, somewhat like the palapalai (a native fern).

Kāluli St. (Kailua) – To sway, bend.

Kalulu Lp. (Waipahu) – Shelter.

Kama Ln. (Honolulu) – Child. Named for original awardee.

Kamaʻaha Ave./Lp. (Kapolei) – To tie sennit, to bind securely, to form a loop to support a netted calabash; the loop itself; a belt.

Kamaʻāina Dr./Pl. (Honolulu) – Native-born, one born in a place, host. Literally: child (of) land.

Kamaehu St./Pl. (ʻEwa Beach) – Strength, energy, firmness of resolution, fixedness of purpose.

Kamāhana Pl. (Mililani) – The constellation Gemini. Literally: the twins.

Kamaka

Kamahaʻo St./Pl. (Pearl City) – Wonderful, astonishing, surprising, remarkable.

Kamahele St./Pl. (Kailua) – A far-reaching, strong or heavy branch, the main branch.

Kamahoi St. (ʻEwa Beach) – Wonderful, marvelous, splendid; delighted.

Kamaile St. (Honolulu) – The maile (vine).

Kamaileʻunu St. (Waiʻanae) – The stripped maile (vine). Named for an Oʻahu mountain ridge and peak (1,312 feet).

Kamaʻilio St. (ʻEwa Beach) – To talk, converse.

Kamaʻiʻo St./Pl. (Mililani) – An unidentified star.

Kamaka Pl. (Kāneʻohe) – The eye.

Kamaka Ln. (Honolulu) – The eye. Named for original awardee.

Kamakaʻaulani Pl. (ʻEwa Beach) – Brother of Kapaʻahulani, who collaborated with him in a scheme which made Kūaliʻi king over all the islands.

Kāmakahala St. (Waialua) – Native shrubs and trees growing in damp, shady forests.

Kamakahi St. (Honolulu, Waipahu) – Only child, single child.

Kamakani

Kamakani Pl. (Honolulu) – The wind.

Kamakeʻe St. (Honolulu) – The desire. Wife of Jonah Piʻikoi. See Piʻikoi. Named for original awardee.

Kamakini St. (Honolulu) – To impose a general kapu. Literally: to tie the multitude.

Kāmākoi Rd./Pl. (Kāneʻohe) – To fish with a pole.

Kāmala Lp. (Honolulu) – Hut. Named for a Kauaʻi promontory.

Kamālalehua Pl. (Honolulu) – Julia Kamalaleha Haʻalehua, the only child of Levi Haʻalehua. Died August 8, 1856.

Kamalani Pl. (Kāneʻohe) – Child of a chief; a petted child. Figuratively: finicky, fussy.

Kamalei St. (Mililani) – An unidentified star. Literally: beloved child.

Kamaliʻi St. (Honolulu) – Children.

Kamalino St. (Mililani) – A sweet pot.

Kamalō St. (Waipahu) – Short for Kamaloʻo: the dry place. Named for a Molokaʻi land division.

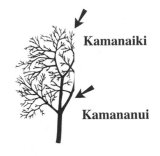

Kamanaiki

Kamananui

Kamāmalu Ave. (Honolulu) – Short for Kamehamalu: protection (of) Kamehameha.

Kamanaiki St. (Honolulu) – The small branch. Named for an Oʻahu stream.

Kamananui Rd. (Wahiawā) – The large branch. Named for an Oʻahu land division.

Kamanaʻoʻiʻo Pl. (Waimānalo) – The faith.

Kamani Ln./St./Pl. (Haleʻiwa, Honolulu) – A large tree with white flowers much like orange blossoms, fragrant when fresh. Its hard, tough wood was shaped into calabashes.

Kamani Kai Pl. (Kailua) – Kamani trees (along the ocean).

Kamaʻole St. (Honolulu) – Childless. Named for a Maui land division.

Kamaʻomaʻo Pl. (Honolulu) – The greenness. Named for a Maui plain.

Kāmau Pl. (Kāneʻohe) – To keep on, continue, persevere.

Kamehame Dr./Pl. (Honolulu) – The hame (tree). Named for an Oʻahu mountain ridge.

Kamehameha Ave./Hwy. (Oʻahu) – The lonely one. Named for King Kamehameha (1758-1819). He built and rebuilt Hawaii Island heiau for spiritual strength to conquer the Hawaiian islands. Used foreign advisors and cannons to win military victories. Conquered all islands through military victories, except Kauaʻi and Niʻihau, which he unified via treaty (1810). First Hawaiian monarch (1795-1819). Upheld traditional kapu separating men and women from eating together, and restricting women from eating certain foods. Proclaimed "Law of the Splintered Paddle" to protect the aged, children, and women (1783).

Kamehameha

Kamehameha IV Rd. (Honolulu) – The lonely one. Named for Alexander Liholiho (1834-1863), crowned King Kamehameha IV (1854-1863). Feared American takeover from U.S. "manifest destiny." He favored British advisors. Supported building Queen's Hospital, named after wife, Queen Emma, to help sick Hawaiian's dying of foreign diseases.

Kamenani St. (Honolulu) – Perhaps should be Kameanani: the beautiful thing.

Kamiki St. (Waipahu) – Ridge on eastern Lāna'i.

Kamila St. (Honolulu) – Camellia (flower).

Kamilo St. (Honolulu) – The milo (tree). A Kaua'i promontory.

Kamiloiki Pl. (Honolulu) – Small Kamilo (milo tree). Named for an O'ahu valley.

Kamilonui Rd./Pl. (Honolulu) – Large Kamilo (milo tree). Named for an O'ahu valley.

Kaminaka Dr. (Honolulu) – Chaminade.

Kamoana Pl. (Kapolei) – The deep sea.

Kamoawa St./Pl. ('Ewa Beach) – A large shark who guarded the entrance to the waters of Ka'ahupahau, the shark goddess of 'Ewa.

Kamohoali'i St. (Honolulu) – The chiefly chosen one. Possibly named for Daniel Kamohoali'i Kaumuali'i (he called himself Kama), an area resident and son of an ancient landowning family. He and his father were named for the shark god, Kamohoali'i (Pele's older brother), their family deity.

Kamoi Pl. (Honolulu) – The threadfish. Named for a Hawai'i Island promontory.

Kamōkila Blvd. (Kapolei) – Majestic, tall, strong, imposing; having poise that commands admiration.

Kamoku St. (Honolulu) – The district. Named for an O'ahu land section.

Kāmole St./Pl. (Honolulu) – Primrose willow, a perennial herb with yellow flowers. Used medicinally.

Kamo'oali'i St. (Kāne'ohe) – The chiefly mo'o (lizard, reptile of any kind). Named for a nearby stream.

Kamo'okoa Pl. (Honolulu) – The brave lizard. Named for a Kaua'i mountain ridge.

Kamo'oali'i

Kamuela Pl. (Honolulu) – Samuel. Named for Samuel Dowsett. See Kimopelekane.

Kamuela Ave. (Honolulu) – Samuel. Named for Samuel Wilder King (1886-1959). Honolulu Supervisor (1933-1939), U.S. Congressman (1935-1942), Territorial Governor (1953-1957), and Bishop Estate Trustee (1957-1959). See Lukepane.

Kana Pl. (Honolulu) – Horizontal support in houses for carrying poles.

Kana'e St. (Mililani) – Very fragrant.

Kanaeha Pl. (Pearl City) – Definition not known.

Kanahā St. (Kailua) – The shattered (thing).

Kanahale Rd. (Wai'anae) – Probably should be Kanahele: the forest.

Kāna'i Pl. (Kāne'ohe) – Smooth, calm, of the sea.

Kana'ina Ave. (Honolulu) – The conquering. Named for High Chief Charles Kana'ina (1802-1855). Father of King Lunalilo, and a Diamond Head area landowner.

Kanaka St./Pl. (Kāne'ohe) – Human being, man, mankind, person, individual.

Kanakanui St. (Honolulu) – Big man. Named for original awardee, Samuel Kanakanui, a civil engineer employed by the territorial government. He surveyed all the Kalihi-kai lands.

**Kanaka
Kāne**

Kanakou Pl. (Honolulu) – Kou (wood) support. Named for a Kaua'i mountain peak.

Kanalani Pl. (Hale'iwa) – In great numbers; abundance.

Kanaloa St. ('Aiea) – God of the ocean. One of the great Hawaiian gods. See Lono.

Kanalu St. (Waialua) – The wave. Named for original grantee.

Kanalui St./Pl. (Honolulu) – St. Louis.

Kaname'e St. (Mililani) – An unidentified star, said to be the guardian star of King Kaumuali'i of Kaua'i.

Kanani Pl. (Honolulu) – The beauty.

Kanapua Pl. (Wai'anae) – Should be Kāne'āpua: Kāne fish trap, a legendary figure who dug part of the Kaupuni Stream.

Kanapu'u Dr. (Kailua) – Uneven, as the surface of a table or road.

Kanā'ū St. (Honolulu) – The nā'ū (a yellow gardenia).

Kanawao St./Pl. (Waipahu) – Small endemic trees with large, oval-toothed leaves.

Kāne Pl. (Waialua) – Male. Named for original grantee.

Kāne'ākī St. (Wai'anae) – Hair-switch Kāne. ('ākī: a knot that fastens hair braids). Named for an O'ahu heiau.

Kāneali'i Ave. (Honolulu) – Chiefly man. Named for original awardee.

Kanalu

Kaneana St. ('Ewa Beach) – Name of a cave on Mokuumeume (Ford Island) once occupied by fishermen.

Kaneapu Pl. (Kailua) – Should be Kāne'āpua: Kāne fish trap. See Kanapua.

Kānehoa Lp. (Kapolei) – Companion (of) Kāne. A god, possibly the father of Pele. Named for an O'ahu land section.

Kānehoalani St. (Wai'anae) – Maternal grandfather of Kākuhihewa.

Kānehūnāmoku Pl. (Waimanalo) – Brother of Kauholokahiki. See Kauholokahiki.

Kāne'īlio St./Pl. (Wai'anae) – Dog Kāne. Named for an O'ahu bay heiau.

Kānekapolei St. (Honolulu) – Definition not known. Name of the wife of Hawai'i Island King Kalani'ōpu'u, who ruled during Captain James Cook's visit (1778-1779).

Kānekōpā Pl. (Honolulu) – A kind of foreign cloth.

Kanela St. (Mililani) – Canal.

Kāneloa Rd. (Honolulu) – Tall Kāne. Named for an O'ahu land section.

Kāneʻohe Bay Dr. (Kāneʻohe, Kailua) – Bamboo husband. Legend says a bamboo knife is as sharp as a
husband's cruelty. Named for an Oʻahu land division.

Kānewai St. (Honolulu) – Water (of) Kāne. Named for
an Oʻahu land section.

Kaniʻahē St./Pl. (Wahiawā) – To giggle or laugh softly,
as with delight.

Kanīʻau Pl. (Waipahu) – The coconut midrib.

Kaniela Pl. (Honolulu) – Daniel.

Kanihaʻalilo St. (Kapolei) – Name of a star.

Kānihi St. (Pearl City) – An arm stroke used in lua fighting.

Kanikani Pl. (Wahiawā) – Jack knife.

Kanikō Pl. (Wahiawā) – Long series of loud bell ringing.

Kānia St. (Kapolei) – A variety of sugar cane.

Kaniʻūʻū St. (Kapolei) – Name of a star.

Kāniko

Kānoa St. (Honolulu) – Bowl, as for kava. Named for Kauaʻi Governor
Paul Kānoa (1802-1855). Member, House of Nobles and the Privy
Council. Received a portion of Kapālama in the 1848 Great Mahele.

Kanoe Pl. (Honolulu) – The mist.

Kanoelani Rd. (Honolulu) – The heavenly mist. One of the names of
Queen Liliʻuokalani.

Kanoelehua Pl. (Wahiawā) – The lehua (blossom) mist.

Kanoena St. (Waialua) – Definition not known. Named for original
grantee.

Kanoenoe St. (Honolulu) – The mist.

Kanoulu St. (Waialua) – The loulu (palm). Named for original grantee.

Kanu St. (Honolulu) – To plant, bury.

Kanuku St./Pl. (ʻAiea) – The mouth, the entrance.

Kanunu St. (Honolulu) – Large physically, both tall and stout; husky.

Kaoea Pl. (Mililani) – An unidentified constellation, said to preside over the
destiny of Hanalei, Kauaʻi.

Kaʻohe Pl. (Honolulu) – The bamboo. Named for Hawaiʻi Island land
divisions.

Kāʻohinani Dr. (Honolulu) – The beautiful harvest (probably for taxes).
Named for Mrs. Mary Kāʻohinani Dowsett Parrish. See Kimopelekane.

Kāʻokoʻa Pl. (ʻAiea) – Whole, entire; separated, independent,
standing apart.

Kaola Way (Honolulu) – Beam, rail, shelf, railing.

Kaolo St. (Honolulu) – Path, trail.

Kaomaʻaikū Pl. (Mililani) – Aldebaran, a star in the horns
of the constellation Alpha Tauri.

Kaomi Lp. (Kapolei) – To press down, squeeze with downward pressure; to massage by pressing firmly with the back
of the palm of the hand; to suppress as a thought or emotion.

Kaomi

Ka'onawai Pl. (Honolulu) − The liquid intoxicant.

Ka'ōnohi St./Pl. ('Aiea) − The eyeball. Named for an O'ahu land section.

Ka'ō'ōpulu Pl./Way (Honolulu) − The wet digging stick.

Kā'ope St. ('Ewa Beach) − Yellowish mother-of-pearl shell.

Ka'ōpua Lp. (Mililani) − An unidentified star.

Kapa Pl. (Honolulu) − Tapa. Named for a Kaua'i reservoir.

Kapa

Kapa'a St. (Kailua) − The solid. Named for an O'ahu land section.

Kapa'ahulani St. ('Ewa Beach) − A favorite of King Kūali'i. Kapa'ahulani and his brother Kamaka'aulani collaborated in a scheme which made Kūali'i king over all the islands.

Kapa'akea Ln. (Honolulu) − The limestone. Named for an O'ahu land section.

Kāpae Pl. (Mililani) − A trade wind at Puna, Hawai'i Island.

Kapaekahi St. (Wai'anae) − The single landing.

Kapahu St. (Honolulu) − 1) The box, the drum, the coffin. 2) The push. Possibly named for Kapahu Ke'ōpua. She was one of the first Hawaiians awarded a house lot in the Hawaiian Homes' Papakōlea homestead (1935). People who worked diligently were called Kapahu.

Kapahulani Pl. ('Aiea) − The heavenly drum.

Kapahulu Ave. (Honolulu) − The worn-out soil. Named for an O'ahu land section.

Kapaia St. (Honolulu) − 1) The wall. 2) The forest clearing. Named for a Kaua'i land section.

Kapakai Pl. (Wai'anae) − Seashore, border of the sea.

Kapahu

Kapakapa Way (Mililani) − An unidentified star.

Kapalai Rd./Pl. (Kāne'ohe) − The palai (fern).

Kapālama Ave. (Honolulu) − The lama (wood) fence. The fence surrounding a house of ali'i women was considered a kapu sign. Named for an O'ahu land division.

Kāpalapala Pl. (Honolulu) − Printing, stamping, to paint or print a design.

Kapaloala Pl. (Honolulu) − Definition not known.

Kapalu St. (Honolulu) − The bait. Named for original awardee.

Kapalulu Pl. (Honolulu) − Roaring, as of an airplane.

Kāpana Pl. ('Ewa Beach) − A slender, attractive native shrub in the Mint family. It has white, purple-tinted, tubular flowers.

Kapanoe St. (Mililani) − Edge of blanket of mist.

Kapāpala Pl. (Honolulu) − The Charpentiera (shrub). Named for a Hawai'i Island land division.

Kāpalapala

Kapapapuhi St. ('Ewa Beach) – Point of land in the West Loch of Pearl Harbor.

Kapawa Pl. (Mililani) – An unidentified star. Literally: the pre-dawn time.

Kape'a St./Pl. (Kāne'ohe) – The Southern Cross, a constellation. Literally: the cross.

Kapi'o

Kapehe St. (Kāne'ohe) – The owl snare. Named for original awardee.

Kapehu St. (Waipahu) – Stream on Hawai'i island. Literally: the swelling.

Kāpiki Rd. (Wai'anae) – Poi made with an inferior grade of soggy taro.

Kapili St. (Honolulu) – 1) The relationship. 2) The pili (grass). Named for Princess Likelike (1851-1887). She lived nearby, and used Kapili as a pen name.

Kapi'o St. (Waipahu) – The arch.

Kapi'olani Blvd. (Honolulu) – The arch (of) heaven. Named for Queen Kapi'olani (1834-1899), wife of King Kalākaua. Established programs to improve the welfare of Hawaiian women. She founded Kapi'olani Maternity Home (1890) which later merged with another hospital, and eventually became Kapi'olani Medical Center for Women and Children.

Kapo Way (Honolulu) – A sister of Pele. One of her adventures resulted in the formation of Pu'u Ma'i (known as Koko Crater).

Kapoho Pl. (Honolulu) – The depression. Named for a Hawai'i Island land division.

Kapolei Parkway (Kapolei) – Cone (166 feet high) on the southeast slope of the Wai'anae mountain range. Literally: beloved Kapo (sister of Pele).

Kapo'o St. (Kāne'ohe) – Cavity, hollow, depression.

Kapouka Pl. (Kapolei) – Upland of Kapo, a sister of Pele.

Kapua Ln. (Honolulu) – The flower.

Kapuahi St./Pl. (Mililani) – An unidentified star. Literally: fireplace.

Kapua'i

Kapua'i Pl. (Hale'iwa) – Sole of the foot, footprint, tread, track.

Kapuhi St./Pl. (Hale'iwa) – Master of an animal; nurse or caretaker of a child; provider in general. Named from the O'ahu custom of taming and feeding a particular eel (puhi) in the sea.

Kapukapu Pl. ('Aiea) – Dignity, regal appearance, entitled to respect and reverence, difficult of access because of rank, dignity, and station.

Kapukawai St. (Waipahu) – Handsome.

Kapulei St. (Honolulu) – Lei sacredness. Possibly named for the land owner when it was subdivided.

Kapulena Lp. (Honolulu) – Definition not known. The king shark of Hāmākua. Named for a Hawai'i Island land division.

Kapunahala Rd. (Kāne'ohe) – The pandanus spring. Named for an O'ahu land section.

Kapunapuna Way (Honolulu) – The windblown. Named for an Oʻahu land area.

Kapuni St. (Honolulu) – The surrounding. Named for an Oʻahu land section.

Kau St. (Waipahu) – Summer.

Kaua St. (Honolulu) – Army; war, battle. Named for original awardee.

Kauaʻi St. (Honolulu, Wahiawā) – Named for the island.

Kauakapuʻu Lp. (Mililani) – An unidentified star associated with Kohala, Hawaiʻi Island.

Kaualio Pl. (Honolulu) – Cavalry, cavalry war. Literally: horse war.

Kauamea Pl. (Mililani) – A constellation, possibly Corona Borealis.

Kauanomeha Pl. (Mililani) – A star, possibly Sirius. Literally: placed in holy stillness.

Kauaʻōpuʻu St. (Waiʻanae) – Whale-tooth pendant war. Named for an Oʻahu land section.

Kauhaʻa Pl. (Kāneʻohe) – To move up and down as the waves, or as in dancing.

Kauhakō St./Pl. (Honolulu) – The dragged large intestines. Named for a Kauaʻi mountain peak.

Kauhale St. (ʻAiea) – Group of houses comprising the ancient Hawaiian home: men's eating house, women's eating house, sleeping house, cook house, canoe house, etc.

Kauhaʻa

Kauhana St./Pl. (Honolulu) – Definition not known.

Kaʻuhane St. (Honolulu) – The spirit. Named for Noble Kaʻuhane (1900-1960). Member, Honolulu Board of Supervisors (1945-1960), and Hawaiian Homes Commission (1935-1945). Encouraged funding to develop the Papakōlea Homestead (1935). Coached St. Louis College track and football teams.

Kauhi St. (Kapolei) – The cover.

Kauhihau Pl. (Pearl City) – The hibiscus covering. Named for an Oʻahu land section.

Kauhola Pl. (Honolulu) – To open, unfold, as a tapa; to expand, as a flower in bloom. Named for a Hawaiʻi Island promontory.

Kauholokahiki St./Pl. (Waimānalo) – Name of the woman stranger in the legend of Muliwaiʻōlena. She bathed only in the waters of this stream.

Kauʻi St. (Waialua) – The beautiful. Named for original grantee.

Kaʻuiki St. (ʻEwa Beach) – The glimmer. Named for a Maui promontory and hill.

Kauila St. (Honolulu) – Three species of native trees. Their wood was shaped into spears, tapa anvils, mallets, beaters, and digging sticks.

Kauʻinohea Pl. (Kāneʻohe) – The beautiful youth.

Kauʻiokalani Pl. (Waiʻanae) – The beauty of heaven.

Ka Uka Blvd. (Waipahu) – The uplands.

Kaukahi Pl. (Waipahu) – Standing alone, solitary, by oneself; persevering, singleness of purpose.

Kauka'i Rd. (Wai'anae) – To depend on; one depended on.

Kaukali'a St. (Mililani) – An unidentified star.

Ka'ukama Rd. (Wai'anae) – Cucumber.

Kaukamana St. (Wai'anae) – Definition not known. Probably a Hawaiianized name.

Kaukini Pl. (Mililani) – Cousin; a ridge in West Maui.

Kaukoe St. (Waipahu) – To continue or persevere in a straight course.

Kaulahao

Kaukolu St./Pl./Way ('Ewa Beach) – Triple, group of three.

Kaukonahua Rd. (Waialua) – Definition not known. Named for an O'ahu stream.

Ka'uku Pl. (Honolulu) – The louse. Named for a Hawai'i Island volcanic cone.

Kaulahao St. ('Aiea) – Chain. Literally: iron rope.

Kaula'ili Rd. (Wai'anae) – Leather rope, lassoing rope, lariat.

Kaula'ināhe'e Pl. ('Aiea) – Dry the octopuses.

Kaulana Way/Pl. (Honolulu) – 1) Famous. 2) Restful, quiet.

Kaulani Way (Kailua) – To rely on the chief, to support the chief, to put confidence in the chief.

Kaulawaha Rd. (Wai'anae) – Bridle, reins. Literally: mouth chain.

Kaulele Pl. (Honolulu) – To take flight; soaring, on the wing.

Kauleo Pl. ('Ewa Beach) – To urge, exhort, enjoin, advise, command.

Kaulia Pl. (Mililani) – An unidentified star, called the chief of the month Ikiiki because it appears in that month.

Kaulike Dr. (Pearl City) – Equality, justice; equal, impartial, just; to make alike, treat fairly and impartially.

Kaulona Way/Pl. ('Ewa Beach) – To observe closely, to direct attention to, aim at.

Ka'ulu St. (Waimānalo) – The breadfruit.

Kaulua St. (Mililani) – 1) Sirius, or according to some accounts, constellation. 2) An ancient Hawaiian lunar month.

Kaula'ili

Kauluikua Pl. (Mililani) – Sirius, a star.

Kaulukanu St./Pl. (Waimānalo) – The garden patch. Named for an O'ahu land section.

Kaululā'au St. (Honolulu) – The forest. Possibly named for John Whitney Kaululā'au Wright, Sr. (1887-1959). Known as the "Mayor of Papakōlea." He was the first person awarded a house lot in the Hawaiian Homes' Papakōlea Homestead (1935).

Kaululena St. (Mililani) – Sirius, a star.

Ka'ululoa Pl. (Honolulu) – The tall breadfruit. Named for an O'ahu land section.

Kauluwela Pl. (Honolulu) – Glowing, bright-colored, colorful. Named for an Oʻahu land section.

Kaumahana Pl. (Pearl City) – Native mistletoes, small, inconspicuous evergreen shrubs which appear to be leafless. Literally: warm perch.

Kaumailuna Pl. (Honolulu) – To appear above.

Kaʻumaka Pl. (Honolulu) – Give me eye. Named for a Kauaʻi land division.

Kaumakani St./Pl. (Honolulu) – Placed (in the) wind. Named for a Kauaʻi land section.

Kaʻūmana Pl. (Kailua) – An unidentified star. Named for Kaʻūmana Widemann, of the Dowsett family. Daughter of Kealiʻimaikaʻi, Kamehameha I's brother who married Piʻia, sister of Kaʻahumanu. See Kimopelekane.

Kaumoku St. (Honolulu) – Definition not known. Named for a Kauaʻi stream.

Kaumoli St./Pl. (Pearl City) – Stick with holes down its middle, for holding gunwales in place while gunwales are sewn on with sennit (cord, rope).

Kaumualiʻi St. (Honolulu) – The royal oven. Reputedly named for Solomon Kama Kaumualiʻi who resided in this area. A descendant of Hawaiʻi Island Chief Keōuakūahuʻula (he was sacrificed by Kamehameha in 1791).

Kaunā St. (Honolulu) – Definition not known. Named for a Hawaiʻi Island promontory. Also called Lae o Kaunā.

Kaunala St./Pl. (Haleʻiwa) – The weaving. Named for an Oʻahu land division.

Kaunaloa Pl. (ʻEwa Beach) – Perseverence, to persevere.

Kaunānā Pl. (ʻEwa Beach) – To discover; perceive.

Kaunaʻoa St. (Honolulu) – A shelled marine worm. It inflicts serious cuts if stepped on, and grows in the flesh if not removed entirely.

Kaunaʻoaʻula St. (Kapolei) – Red kaunaʻoa vine.

Kaunoʻa St. (ʻEwa Beach) – A mollusk. In its adult stage it becomes solidly attached to rocks.

Kaunolū St. (ʻEwa Beach) – Definition not known. Named for a Lānaʻi land division.

Kauoha St./Pl.Way (ʻEwa Beach) – Order, command.

Kauʻolu Pl. (Waipahu) – Place or time of pleasantness or ease.

Kauʻōpae Pl. (Mililani) – Sirius, said to be the patron star of shrimp fishing. ʻŌpae: shrimp.

Kauʻōpua St. (Mililani) – An unidentified star.

Kaupaku Pl. (Honolulu) – Ridgepole, highest point, roof, attic. Figuratively: greatest. Named for a Kauaʻi stream.

Kaupalena St. (Honolulu) – To limit, mark a border, set a deadline; limitation, deadline.

Kaupau Pl. (Hauʻula) – An edible brown seaweed, with many slender branches.

Kaupē Rd. (Waialua) – To put forward, of a paddle.

Kaupili Pl. ('Aiea) – Beloved wife or friend, beloved friendship united in close relationship. Literally: place clinging.

Kaupuni St./Pl. (Wai'anae) – Place around. Named for an O'ahu stream.

Kauwā St. ('Aiea) – Untouchable, outcast, pariah, slave; servant. Possibly named for an original awardee.

Kauwahi Ave. (Wai'anae) – Some, a litter, a few; something; some place.

Kauweke Pl. (Waipahu) – Southwest.

Kauwili St. ('Ewa Beach) – To mingle, mix.

Kawa St. (Kāne'ohe) – Leaping place, as a precipice where a swimmer leaps into a pool. Named for an O'ahu stream.

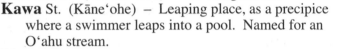

Kawa

Kawa'ekū St. (Hau'ula) – A lua fighting stroke.

Kawaena Pl. (Honolulu) – The garden.

Kāwa'ewa'e Way/Pl. (Hau'ula) – A kind of stone or coral, as used to polish canoes, or to rub bristles off pigs destined for the imu (underground oven).

Kawahine Pl. (Waimānalo) – The woman.

Kawaiaha'o St. (Honolulu) – The water of Ha'o. Ha'o: a chiefess who bathed in a nearby spring. Named for Kawaiaha'o Church (dedicated in 1842 on land donated by Kamehameha III). The church is named for an O'ahu land section.

Kawaihae St./Pl. (Honolulu) – The water (of) wrath. Named for Hawai'i Island land divisions.

Kāwaihemo Pl. (Hau'ula) – Extremely watery kāwai. Kāwai: last liquor yielded in distillation, extremely thin and watery.

Kawaihoa Way (Honolulu) – The companion's water. Named for an O'ahu promontory.

Kawaiholo St. (Honolulu) – The running water.

Kawaiiki Pl. (Honolulu) – The small stream. Named for an O'ahu land section.

Kawaiki Pl. (Honolulu) – Perhaps should be Keawaiki: the small bay. Named for a Hawai'i Island bay.

Kawaikini St. (Hau'ula) – The many waters.

Kawaiku'i St./Pl. (Honolulu) – The pounded water. Named for an O'ahu land section which is named for a spring.

Kawailoa Rd. (Kailua) – The big water. Named for an O'ahu land section.

Kawailoa Dr./Rd. (Hale'iwa) – The big water. Named for an O'ahu land division.

Kawainui St. (Kailua) – The big water. Named for an O'ahu fishpond.

Kawaipapa St. (Hau'ula) – The level water. Named for an O'ahu gulch.

Kawaipuna St./Pl. (Hau'ula) – The spring water.

Kawānanakoa Pl. (Honolulu) – The fearless prophecy; the warrior's prophecy. Named for an O'ahu land section.

Kawanui St. (Waipahu) – Big leaping place.

Kawao Ave. (Wai'anae) – The inland region.

Kāwa'u St. (Mililani) – An unidentified star.

Kawēkiu Pl. (Honolulu) – The summit.

Kawela Camp Rd. (Kahuku) – The heat. Named for
an O'ahu land division.

Kaweloali'i St./Pl. (Mililani) – An unidentified star,
the companion of Kamalama. Literally: the royal family.

Kāwili

Kāwelokā St./Pl. (Pearl City) – To trail or drag, as a dress train.

Kawelolani Pl. (Honolulu) – The royal breed.

Kāwelu St. (Pearl City) – Love grass, a clumpy endemic grass. Conspicuous
wind-blown grass at the Nu'uanu pali, famous in song.

Kaweo Pl. (Mililani) – An unidentified star.

Kāwika Pl. (Honolulu) – David.

Kāwili St./Pl. (Wai'anae) – To mix ingredients, blend; entwined, interwoven,
interlaced.

Kawiwi Way. (Wai'anae) – Mountain in the Wai'anae region, believed to
have been a place of refuge in war.

Kawoa Way/Pl. (Hale'iwa) – Savoy, a cabbage with curled leaves.

Kawohi Pl. (Honolulu) – The wohi. Wohi: a high chief exempt from the
prostration kapu (lying on the stomach in the king's presence).

Kawowo Rd./Pl. (Hale'iwa) – Seedling; sucker, shoot from a parent stalk;
to multiply and thrive, as a plant or people. Figuratively: progeny.

Kea Pl. (Waialua) – White (color). Named for original awardee.

Kea'ahala Rd./Pl. (Kāne'ohe) – The pandanus root. Named for an O'ahu
land section.

Keaāhua Lp. (Waipahu) – Stream at Hanalei, Kaua'i; land division,
village, road on Maui. Literally: the mound.

Kea'alau Pl. (Kāne'ohe) – The many roots. Named for an O'ahu land
section.

Keaali'i Way/Pl. ('Ewa Beach) – A cave in the sea at the entrance to Puuloa
Harbor, home of a large shark named Kamoawa.

Kea'eloa Ln. (Honolulu) – The trade wind.

Keahi St./Pl. (Honolulu) – A native tree with milky sap.

Keahia Rd. (Honolulu) – The faded. Named for an O'ahu land division.

Keahilele St./Pl. (Mililani) – An unidentified star, the companion of
Ke'alohilani. Literally: the firebrand.

Keahipaka Ln. (Hale'iwa) – The tobacco fire.

Keāhole St./Pl. (Honolulu) – The āhole. Āhole: mature stage of
āholehole (fish). See Āholehole. Named for Hawai'i Island land
sections.

Keaka Dr. (Honolulu) – Jack.

Keaka'ula Pl. ('Ewa Beach) – The red sunset.

Keākealani St. (Honolulu) – The breadth (of) heaven.

Keakula St. (Waialua) – Pine; box tree, a shrub.

Keala Rd. (Hau'ula) – The path.

Kealahou Pl. (Kailua) – The new pathway.

Kealahou St. (Honolulu) – The new pathway. Named for Maui land divisions.

Kealaka'a St./Pl. (Mililani) – An unidentified star. Literally: the rolling pathway.

Kealakaha Dr. ('Aiea) – The turning road.

Kealaka'i St. (Honolulu) – The leader.

Kealalani Pl. (Hau'ula) – The heavenly road, the royal road.

Kealaluina Dr. ('Aiea) – The sailor's road.

Kealamāka'i St. (Honolulu) – Police road.

Ke Ala Manō St. (Honolulu) – The shark's road.

Kealanani Ave. (Kapolei) – The beautiful street.

Keala'olu Ave./Pl. (Honolulu) – The pleasant road, the cool road.

Keālia Dr. (Honolulu) – The salt bed. Named for an O'ahu land section.

Kealoha St./Pl. (Honolulu) – The compassion. Named for original awardee.

Kealohanui St. (Waialua) – The great affection. Named for original grantee.

Ke'alohi St./Pl./Way (Mililani) – An unidentified star. Literally: the brightness.

Ke'alohilani Ave. (Honolulu) – The royal brightness. Named for the Waikīkī cottage of Queen Lili'uokalani, which used to be here.

Keama Pl. (Honolulu) – The outrigger float.

Keana Rd. (Kāne'ohe) – The cave. Named for an O'ahu land section.

Ke'anae St. ('Aiea) – The 'anae (full-sized mullet fish). Named for a Maui land division.

Keaniani St./Pl. (Kailua) – The refreshing (breeze).

Keanu St./Pl./Way (Honolulu) – The coolness. A family name.

Keaolani St./Pl. (Mililani) – The heavenly cloud.

Keaolele Pl. (Honolulu) – The flying cloud.

Keao'ōpua St./Pl. (Mililani) – The horizon cloud bank.

Ke'apua St./Pl. ('Aiea) – To shoot or slide arrows made of sugar cane tassel stems.

Keauhou St. (Honolulu) – The new era. Named for an O'ahu land section.

Keaukaha Pl. (Waipahu) – Hawaiian homestead area, elementary school, waterfront park and residential district in Hilo. Literally: the passing current.

Keaulana Ave. (Wai'anae) – The calm tide.

Keaunui Dr. ('Ewa Beach) – Head of the powerful and celebrated 'Ewa chiefs.

Keawe St. (Honolulu) – Definition not known. Possibly named for original awardee.

Keawemauhili Pl. (Kahuku) – Name of a former Kahuku Plantation employee.

Keʻeaumoku St./Pl. (Honolulu) – Definition not known. Named for High Chief Keʻeaumoku (1784?-1824). Brother of Queen Kaʻahumanu and John Adams Kuakini. Maui governor, ally and father-in-law of Kamehameha I. Wanted to abolish the ancient Hawaiian religion before 1819 kapu. Ceremonially started the first printing press at Kawaiahaʻo Mission (1822).

Keʻehau St. (Mililani) – To farm at night, especially during moonlight nights.

Keʻehi Pl. (Honolulu) – Tread upon. Hawaiian name of the adjacent lagoon.

Keʻehuhiwa St./Pl. (Mililani) – An unidentified star, the companion of Luahoʻomoe.

Keʻele Pl. (ʻEwa Beach) – Great, excessive.

Keʻena Pl. (ʻEwa Beach) – Office, room.

Keha Pl. (Honolulu) – Height, pride, dignity; lofty, prominent; majestic.

Kēhau Pl. (Honolulu) – Dew, mist, dewdrop.

Kēhaulani Dr. (Kailua) – Heavenly dew.

Kēhela St./Pl. (Waipahu) – An unidentified star.

Kehena Pl. (Honolulu) – Place where refuse is thrown and burned; dump.

Kehepue Lp./Pl. (Mililani) – Should be Kēkēpue: an unidentified star.

Kehoʻoea Pl. (Mililani) – Lyra, a constellation.

Kēhue St./Pl. (ʻEwa Beach) – Yellowish, of soil.

Kei Pl. (ʻEwa Beach) – To glory in, take pride in; dignified, proud.

Keiki Ln./Pl. (Honolulu, Haleʻiwa) – Child, offspring, boy, youngster, son, lad, nephew, son of a dear friend.

Kē Iki Rd. (Haleʻiwa) – Small Kē. Kē: protest, complaint.

Keikialiʻi St. (ʻAiea) – Prince, child of a chief.

Keikikāne Lp./Pl. (Kāneʻohe) – Boy, lad, son.

Keikilani Cir. (Honolulu) – Royal child.

Kekaʻa St. (Honolulu) – The rumble. Named for a Maui promontory.

Kekaha Pl. (Honolulu) – The place. Named for a Kauaʻi land section.

Kekahi St. (Mililani) – Companion.

Kekai Pl. (Kapolei) – The ocean.

Kekaihili Pl. (ʻEwa Beach) – An unidentified southern star.

Kekaiholo St. (ʻEwa Beach) – Running sea or current.

Kekakia Pl. (ʻEwa Beach) – Stadia, in surveying; furlong.

Kekau Pl. (Honolulu) – The summer season.

Kekaulike St. (Honolulu) – The equality. Named for Kekaulike (1843-1884). Mother of David Kawānanakoa and Jonah Kūhiō Kalanianaʻole. Wife of High Chief Piʻikoi. Sister of Kapiʻolani.

Keiki

Kekāuluohi St. (Honolulu) – The vine growing (with) shoots. Named for Kekāuluohi (1794?-1845). Also known as Auhea. Kuhina Nui (1839-1845). Wife of Kamehameha I, Kamehameha II, and Kanaʻina. Mother of Lunalilo. Named for daughter of Kamehameha's half-brother Kaleimamahū, and Kaʻahumanu's sister Kalakua. After she arrested Catholics (1839), she signed a treaty of demands with French warship Captain LaPlace. She paid him $20,000 penalty to ensure religious freedom in Hawaiʻi. Established penal settlements on Kahoʻolawe and Lānaʻi.

Kekauoha St. (Kahuku) – Name of a former Kahuku Plantation employee.

Kekauwā St. (Waialua) – The slave. Named for original awardee.

Kekepania Pl. (Kapolei) – Stephanie.

Kekiʻo Rd. (Kaʻaʻawa) – The pool.

Kekoa Pl. (ʻAiea) – The soldier.

Kekona Pl. (Honolulu) – Second (a unit of time).

Kekuanoni St./Pl. (Honolulu) – The noni (tree) god. Named for original awardee.

Kekūilani Lp. (Kapolei) – A place resembling heaven.

Kekumu Pl. (Waimānalo) – The tree, the source.

Kekupua St./Pl. (Honolulu) – The demigod. Named for a Kauaʻi valley.

Kela Pl. (ʻEwa Beach) – Sailor.

Kelakela St./Pl. (Mililani) – Excelling, exceeding beyond.

Kēlau St. (Kapolei) – To put out first leaves.

Keleawe Pl. (ʻEwa Beach) – General name for metals, as brass, copper, bronze, tin, steel, lead.

Kelewaʻa St./Pl. (Mililani) – Sirius, a star. Literally: sailing (by) canoe.

Kelewina St./Pl. (Kailua) – Kelvin.

Keliʻikipi St. (Waiʻanae) – The rebel chief.

Kelikoi St. (Honolulu) – Should be Kelikoli: territory.

Keluka Pl. (Kāneʻohe) – Thrush (bird).

Kemika Pl. (ʻEwa Beach) – Chemist, chemical.

Kemole Ln. (Honolulu) – The main root.

Kemu Pl. (Mililani) – To absorb, consume.

Keneke St./Pl. (Kāneʻohe) – Kenneth.

Kenela St. (Kāneʻohe) – General. Usually: Kenelala.

Keni St./Pl. (Mililani) – To walk softly so as to make no noise.

Kenola Pl. (Waipahu) – Tern (bird).

Kē Nui Rd. (Haleʻiwa) – Big Kē. Kē: protest, complaint.

Keʻo Pl. (Kaʻaʻawa) – White, clear.

Keoʻahu Rd. (Waialua) – The Oʻahu resident. Named for original grantee.

Kēlau

Kekoa

Kela

Keoe Way/Pl. (Kāneʻohe) – Lyra, a constellation.

Keōhapa Pl. (Kāneʻohe) – Perhaps: Joe Harper (1904-1988). A vocational agriculture instructor, Oʻahu Prison warden (1946-1961), and Kahaluʻu community planning advocate.

Keōkea Pl. (Honolulu) – The white sand. Named for Hawaiʻi Island land divisions, a bay or a promontory.

Keoki Pl. (Honolulu) – George.

Keokolo St. (Kapolei) – Theodore.

Keola St. (Honolulu) – The life. Named for original awardee.

Kōʻole St./Pl. (Kāneʻohe) – Without protest. Named for an Oʻahu land section.

Kēolewa Pl. (Honolulu) – 1) The floating cloud. 2) An unidentified star. Named for original awardee.

Keolu Dr. (Kailua) – Definition not known. Named for an Oʻahu land section.

Keonaona St. (Honolulu) – The soft fragrance.

Keoneʻae Pl. (ʻEwa Beach) – A plain in Honouliuli on the way to Puʻukapolei.

Kē Waena

Keonekapu St./Pl. (ʻEwa Beach) – Named for J. Keonekapu, one of two ʻEwa "racing sons" who owned fast and famous horses that were often wagered on.

Keoneʻula Blvd. (ʻEwa Beach) – Red sands.

Keoni St. (Honolulu) – John.

Keoniana St. (Honolulu) – Named for John Young II (1810-1857). Son of John Young (see Olohana) and Chiefess Kaʻoanaʻeha. Kuhina Nui (1845-1854), Maui governor, Supreme Court Justice, and Minister of Foreign Relations.

Keoʻo St. (Waialua) – The ripe one. Named for original grantee.

Keʻōpua St. (Honolulu) – The cloud bank. Possibly named for early Hawaiian residents of the Papokōlea Homestead (1935).

Kēpā St. (Honolulu) – Spur, as used by horseback riders. Possibly Kepa: Hawaiianization of Cephas.

Kepakepa St./Pl. (Waipahu) – Conversational chant, fast rhythmic chant or recitation, with every syllable clearly pronounced.

Kepaniwai St. (Honolulu) – The water dam. Named for a battle in ʻIao Valley, Maui won by Kamehameha (1790).

Kepāʻuala St./Pl. (Waiʻanae) – The sweet potato enclosure. Probably should be Kēpauʻula: red gum. Puʻu Kēpauʻula: name of an Oʻahu mountain peak (2,678 feet).

Kepola Pl. (Honolulu) – Deborah.

Kepuʻe St./Pl. (Waiʻanae) – The hill.

Kepuhi St. (Honolulu) – The eel. Possibly a place name.

Keuwai St. (Waialua) – Too much water. Named for original grantee.

Kē Waena Rd. (Haleʻiwa) – Middle Kē. Kē: protest, complaint.

Kēwai Pl. (Waialua) – Misty.

Kewalo Ln. (Haleʻiwa) – The calling.

Kewalo St. (Honolulu) – The calling. Named for an
Oʻahu land section.

Kīʻaha

Kīʻaʻala Pl. (Honolulu) – Sweet basil, an aromatic
herb in the Mint family. Literally: fragrant tī.

Kīʻaha Lp./Pl. (Mililani) – Modern name for the Big
Dipper. Literally: cup.

Kiaʻi Pl. (Honolulu) – To watch, guard; to overlook, as a bluff.

Kialua St. (Kāneʻohe) – Brig, two-masted vessel, two-masted schooner.

Kiana Pl. (Waiʻanae) – Diana.

Kiani St. (Kāneʻohe) – To flick, flip, wave gently, as the hand overhead in a
hula gesture.

Kiapā Pl. (Waiʻanae) – Swift-sailing canoe.

Kiapaʻakai Pl. (Mililani) – Polaris, the North Star. Literally: pillar of salt
(it was immovable, like the Biblical Lot's wife).

Kiapoko St./Pl. (Waialua) – A short canoe with a rounded hull, used for
fishing near shore.

Kīʻapu Pl. (Honolulu) – Tī leaf folded into a cup and used for dipping water.

Kīau Pl. (Waipahu) – To gallop; to walk lightly and swiftly.

Kiawa Pl. (Honolulu) – Should be Kuawa: guava, or kiawe (tree). See
Kiawe.

Kiawe St./Pl./Way (ʻAiea, Honolulu) – The algaroba (mesquite) tree. First
planted in dry areas of Hawaiʻi (1828). A common and valuable tree with
many uses: pods for animal food, wood for fuel, lumber for house poles,
and flowers for honey.

Kiʻekiʻe Pl. (Wahiawā) – High, lofty, exalted, majestic, superior.

Kiʻekōnea Way (Waialua) – Definition not known. Named for original
awardee.

Kiela Pl. (Wahiawā) – Should be Kiele. See Kiele.

Kiele Ave./Pl. (Honolulu) – Gardenia, a shrub grown
for its handsome, fragrant flowers.

Kīhale St./Pl. (ʻAiea) – House key.

Kīhāpai St./Pl. (Kailua) – Cultivated patch, garden,
orchard, field.

Kīhei Pl. (Honolulu) – Rectangular tapa garment worn
over one shoulder and tied in a knot; bed spread; shawl;
cloak of makaloa matting.

Kīhale

Kīhene St. (Mililani) – Bundle or basket of tī or other leaves, as used to
carry sweet potato, flowers, etc.

Kīhewa Pl. (ʻAiea) – Short for Kiʻi hewa: fault-finding.

Kihi St. (Honolulu, ʻEwa Beach) – Outside corner, edge, tip; to turn aside.

Kihikihi St./Pl. (Waipahu) – A variety of sweet potato.

Kīholo St. (Honolulu) – Fishhook. Named for a Hawai'i Island bay.

Kīhonua Pl. (Wai'anae) – Side or bank of a canal or ditch.

Ki'i Rd. (Kahuku) – Image. Named for an O'ahu land section.

Ki'i St./Pl. (Honolulu) – Image. Named for a Hawai'i Island bay or promontory.

Ki'ilani St./Pl. (Mililani) – Heavenly image.

Ki'i'oni'oni Lp./Pl. (Honolulu) – Moving picture, movie, cinema.

Ki'ipōhaku Way (Honolulu) – Petroglyph. Refers to a nearby petroglyph cave.

Ki'ipōhaku

Kika St./Pl. (Kailua) – Kirk.

Kīkaha St. (Kapolei) – To soar, glide, poise, wheel, skim along, as a frigate bird; to walk along absent-mindedly, ignoring everyone.

Kikala St. ('Aiea) – Pine tree, fir tree.

Kīkalakē Pl. (Mililani) – A kind of fishhook.

Kikanai Lp. (Honolulu) – Should be Kīkānia. See Kīkānia.

Kīkānia St. ('Aiea) – Short for Kīkānia-lei, a kind of nightshade (plant), with round, scarlet fruits strung for leis.

Kikaweo St. (Wahiawā) – Should be Kikawaiō: a native fern.

Kīkēkē Ave. (Honolulu) – To knock, rap, tap, pound.

Kīkepa St./Pl. (Waipahu) – Tapa or sarong worn by women under one arm and over the shoulder of the opposite arm.

Kīkīao St. (Kapolei) – Sudden wind gust.

Kikilia Pl. (Honolulu) – Cecelia.

Kīkī'ula Lp./Pl./Way (Mililani) – An unidentified star. Literally: emitting red.

Kīko'o St./Pl. ('Ewa Beach, Honolulu) – Span; a measure from the end of the thumb to the end of the index finger. Named for a Kaua'i hill.

Kīko'u St. (Waialua) – To cultivate with a hoe or digging stick; to rap or strike with a club; to tap.

Kikowaena St./Pl. (Wahiawā, Honolulu) – Center of a circle; headquarters; central, telephone operator; bull's eye.

Kikowaena

Kila Way (Waialua) – High place. Named for original grantee.

Kīlaha St./Pl. ('Ewa Beach) – Broad, wide, ample.

Kilakila Dr. (Honolulu) – Majestic, tall, strong, imposing; having poise that commands admiration.

Kilani Ave./Pl. (Wahiawā) – Zealand.

Kīlau Pl. (Wahiawā) – Bracken or brake, a stiff, weedy native fern with creeping underground stems.

Kīlauea Ave./Pl. (Honolulu) – Spewing, much spreading. Named for a Hawai'i Island volcano (4,090 feet).

Kīlea Pl. (Wahiawā) – Small but conspicuous hill.

Kileka Pl. ('Aiea) – Holm tree, cypress.

Kīlepa Pl. ('Aiea) – To float in the wind, to flutter, flap, flip.

Kili Dr. (Wai'anae) – Raindrops; fine rain; to rain gently.

Kilihau St. (Honolulu) – Ice-cold shower. Named for a former O'ahu fishpond.

Kilihē Way ('Aiea) – Drenched, by sea spray or fragrance.

Kilihe'a Way ('Aiea) – Stained with color, as a sky at sunset.

Kilihune Pl. (Honolulu) – Fine, light rain, wind-blown spray, drizzle; to shower lightly.

Kilika Pl. ('Aiea) – The black mulberry tree, brought to Hawai'i to establish a silk-producing industry in the early 1900s. Its leaves are fed to silkworms. The tree comes from the Far East.

Kilinahe St./Pl. ('Ewa Beach) – Light, soft, gentle rain.

Kilinoe St. ('Aiea) – Fine, misty rain.

Kilioe Pl. (Hale'iwa) – A native climbing shrub. Named for original awardee.

Kili'ohu Lp. ('Aiea) – Fine rain and light mist.

Kilipoe St. ('Ewa Beach) – Name of a wind.

Kilipohe St. ('Aiea) – Well-shaped and moist, as a flower wet with dew or fine raindrops.

Kīloa Pl. (Mililani) – To put away for safe keeping, as bundles on a shelf.

Kilohana St. (Honolulu) – Best, superior, excellent.

Kilohi St. (Honolulu) – To glance, gaze, into a mirror.

Kilohōkū St. (Mililani) – Astrologer, astronomer; to observe and study the stars.

Kilolani Pl. (Honolulu) – Soothsayer who predicts the future by observing the sky; astronomer, astronomy, astrologer.

Kilolani

Kiloni St. (Honolulu) – Origin not known. Probably a Hawaiianized name.

Kilou Pl. (Mililani) – Quiet nook, lonely spot; silent.

Kilo'uhane Pl. (Wai'anae) – Spirituality.

Kīlua Pl. (Honolulu) – Determined.

Kime St./Pl. (Waipahu) – Team.

Kimo St. (Wai'anae) – James. Possibly named for James McCandless, brother of Lincoln McCandless. See Linakola.

Kimo Dr. (Honolulu) – James. Named for James Isaac Dowsett, Jr. See Kimopelekane.

Kimokeo St. (Honolulu) – Timothy.

Kimopelekane Rd. ('Ewa Beach) – British James. Named for James Isaac Dowsett (1829-1898). The first nonmissionary Caucasian born in Hawai'i. Playmate of the young Kamehamehas. Member of House of Nobles. Extensive ranching, whaling, and landholding businesses. Supported 1893 overthrow. Founder of one side of Dowsett family. Son of Captain Samuel James (Ala Kimo). Married Annie Ragsdale. Father of 13 children, including James Isaac, Jr. (Pelekane), Rowena (Niolopua), Mary (Kā'ohinani), Phoebe (Kahawalu), Samuel (Kamuela) and Alexander Cartwright ('Alika). Other relatives include Herbert Melville (see Hulakai), and Ka'umanu Widemann.

Kina St. (Kailua) – China.

Kinalau Pl. (Honolulu) – Probably should be Kinolau: many forms taken by a supernatural body, as Pele, who could transform into a flame of fire, a young girl, or an old hag.

Kīnana Way (Kāne'ohe) – Mother hen or bird and her brood; a brooding place, chicken house.

Kīnana

Kīna'u St. (Honolulu) – Blemish. Named for High Chiefess Kīna'u (1805-1839). Daughter of Kamehameha I. Mother of Princess Kamāmalu, and Kamehameha IV-V. One of five primary wives of Kamehameha II. Kuhina Nui (1832-1839). An early Christian convert, she enforced missionary-inspired laws. Argued with Kamehameha III, who disliked her authority, and the American missionaries.

Kini Pl. (Honolulu) – 1) Jane. 2) Jean.

Kinikohu St. (Wahiawā) – Extremely well-suited, fine-looking. Literally: many suitable.

Kinipōpō St. (Wahiawā) – Ball, baseball; to play ball.

Kino St. (Honolulu) – Body.

Kinohi Pl. (Kapolei) – Beginning, origin, genesis.

Kinohou Pl. (Honolulu) – Beginning, first. Literally: new body.

Kinipōpō

Kino'ole Pl. ('Aiea) – Frail and thin, of animate things.

Kīoe St. (Waialua) – Small surfboard. Named for original grantee.

Kio'ele Pl. (Mililani) – A small native shrub belonging to the Coffee family, a rare or extinct species.

Kiokio Pl. (Waipahu) – Young, immature, as flora or fauna.

Ki'olena Pl. (Waipahu) – Tapa-drying and bleaching place; to dry and bleach tapa; to dye tapa.

Ki'ona'ole Rd. (Kāne'ohe) – Without dung heaps. Named for an O'ahu land section.

Kiopa'a Pl. (Mililani) – Polaris, the North Star. Literally: fixed projection.

Ki'owai St. (Kāne'ohe) – Pool of water, water hydrant, water hole, fountain.

Ki'owainui Pl (Kapolei) – Great shallow fresh water spring.

Ki'owao Pl. (Kapolei) – Cool mountain rain accompanied by wind and fog.

Kīpa'a Pl. (Waipahu) – A style of playing slack-key guitar.

Kīpaepae St. ('Aiea) – Stone pavement or steps for entering a house.

Kipahele St./Pl. (Wai'anae) – To go visiting from place to place.

Kīpahulu Pl. (Wai'anae) – Place where soil is worn out from constant farming; worn-out soil.

Kīpaipai St./Pl. (Wai'anae, Pearl City) – To encourage, inspire.

Kīpalalē Pl. (Wai'anae) – Disorder, jumble, tumult; rapid flow, as a swollen stream; to spread, extend in a disorderly fashion.

Kīpaoa Pl. (Wai'anae) – Sweet basil.

Kīpapa Dr./St./Pl. (Mililani) – Pavement, level terrace. Named for an O'ahu stream and gulch.

Kipapani Pl. (Wai'anae) – To flock.

Kipawale Pl. (Kāne'ohe) – To call without being asked; to intrude; to visit by chance.

Kipikua St. ('Aiea) – Pickaxe. Literally: dig, hew.

Kipona Pl. (Honolulu) – Mixed, mingled; varying in color or texture, as the sea.

Kipikua

Kīpou St./Pl. (Waipahu) – To drive down, as a stake into the ground; to go downward; descend.

Kīpū Pl. (Honolulu) – Hold back. Named for a Kaua'i land division.

Kīpuka St./Dr./Pl. (Wahiawā, Kailua) – Variation or change of form, as a calm place in a high sea, deep place in a shoal, opening in a forest, and especially a clear place or oasis within a lava bed where there may be vegetation.

Kīpūkai Pl. (Honolulu) – Seaside heliotrope, an herb found near the sea or salt marshes. Dried and brewed for tea (used as a tonic).

Kiu Pl. (Kahuku) – A strong, moderately cold northwesterly wind.

Kiuke'e Pl. (Kailua) – Name of a wind associated with Nāwiliwili, Kaua'i.

Kiwi St. ('Ewa Beach) – Animal horn, antler; horn of the kala (fish).

Kīwila St. (Honolulu) – Civic, civil; civilian.

Kiwi

Kīwini Pl. (Waipahu) – Brazen.

Kō St./Pl. (Kāne'ohe) – Sugar cane. Brought to Hawai'i by early Polynesians.

Koa Ave. (Honolulu) – Warrior. A name of Prince David Kawānanakoa (1868-1908). Older brother of Jonah Kūhiō Kalaniana'ole. Son of High Chief Pi'ikoi. Proclaimed prince by King Kalākaua (1883). Jailed one year for participating in 1895 counterrevolution to restore monarchy. A Democrat, he lost 1902 congressional election to his brother, Kūhiō, a Republican.

Koa Ln./Pl./St. (Honolulu, Wahiawā) – The largest native forest tree. Its fine red wood was shaped into canoes, surfboards, and calabashes. Now used for furniture, woodwork, and 'ukuleles.

Koaʻe St./Pl. (Honolulu) – The tropic or boatswain bird, particularly the white-tailed tropic bird, which inhabits island cliffs. It breeds at Mokoliʻi (known as Chinaman's Hat).

Koaʻena St./Pl. (Kāneʻohe) – Abundant koa (tree). Named for an Oʻahu land section.

Koaha Pl./Way (ʻAiea) – Young shoots of the mulberry plant used for medicine. The soft mulberry fiber was used for making fine white tapa.

Kōaheahe St./Pl. (Pearl City) – Blowing gently, as the wind.

Koahi St. (ʻEwa Beach) – Should be Kōʻaki: sugar cane.

Koaiʻe Pl. (Kāneʻohe) – An endangered native tree, like the koa but smaller. Its hard wood was shaped into fancy paddles, spears, house timbers, tapa beaters, calabashes, and shark hooks. Figuratively: person from the upland country.

Koa Kahiko St./Pl. (Kāneʻohe) – Veteran, old soldier.

Kōʻaki St. (Waipahu) – Sugar cane.

Koalele St. (Honolulu) – Leaping soldier. Named for original awardee.

Koali Ct./Rd. (Wahiawā, Honolulu) – Some kinds of morning-glory (vines). Used for swings and nets.

Koalipehu St./Pl. (ʻEwa Beach) – The moonflower, a morning-glory (vine) with fragrant, white, night-blooming flowers.

Koʻamanō St. (Honolulu) – Shark shrine. Named for a Kauaʻi land division.

Koa Moali Pl. (Waimānalo) – Probably should be Koa Maoli: native koa (tree).

Kōaniani Way (Honolulu) – To move lightly and smoothly, as a soft cool breeze; to make a breeze with a fan; cooled by a breeze.

Koanimakani St./Pl. (Kapolei) – Blowing breeze.

Koapaka St. (Honolulu) – Valiant, brave, especially in war.

Kōāuka St./Lp. (ʻAiea) – Upland dweller, belonging to the uplands.

Kōʻele Way (Wahiawā) – Small land unit farmed by a tenant for the chief.

Koena Way (Wahiawā) – Remainder, residue, remnant, ruins.

Kohai Pl. (Waiʻanae) – To sway in the breeze, as a tree.

Kohea Pl./Way (Kapolei) – Warm, clear, serene weather.

Kōhi St./Pl. (Kapolei) – To gather, as fruit.

Kōhina St. (Kāneʻohe) – Part of taro where the corm is cut away from the top.

Kohomua St. (ʻAiea) – First choice, primary election, first guess; hypothesis.

Kohomua

Kōhou St. (Honolulu) – New sugar cane.

Kohupono St. (Kapolei) – Decent, upright.

Koʻiawe Way (Kāneʻohe) – Light, moving rain; to shower.

Kōīhala Pl. ('Ewa Beach) – Grandmother of Ka'ahupahau, the shark queen of 'Ewa legend.

Ko'iko'i St. (Wahiawā) – Weight, responsibility; prominent, influential; emphatic, stressed; harsh, severe.

Kō'i'o Dr. (Kapolei) – Accomplished, come to pass, come true, as a prophecy. Literally: truly accomplished.

Koke

Ko'i'ula Pl. (Mililani) – Rainbow-hued rain, mist, cloud.

Koka St. ('Ewa Beach) – Soda.

Koke Pl. (Waipahu) – Quick; swift runner.

Kōkea St./Pl. (Honolulu) – A well-known variety of sugar cane, frequently used for medicinal purposes by ancient Hawaiians.

Kōke'e Pl. (Honolulu) – To wind, bend. Named for a Kaua'i stream.

Kōkī St. (Honolulu) – Upper limit. Named for a Kaua'i promontory.

Koki'o Lp. ('Aiea) – A native shrubby hibiscus with red flowers. Its wood produced good charcoal.

Koko Dr./Head Ave./Head Pk. Rd./Isle Cir. (Honolulu) – Blood. Named for an O'ahu canoe landing and promontory.

Kokoiki Pl. (Mililani) – A star named for Kamehameha I's birthplace in Kohala, seen at the time of his birth in 1758. (The star might have been Halley's comet).

Kokokahi Pl. (Kāne'ohe) – One blood.

Koko Kai Pl. (Honolulu) – Koko near the sea.

Kokokāne St. (Kāne'ohe) – Male blood. Perhaps an effort to Hawaiianize the phrase "blood brother."

Kokole St./Pl. (Kapolei) – Taro of the fifth generation.

Kokoloea Pl. (Wahiawā) – Breeze creeping.

Kokololio Pl. (Honolulu) – Sharp, swift wind gust.

Kokomo Pl. (Honolulu) – Named for a Kaua'i mountain peak, said to have been originally koa komo: koa (tree) entering.

Kokonani St. (Honolulu) – Beautiful koko.

Koko Uka Pk. (Honolulu) – Koko near the mountain.

Kōlani Pl. (Kāne'ohe) – Sitting hula in honor of lani (a chief).

Kōlea St./Pl. (Waipahu) – Pacific golden plover (bird).

Koleaka St. (Waipahu) – Perhaps: shadowed reddishness. Named for original awardee.

Kōleali'ili'i St. (Wai'anae) – A hill (elevation 1,254 feet) at back of Wai'anae Valley.

Kolekole Ave./Dr./Rd. (Wahiawā, Wai'anae) – Red, raw. Named for an O'ahu mountain pass.

Koliana St./Pl. (Waipahu) – Accordian.

Kolili St./Pl. (Kapolei) – To flutter, as a flag.

Kōlīliko St. (Mililani) – To sparkle.

Kolo Pl. (Honolulu) – To creep, crawl; to move along, as a gentle breeze or shower.

Koliana

Koloa St. (Honolulu) – Hawaiian duck, a small brown waterbird, formerly common at Waikīkī ponds, now endangered.

Kolohala St. (Honolulu) – Chinese pheasant, the showy ring-necked pheasant.

Kolokio St./Pl. (Kāneʻohe) – A bird catcher.

Kolokolo Cir. (Wahiawā) – Any creeping vine.

Kolokolo St./Pl. (Honolulu) – Creeping. Named for a Kauaʻi promontory.

Kololio St. (Kapolei) – Sharp, swift wind gust.

Kolomona Pl. (Honolulu) – Solomon.

Kolonahe Pl. (Honolulu) – Gentle, pleasant breeze; gentle, mild; softly blowing. Literally: gentle creeping.

Kolopao Pl. (Kāneʻohe) – An unidentified bird.

Kolopua St. (Honolulu) – Fragrant, as air scented with the perfume of flowers. Literally: creeping flowers.

Kolowaka Dr. (ʻEwa Beach) – Soda water.

Kolowalu St. (Honolulu) – Name of a humanitarian law safeguarding the rights of commoners, in time of Oʻahu King Kūaliʻi. Named for an Oʻahu land section.

Kolū Pl. (Waialua) – A thorny, weedy shrub, with fragrant, round, orange flower heads. In Hawaiʻi, the pods yield a gum that was used as glue. In France, the shrub is used for making perfume. Literally: glue.

Kōmaiʻa Dr./Pl. (Honolulu) – Dragging bananas. Named for original grantee.

Komana St. (ʻEwa Beach) – Stone sinker, used with octopus lures.

Komo St. (Waialua) – To enter. Named for original grantee.

Komoʻaina St. (ʻEwa Beach) – To take possession of a land; to acquire land.

Komohana St. (Kapolei) – West.

Komo Mai Dr./Pl. (ʻAiea, Pearl City) – Come in.

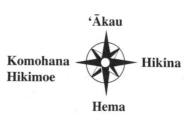

Kona Rd. (Wahiawā) – Leeward sides of the Hawaiian Islands.

Kona St. (Honolulu) – Leeward sides of the Hawaiian Islands. Named for a Hawaiʻi Island district.

Kona Iki St. (Honolulu) – Small Kona.

Konakū St. (Mililani) – Posts on each side of the two center posts at the back wall of a grass house.

Kōnale Pl. (Kāneʻohe) – Quiet, tranquil, peaceful.

Kōnane Pl. (Kāneʻohe) – Bright moonlight.

Konani Ln. (Honolulu) – Probably should be Konane: bright moonlight; to shine, as the moon.

Konia St. (Honolulu) – Definition not known. Named for High Chiefess Konia (1807-1857). Said to be granddaughter of Kamehameha I. Wife of

Abner Pākī. Mother of Bernice Pauahi Bishop, and foster mother of Queen Liliuʻokalani. Member, House of Nobles (1840-1847).

Koniaka Pl. (Waipahu) – All kinds of asters. They are herbs grown ornamentally for their attractive flowers.

Kono St./Pl. (Honolulu) – To invite, ask in, entice.

Konohiki St. (Kāneʻohe) – Head man of an ahupuaʻa (land division) under the chief.

Koʻohoʻō Pl. (Kailua) – Inserted post. Probably should be Koʻokoʻo: cane, staff, rod.

Koʻokū Pl. (Kailua) – Hillside, slope, mountain slope; hillside road or path.

Koʻolani Dr. (Mililani) – Help given to a chief.

Koʻolau Rd./View Dr. (Hauʻula, Kāneʻohe) – Windward sides of the Hawaiian Islands. Named for Oʻahu land districts.

Koʻolau Hale Pl. (Kāneʻohe) – Should be Hale Koʻolau: Koʻolau homes. See Koʻolau.

Koʻolina St. (Waiʻanae) – Definition not known. Named for an Oʻahu land section where the legendary eel Puhinalo was attacked and killed.

Koʻolua Way/Pl. (Mililani) – Name of a star.

Kōpaʻa St. (Waipahu) – Sugar. Literally: hard sugar cane. Probably a garble for Kapaʻa. Named for original awardee.

Kōpākē St. (Waipahu) – A variety of sugar cane imported by the Chinese.

Kope Pl. (Honolulu) – Coffee, coffee beans.

Kōpili Pl. (Kāneʻohe) – Thin, transparent tapa made of mulberry bark.

Kou Pl. (Honolulu, Kāneʻohe, Mililani) – A Cordia tree, probably brought to Hawaiʻi by Polynesians. Its beautifully grained soft wood was shaped into cups, dishes, and calabashes. A popular shade tree, with continuously blossoming orange flowers. It requires little water, and grows very well near the sea.

Kōʻula St. (Honolulu) – Red sugar cane. Named for an Oʻahu land section.

Kōwā St. (Mililani) – Name of a star.

Kōwelo Ave. (Kapolei) – To stream, flutter, wave.

Kū Pl. (Waialua) – Standing. Named for original grantee.

Kuaʻāina Way (Kailua) – Country (as distinct from the city); person from the country, rustic; rural. Literally: back land.

Kuaʻeʻewa Pl. (ʻEwa Beach) – Name of one of two stones, now destroyed, that once marked the boundary between the chief's land and that of the commoners in ʻEwa.

Kuaehu St. (Honolulu) – Silent, still, lonely.

Kuahaka St. (Pearl City) – Surging, swelling, as waves.

Kuahao Pl. (Pearl City) – Anvil, used by blacksmiths.

Kuahaua Pl. (Mililani) – Proclamation, declaration.

Kope

Kuahaua

Kuahea St./Pl. (Honolulu) – Mountain area where trees are stunted, due to altitude.

Kuahelani Ave. (Mililani) – Should be Kuaihelani: a legendary place in the high heavens.

Kuahewa St. (Mililani) – Huge, vast.

Kuahine Dr. (Honolulu) – Term of address for a male's sister or female cousin. Named for legendary sister who brings rains to Mānoa.

Kuahiwi Ave./Way (Wahiawā, Honolulu) – Mountain, high hill.

Kuahono St. (Honolulu) – Should be Kuahonu: a large spotted-back crab, commonly found on coral reefs. Literally: turtle back. Named for a Kaua'i promontory.

Kūāhua Ave. (Honolulu) – Heap, pile; heaped, piled up; rising up, as a whale's back above water. Literally: back heap.

Kuahui St. (Waipahu) – To cooperate, work together.

Kuahulu Pl./Way (Kāne'ohe) – A kind of morning-glory, with white flowers.

Kua'ie St./Pl. (Mililani) – An unidentified star.

Kua'ilima Dr. (Kailua) – Chopping 'ilima (plant). Named for an O'ahu land section.

Kuahui

Kuaiwi Pl. (Honolulu) – Long, straight stone wall.

Kuakahi St./Pl. (Waipahu) – Three generations removed, as between a person and his great-grandparent.

Kuakini St. (Honolulu) – Multitudinous (high ancestors) behind. Named for High Chief John Adams Kuakini (1791-1844). Brother of Ka'ahumanu. Hawai'i Island governor (1820-1844). One of the first chiefs to read and write both English and Hawaiian. The name of U.S. President John Adams was tattooed on his arm.

Kuakoa Pl. (Kāne'ohe) – Should be Kū'oko'a: independence, liberty, freedom.

Kuakolu Pl. (Waipahu) – Five generations removed, as between a person and his great-great-great-grandparent.

Kuakua Pl. (Kāne'ohe) – Strip; embankment between taro patches; narrow land strip; ridged cloth, as corduroy.

Kuala St. (Pearl City) – Pure white mother-of-pearl shell, much prized because of its rarity, as used for fishhooks or lures.

Kualapa St. (Mililani) – Ridge.

Kualau Pl. (Waimānalo) – Shower accompanied by sea wind.

Kuali St. ('Ewa Beach) – White, glistening, sparkling, shining.

Kuali'i St./Pl. ('Ewa Beach) – A celebrated chief noted for his strength and bravery.

Kualoa Rd. (Kāne'ohe) – Long back. Named for an O'ahu land division.

Kualono St. (Honolulu) – Region near the mountaintop, ridge.

Kualua Pl. (Waipahu) – Four generations removed, as between a person and his great-great-grandparent.

Kuamauna St. (Honolulu) – Mountain top.

Kuamoʻo St. (Honolulu) – Backbone. Named for High Chiefess Mary Kuamoʻo (?-1850). A niece of Kamehameha I. Wife of John Young (see Olohana).

Kuamū St./Pl. (Kapolei) – Name of a wind accompanied by heavy rain.

Kuana St. (Honolulu) – Position, attitude; standing.

Kuanalio Lp./Pl./Way (Mililani) – Northern heavens and its stars.

Kuanalu Pl. (Honolulu) – Surf just before it breaks, wave crest.

Kūanoni Way/Pl. (Mililani) – To change, as color.

Kuaōʻa St. (Mililani) – To fit in place.

Kuaola St. (Honolulu) – Verdant mountain, where all thrives and grows.

Kuapapa Pl. (Honolulu) – Peace, quiet, tranquility.

Kūāpōhaku Dr. (Honolulu) – To turn into stone, to transform into stone.

Kuapuiwi Pl. (Kāneʻohe) – Native land, homeland.

Kuapuʻu St. (ʻEwa Beach) – Hunchback; hunch-backed; hump, as of a camel.

Kuanalio

Kūʻau St. (Kailua) – Handle. Named for a legendary rock at Mōkapu (now called Pyramid Rock), believed to give birth to stones.

Kuāua Way (Kāneʻohe) – Shower (rain); to shower.

Kuauli St. (Mililani) – Verdant or green countryside.

Kuāuna Pl. (Mililani) – Bank or border of a taro patch; stream bank.

Kuawa St. (ʻAiea) – Guava.

Kūea St (Kapolei) – Name of a star.

Kuekue St. (Honolulu) – Sound of a tapping, tap, as of a mallet on a tapa anvil.

Kuemanu St. (Waialua) – To attract ʻuaʻu (petrel birds) to a net by imitating their call. Named for original awardee.

Kūʻena St. (Mililani) – Glowing, burning.

Kuapuʻu

Kuewa Dr. (Waialua) – Vagabond, exile, wanderer; wandering, friendless, homeless, unstable.

Kuhaimoana Pl. (ʻEwa Beach) – Mother of Kupiapia and Lukahiʻu, whose sons came to the aid of Kaʻahupahau, the shark goddess of ʻEwa.

Kūhana Pl. (Waipahu) – Each of the two gable posts in the old Hawaiian house.

Kūhaʻo St./Pl. (ʻAiea) – Standing alone, independent. Figuratively: unusual, extraordinary, as rain from a clear sky.

Kuhaulua St./Pl. (Waipahu) – Children of a high chief by a secondary wife. Named for Jesse Kuhaulua, Maui sumo wrestler who achieved fame in

Japan under adopted name Daigoro Takamiyama. Retired in 1985 after 21-year career, with seven major records, including most career matches (1,651) and most career bouts in top division (1,231). The first foreigner to win sumo's highest prize, the Emperor's Cup (1972). First recipient of University of Hawai'i East-West Center award for inter-cultural activity (1972). Now operates a sumo stable under name of Azumazeki.

Kuhe Pl. (Waialua) – A variety of 'o'opu (fish). Named for original grantee.

Kūhea St. (Mililani) – To call.

Kūhela St. (Kapolei) – An unbroken swell of the sea, drifting in without breaking; to sweep along as the sea.

Kuhi St./Pl. (Waialua) – To point, gesture, as in speaking, or dancing the hula; gesture, pointing. Named for original grantee.

Kuhia Pl. ('Ewa Beach) – A former konohiki (headman) of the 'Ewa ahupua'a (land division).

Kuhi

Kuhialoko St./Pl. ('Ewa Beach) – An 'Ewa site named after Kuhia, one of the butlers or providers to Ka'ahupahu, the shark queen of 'Ewa.

Kuhilani St. (Honolulu) – To point out and interpret signs in the sky; a reader of signs in the sky.

Kuhiawaho Pl. ('Ewa Beach) – A former konohiki (headman) of the 'Ewa ahupua'a (land division).

Kuhimana St./Pl. (Waimānalo) – To point with the hand. Named for an O'ahu land section.

Kuhimana

Kuhina St. ('Ewa Beach) – Minister, premier, regent, ambassador; highest officer next to the king.

Kūhiō Ave. (Honolulu) – Literally: standing diagonally. Named for Jonah Kūhiō Kalaniana'ole. See Kalaniana'ole.

Kūhonu Pl. (Kāne'ohe) – A large spotted-back crab, commonly found on coral reefs. Literally: turtle back.

Kui Pl. (Honolulu) – To string pierced objects, as flowers in a lei, or fish.

Ku'ikahi St. (Honolulu) – Treaty, covenant, agreement, feeling of unity.

Kuikele St./Pl. (Honolulu) – Large needle, for darning or a sewing machine. Literally: steering instrument.

Ku'ikepa Pl. (Mililani) – Sculpturing; to carve and shape an image.

Kuiki Pl. (Waipahu) – Quilting; to quilt.

Kuilei St. (Honolulu) – To string flowers, beads, seeds, shells into leis. Named for an O'ahu land section.

Kuilima Dr. (Kahuku) – To go arm in arm, to hold hands; arm in arm.

Kū'īlioloa Pl. ('Ewa Beach) – Long dog Kū (a legendary

Kuikele

dog protecting travelers). Named for the heiau at tip of Kāneʻīlio Point, Waiʻanae.

Kuina St./Pl. (ʻEwa Beach) – A stringing together, as of leis.

Kuʻinē Pl. (Honolulu) – Roaring, as of the sea.

Kuʻinehe Pl. (Mililani) – Quiet and still, without rustling.

Kuini St. (ʻAiea) – Queen.

Kūʻiʻo Pl. (ʻEwa Beach) – Fact, a true statement.

Kuʻipaʻakea Ln. (Honolulu) – Crushing limestone. Named for an Oʻahu land section.

Kuipuakukui St. (Kapolei) – Stringing flowers of the kukui tree into a lei.

Kūkahi St. (Honolulu) – Standing alone, outstanding. Named for an Oʻahu land section.

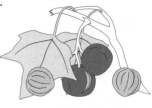

Kukui

Kūkaʻi Pl. (Waiʻanae) – Name of a stream which feeds into Kaupuni Stream in the back of Waiʻanae Valley.

Kukana Way/Pl. (Kailua) – Susan.

Kukane St. (Kāneʻohe) – A rough lemon, with fragrant skin, but too sour to eat.

Kūkaniloko Walk (Haka Dr.) (Honolulu) – Kū sounding inside. Named for an Oʻahu chiefess who lived ten generations before Kamehameha. Granddaughter of Kalonaiki. See Haka.

Kūkea Cir. (Waialua) – Appearing white. Named for original grantee.

Kūkia St. (Kāneʻohe) – Firm, steady.

Kūkiʻi St. (Honolulu) – Standing image. Named for a Kauaʻi promontory.

Kūkila St./Pl. (Honolulu) – Majestic, regal.

Kūkolu St. (Mililani) – Name of the fifth day in the ancient month.

Kūkūau Pl. (Honolulu) – A large deep-sea crab with brown spots. Named for Hawaiʻi Island land divisions.

Kukui Dr./Pl./St. (Honolulu, Wahiawā) – Candlenut tree. Official state tree. Ancient Hawaiians used kukui for dye, lamps, fuel, medicine, relish, and leis. The downtown street is named for kukui trees that grow on royal grounds.

Kukuiʻula Lp./Pl. (Honolulu) – Red light. Named for a Kauaʻi land section.

Kukula St. (Lāʻie) – To go to school.

Kukuna Rd. (Hauʻula) – Ray, of the sun; spoke of a wheel; pistil of a flower.

Kula Ct. (Wahiawā) – Plain; open country.

Kula St. (Honolulu) – Plain; open country. Named for a former Maui land district.

Kukula

Kulaaupuni St. (Waiʻanae) – Public school, government school.

Kulahānai St./Pl. (Waiʻanae) – Boarding school.

Kulahelelā Pl. (Waiʻanae) – Day school.

Kulāiwi St. (Waimānalo) – Native land, homeland; native.

Kulakoa St./Pl. (Wai'anae) – Military academy.

Kula Kōlea Dr./Pl. (Honolulu) – Kōlea (bird) plain.

Kulakumu Pl. (Wai'anae) – Teacher's training school, normal school.

Kūlālā Pl. (Wai'anae) – Plant propagated by slips, shoots or twigs.

Kulamanu St./Pl. (Honolulu) – Bird plain. Possibly named for Kulamanu Beatrice McWayne who lived here.

Kūlana Ct./Pl. ('Ewa Beach) – Station, rank, title, condition, position, place, situation; patch, site; outstanding, prominent.

Kūlani St. (Honolulu) – Of chiefly nature. Named for a Hawai'i Island volcanic cone.

Kulanui St./Ln. (Lā'ie) – University, college; formerly high school. Literally: big school.

Kulapa Pl. (Wai'anae) – To frolic, jump or skip about in sport.

Kula'uala Way (Honolulu) – Sweet potato plain. Sweet potatoes were grown on farms that used to be here.

Kulauku St. (Wai'anae) – Private school.

Kulauli St. (Kāne'ohe) – Green plain.

Kulawae St./Pl. (Wai'anae) – Select school.

Kulawai St./Pl. ('Aiea) – Watering trough, water source.

Kulawea St./Pl. ('Aiea) – Should be Kulawae: select school.

Kūle'a Pl. ('Aiea) – Successful, competent; happily.

Kuleana Rd./Pl. (Pearl City) – Right, privilege, concern, responsibility, property ownership; small piece of property.

Kulekule Pl. (Waipahu) – Secure, permanent.

Kūlewa Lp. (Waipahu) – Moving slowly through space, as clouds; swaying, dangling, hanging.

Kūlia St. (Wahiawā) – To stand, halt; to try, strive.

Kūlike Pl. (Kapolei) – Alike, identical, conforming, resembling.

Kūlina St. ('Aiea) – Corn. Named for an O'ahu land section.

Kuli'ou'ou Rd./Pl. (Honolulu) – Sounding knee. Named for an O'ahu land section.

Kūloa Ave. (Kapolei) – Name of a star, perhaps Venus when seen in the morning.

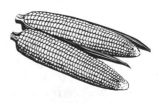

Kūlina

Kūloa'a Pl. (Kailua) – Prosperous, well-supplied with needs.

Kūloko St. (Pearl City) – Local, domestic. Literally: state of being inside.

Kūlua Pl. (Mililani) – Name of the fourth and seventeenth nights of the ancient Hawaiian lunar month.

Kulu'ī Pl. (Honolulu) – Small, endemic trees and shrubs, almost all are endangered or extinct.

Kulukeoe St./Pl. (Kāne'ohe) – Perfect, without error, as a prayer.

Kūmaipō St. (Wai'anae) – Kū from night. Named for
an O'ahu land section.

Kūmakani Lp./Pl. (Honolulu) – Windbreak; wind-
resisting.

Kūmakua Pl. (Kāne'ohe) – Name of a strong wind.

Kūmano St. (Pearl City) – Water dam, reservoir.

Kūmau Pl. (Waipahu) – Customary, usual, regular.

Kumua'o

Kūmauna Pl. (Waimānalo) – Standing (on the) mountain.

Kumepala Pl. (Waipahu) – Cymbal.

Kūmimi St. ('Ewa Beach) – Various kinds of small crabs.

Kūmoana St. (Pearl City) – An unidentified large deep-water crab.

Kūmo'o Lp./Pl. (Kāne'ohe) – Lineage, as of chiefs or priests.

Kumu St./Pl. (Honolulu) – Tree.

Kumua'o St. (Waipahu) – Teacher.

Kumuhau St. (Waimānalo) – Hau tree. Named for an O'ahu land section.

Kumuiki St. (Kapolei) – Small beginning.

Kumukahi St. ('Ewa Beach) – Origin, beginning.

Kumukahi Pl./Way (Honolulu) – Beginning. Named for a Hawai'i Island
promontory.

Kumuko'a St./Pl. (Honolulu) – An unidentified star.

Kumukula St. (Waipahu) – School teacher.

Kumukumu St. (Honolulu) – Stubs. Named for a Kaua'i land division.

Kumulani St./Pl. (Honolulu) – Base of the sky; horizon.

Kumulipo St. (Kapolei) – Origin, genesis, source of life, mystery; name of
the Hawaiian creation chant.

Kumuma'o Pl. (Mililani) – Any type of green Hawaiian stone, as used for
maika stones in the ancient Hawaiian game suggesting bowling. Literally:
green base.

Kumuone St. (Honolulu) – Sandbank; sandstone, used for maika stones in
the ancient Hawaiian game suggesting bowling. Literally: sand base.

Kumupali Rd. (Hale'iwa) – Foot of a cliff.

Kūmū'ula St. (Waimānalo) – Red kūmū (fish).

Kumuwai Pl. (Honolulu) – Source of a stream, spring.

Kunawai Ln. (Honolulu) – Freshwater eel pool. Name of a supernatural
eel. Named for an O'ahu land section.

Kuneki St./Pl./Way (Kāne'ohe) – Filled to overflowing; to flow away.

Kunia Dr./Rd. (Kunia) – Burned. Named for an O'ahu land section.

Kūnihi Pl. (Honolulu) – Steep, sheer, precarious.

Kuoha St. (Waialua) – Love prayer used by a kahuna hana aloha (love
magic priest) to invoke love in someone of the opposite sex. Named for
original grantee.

Kū'oko'a St. (Pearl City) – Independence, liberty, freedom; independent,
free.

Kūola Pl. (Honolulu) – Alive and safe, as after escaping from danger.

Kū'ono Pl. (Kāne'ohe) – Nook, cranny, gulf, bay, cove, indentation.

Kuo'o St. (Waipahu) – Serious, dignified.

Kūpa'a Dr. (Honolulu) – Steadfast, firm; reliable, loyal.

Kūpahu St. (Waialua) – To brace oneself, while being pushed. Named for original grantee.

Kūpale St. (Kāne'ohe) – Defense; to defend, ward off.

Kupali'i Lp. ('Aiea) – All species of Peperomia, small native succulent forest herbs, related to kava.

Kupanaha Pl. (Kapolei) – Surprising, strange, wonderful, extraordinary.

Kūpaoa Pl. (Hale'iwa) – Night cestrum (plants) and other fragrant or strong-smelling plants, including one used to scent tapa.

Kūpau St./Pl. (Kailua) – Entirely finished.

Kūpaua Pl. (Honolulu) – Name of the valley where this development is located. Literally: upright clam.

Kupehau Rd. (Kunia) – Mother-of-pearl shell.

Kūpehe Ln. (Waipahu) – To walk slowly, unsteadily, as a sick person.

Kupekala St. ('Ewa Beach) – An edible bivalve shell-fish found at Pearl Harbor.

Kūpaoa

Kupeleko Pl. ('Ewa Beach) – Cypress; found near the Soto Mission in Tenney Village.

Kupiapia Pl. ('Ewa Beach) – Son of Kuhaimoana, who with his brother Lukahi'u, came to the aid of Ka'ahupahau, shark goddess of 'Ewa.

Kupipi Pl. ('Ewa Beach) – Son of Ka'ahupahau, the shark goddess of 'Ewa.

Kūpohu St. (Kāne'ohe) – Should be Kūpoho: calm.

Kūpono Pl. ('Aiea) – Upright, honest, proper, right, just, fair.

Kupu Pl. (Honolulu) – Sprout, growth; offspring; to sprout, grow, increase.

Kūpuku Cir. (Mililani) – A constellation of seven stars, probably the Pleiades. Literally: cluster.

Kupukupu Cir./Pl./St. (Wahiawā, 'Aiea) – General name for ferns on a single stem.

Kupulau Pl. (Mililani) – Spring season. Literally: leaf sprouting.

Kupuna Lp. (Waipahu) – Starting point, source; growing.

Kupuohi St./Pl. (Waipahu) – To flourish, grow vigorously, mature early, as an adolescent.

Kupu'eu Pl. (Waipahu) – Hero, wondrous one.

Kupuwao Pl. ('Aiea) – An endemic class of small trees. Literally: mountain sprout.

Kūuaki Pl. (Waipahu) – Watchman, sentinel, guard.

Ku'uala St. (Kailua) – My street.

Ku'ualoha Rd. (Wai'anae) – My affection.

Ku'uhale St. (Kailua) – My house.

Ku'uhoa Pl. (Kailua) – My companion.

Ku'u Home Pl. (Kāne'ohe) – My home.

Ku'uhale

Kuʻuipo Pl. (Kāneʻohe) – My sweetheart.
Kuʻukama St. (Kailua) – My child.
Kuʻulei Rd. (Kailua) – My lei; my beloved.
Kuʻumele Pl. (Kailua) – My song.
Kuʻuna St./Pl. (Kailua) – Slope of a hill. Figuratively: traditional, hereditary.
Kuʻuniu St. (Kailua) – My coconut.
Kuʻupua St. (Kailua) – My flower.

Kuʻuipo

Kuuwelu St./Pl. (ʻEwa Beach) – Should be Kūwelu: an unidentified woody shrub.
Kūwale Rd./Pl. (Waiʻanae) – Standing alone. Named for Mauna Kūwale, a nearby peak.
Kūwili St. (Honolulu) – Stand swirling. Named for an Oʻahu land section.
Laʻa Ln. (Honolulu) – Sacred, holy, devoted, consecrated, dedicated.
Laahaina Pl. (Kapolei) – Should be Lāʻahaʻaina: feast day.
Laʻakea St./Pl. (Honolulu) – Sacred light, sacred things of day, as sunshine, knowledge, happiness. Literally: light sacredness.
Laʻakona St. (ʻEwa Beach) – Name of a prosperous ʻEwa chief.
Laʻaloa St./Pl. (Kapolei) – A variety of hard taro.
Laʻamia St./Pl. (Honolulu) – Calabash tree. The pulp and seeds are removed from the shells, which are polished. Seeds of aliʻipoe are placed inside the shells to make hula rattles. See Aliʻipoe.
Laʻanui St. (Waiʻanae) – Last name of Princess Kahanu's mother, Mūʻolo Laʻanui.
Lāʻau St. (Honolulu) – Tree, plant, wood, forest, stick, pole, rod, club.
Lāʻauhuahua Way/Pl. (Pearl City) – Fruitful tree.
Laʻaʻula Pl. (Mililani) – Autumn.
Laʻaulu St./Pl. (ʻEwa Beach) – Spring, time of growth.
Lāʻaunoni Pl. (Waiʻanae) – Noni tree. The Indian mulberry, with large shiny leaves, small flowers, and distasteful fruit. Many parts of the tree were used for dyes and medicine.
Lāʻau Paina Pl. (Waialua) – Pine tree.
Lae St. (Honolulu) – Forehead. Named for original awardee.
Laʻelaʻe Way (Honolulu) – Bright, shiny, clear, serene, calm, pleasant.
Laelua Pl. (ʻAiea) – Prominent, as a ridge. Literally: double brow.
Laenani Dr. (Kāneʻohe) – Beautiful promontory.

Kuʻuniu

Laenui St. (Waipahu) – Large promontory.
Laha St./Pl. (Kāneʻohe) – Extended, spread out, broad, widespread.
Lāhai St. (Mililani) – To poise aloft, as a kite.
Lahaina St. (Waiʻanae) – Named for a Maui district, said to have been Lāhainā: cruel sun.

Laha'ole Pl. (Waipahu) – Rare, choice, unique; not spread, not common.
Lahe St. (Mililani) – Soft.
Lahi St. (Kapolei) – A variety of sugar cane, the yellow variation of laukona.
Lāhiki Cir. ('Aiea) – Eastern sun, rising sun; eastern.
Lāhikiola Pl. (Wai'anae) – Life bringing sun.
Lāhilahi St./Pl. (Wai'anae) – Thin. Named for Mauna Lahilahi, a nearby hill.
Lāhui St./Pl. (Mililani) – Nation, race, tribe, people, nationality.
Lā-'Ī Rd. (Honolulu) – Tī leaf.

Laiki

Lā'ielua Pl. (Honolulu) – Two 'ie-vine leaves.
Laiki Pl. (Kailua) – Rice. Named for Arthur Rice (1878-1955). Son of Kaua'i Governor William Rice. Kaua'i County Treasurer (1912). Site of his former country home (built 1915). Coconut palms were planted for a copra plantation, which failed. The property has been subdivided.
La'ikū St./Pl. (Wai'anae) – Great calm, quiet, peace, serenity.
Lā'imi Rd. (Honolulu) – Day of seeking. Named for an O'ahu land section.
La'ipū St./Pl. (Mililani) – To be peaceful.
Laka Pl. ('Aiea) – Tame, domesticated, gentle, docile.
Lākana Pl. ('Ewa Beach) – Lantana, a thorny tropical American bush with colorful flowers.

Lākapu St. (Honolulu) – Kapu day.
Lākau Pl. (Waipahu) – Setting sun.
Lākī Rd. (Honolulu) – Tī leaf.
Lakimau St. (Honolulu) – Always lucky.
Lakimela Ln. (Honolulu) – Origin not known.
Lākau

Lākō St. ('Ewa Beach) – Sugarcane leaf.
Lakoloa Pl. (Honolulu) – Very rich; very prosperous.
Lakona Walk (Honolulu) – Definition not known. Named for an ancient O'ahu chief known for his peaceful reign, 15 generations before Kamehameha. See Haka.
Lālā Pl. (Kailua) – Branch, limb.
Lālahi St. (Kapolei) – Thin, delicate.
Lala'i St./Pl. (Mililani) – Calm, stillness, quiet, as of sea, sky, wind.
Lālama Lp. (Waipahu) – Daring, fearless, clever, as a climber of precipices or trees.

Lālāmilo St./Pl. (Honolulu) – Milo (tree) branch.
Lālani St. ('Aiea) – Row, rank, line.
Lālāwai Dr./St. ('Aiea, Wahiawā) – Prosperous, successful, well-to-do, rich.

Lakoloa
Lālāwai

Lale St. (Kailua) – To hasten, hurry, push on; to encourage, urge on, stir up to action.

Lālea Pl. (Honolulu) – Buoy, beacon; prominent object or landmark ashore to steer by.

Lālei Pl. (Mililani) – Assembled together, as flowers in a lei.

Lalo Kuilima Way/Pl. (Kahuku) – Should be Kuilima Hema: south Kuilima. See Kuilima.

Lama

Lama Pl. (Kailua) – Torch, light, lamp.

Lamakū Pl. (Honolulu) – Large torch, giving light from burning kukui nuts strung on a coconut midrib, wrapped in dried tī leaves, and placed at the tips of bamboo handles.

Lamalama Pl. (Kāneʻohe) – Torch fishing; to go torch fishing.

Lamaloa Pl. (Honolulu) – Long torch.

Lamaʻula Rd./Pl. (Kāneʻohe) – Red torch.

Lana Ln. (Honolulu) – Floating, buoyant; to lie at anchor, as a fishing canoe.

Lānaʻe Way (Kailua) – Windward day.

Lānaʻi St. (Honolulu, Wahiawā) – Day of conquest. Named for the island.

Lanakila Ave./Pl. (Honolulu, Pearl City) – Victory. Named for an Oʻahu land section.

Lanakoi St. (Kapolei) – To desire greatly.

Lani St./Pl. (Honolulu) – 1) Sky, heaven. 2) Very high chief, majesty.

Lānia Way/Pl. (ʻAiea) – To warm, toast, or wilt over a fire, as young pandanus leaves.

Lanialiʻi St./Ct. (Wahiawā) – A climbing shrub with yellow flowers. Literally: royal chief.

Lanihale Pl. (Honolulu) – Chief's house.

Lanihuli St./Pl. (Lāʻie) – Changing heaven. Named for a Mormon missionary home built in Lāʻie and dedicated in 1894. It was razed in 1960.

Lanihuli Dr. (Honolulu) – Changing heaven. Probably named for an Oʻahu mountain peak.

Lanikāula St. (Honolulu) – Priest aristocrat. Possibly named for a Molokaʻi prophet who warned Maui King Kamalālāwalu not to invade Hawaiʻi Island. The king ignored the advice, and was killed in the attack.

Lanikeha Way/Pl. (Pearl City) – Lofty heaven. Name of a legendary part of heaven. Frequent name of residences of high chiefs, as that of Kamehameha III at Lahaina, Maui.

Lanikuakaʻa St. (ʻAiea) – Sky with rolling ridge. Poetic name for a very high chief or the highest heaven.

Lanikūhana Ave./Pl. (Mililani) – An unidentified star. Literally: chief standing (at) work.

Laniloa Pl./Rd. (Wahiawā, Honolulu) – Tall majesty.

Lanipaʻa St. (Mililani) – Firmament. Literally: solid heaven.

Lanipili Pl. (Honolulu) – A heavy rain, lasting many days, or a cloudburst.

Lanipō Dr. (Kailua) – Dense, dark, as plants, rain; said of luxuriant growth.

Lanipoko Pl. (Honolulu) – Short heaven.

Lanipola Pl. (Kāneʻohe) – Perhaps should be Lanipōlua: rain name.

Lanipūʻao St. (Honolulu) – Womb sky. Named for a sea rock near Kalāheo, Kauaʻi. Also called Kalanipūʻao.

Laniuma Lp./Rd./Pl. (Honolulu, Wahiawā) – The rose geranium. Its fragrant leaves are used in leis with odorless flowers.

Laniwai Ave. (Pearl City) – A kind of water lemon or sweet granadilla (passion fruit).

Laniwela Way (Kāneʻohe) – Canada fleabane, a weedy herb.

Lānui Pl. (Honolulu) – Holiday, important or big day.

Lāola Pl. (Honolulu) – Day of health.

Lapa Pl. (Kailua) – Ridge, steep side of a ravine.

Lapaiki St. (Mililani) – Small drum.

Lāpine Pl. (ʻEwa Beach) – Lemon grass, a plant with rough, fragrant leaves. The leaves are dried and used for cooking.

Lau Pl. (Kaʻaʻawa) – Leaf, frond; to leaf out.

Lauaʻe St. (Mililani) – A fragrant fern; beloved.

Lauaki St./Pl. (Mililani) – To cooperate, work together, as experts; to concentrate on the same task; to pool talents.

Lauaʻe

Lauʻawa St./Pl. (Mililani) – Pagoda flower, a low shrub with clusters of scarlet flowers.

Lauhala Rd./St. (Wahiawā, Honolulu) – Pandanus leaf, especially as used in weaving. See Hala.

Lauhoe Pl. (Honolulu) – Blade of a canoe paddle.

Lauhulu St. (ʻAiea) – Dry banana leaf.

Lauia St. (Kapolei) – A parrot fish.

Lauiki St. (Honolulu) – Little leaf.

Laukahi St./Pl. (Honolulu) – Broad-leafed plantain, a stemless weed with thick, broad leaves and tiny flowers. Used medicinally.

Laukalo St. (Waimānalo) – Taro leaf. Named for an Oʻahu land section.

Lauhoe

Laukani St. (Honolulu) – Tough, hardy.

Laukea St. (Waipahu) – A small tree or shrub on Kauaʻi only in the euphorbia family, having small clustered flowers.

Laukō St. (Waipahu) – Sugar cane leaf.

Laukoa Pl. (Honolulu) – Leaf of a koa tree.

Laukona Lp. (ʻEwa Beach) – A variety of sugar cane with green and yellow striped canes and leaves. Used in sorcery.

Laukupu Way (Honolulu) – Growing leaf. Named for the moʻo or supernatural lizard guardian of Kuapā fishpond.

Laulā Way (Honolulu) – Broad, wide; liberal; widely known.

Laulani St. (Honolulu) – Heavenly leaf.

Laulauna St. ('Ewa Beach) – Friendly, sociable.

Laulaunui St. ('Ewa Beach) – Islet in the West Loch of Pearl Harbor. Literally: large leaf package.

Laulē'a Pl. (Kāne'ohe) – Peace, happiness, friendship; restoration of a disrupted friendship; happy, glad, courteous, peaceful.

Laulele St. (Wai'anae) – Net fishing with small nets, in shallow water.

Laulele

Lauli'i Way (Waimānalo) – Small leafed.

Laulima St. ('Aiea) – Cooperation; group of people working together. Literally: many hands.

Lauloa St. (Kailua) – Long wave or surf, extending from one end of the beach to the other.

Laumaile St. (Honolulu) – Maile leaf. See Maile.

Laumaka St. (Honolulu) – Budding leaf. Named for Great Mahele awardee who received Hāunapō, an O'ahu land section.

Laumania Ave. (Wai'anae) – Smooth, sheer, steep, even.

Laumiki Pl. (Kāne'ohe) – Shriveling leaf.

Laumilo St. (Waimānalo) – A rare and tasty eel. Literally: milo leaf.

Launa Pl. (Honolulu) – Friendly, sociable; to associate with, fraternize with.

Launa Aloha Pl. (Kailua) – Friendly association, fellowship.

Launahele St. ('Ewa Beach) – Plants, forest growth or leaves, herbs, greenery.

Launiu St. (Honolulu) – Coconut leaf, frond.

Lau'o St. ('Ewa Beach) – Sugar cane leaf.

Lauoha Pl. (Honolulu) – Sail of a vessel.

Lau'ole St. ('Aiea) – Leafless.

Lauone Lp./Pl. (Wahiawā) – Light, fertile soil, easy to cultivate. Literally: sand surface.

Laupa'i St./Way/Pl. ('Ewa Beach) – A great many, multitude, great quantity.

Lauoha

Laupalai Pl. (Waipahu) – To shine, glitter, sparkle, as dew in the sun.

Laupapa St./Pl. ('Ewa Beach) – A broad flat, as coral, lava, or reef.

Lau'ula St. (Honolulu) – Red leaf.

Lauwī Pl. (Waipahu) – A Hawaiian honeycreeper, a small, endemic, endangered forest bird.

Lauwiliwili St. (Kapolei) – A butterfly fish.

Lawa Pl. (Honolulu) – Enough, sufficient, ample.

Lāwa'i St. (Honolulu) – Definition not known. Named for a Kaua'i land division.

Lawaiʻa St. (Waiʻanae) – Fisherman; to fish, to catch fish.

Lawakua Lp. (Waipahu) – Strong-backed, muscular, of strong physique, bulging with muscles.

Lāwalu Pl. (ʻEwa Beach) – Fish or meat bound in tī leaves for cooking; to cook thus.

Lawehana St. (Honolulu) – Workman, laborer; industrious; to do labor, work.

Lawelawe St./Pl. (Honolulu) – To serve, work for, attend to; to wait, on tables; to handle.

Lawakua

Lawena St. (Mililani) – Getting, acquiring, taking; movement, as dancing hands.

Lea Pl. (Mililani) – An unidentified star.

Lēʻahi Ave. (Honolulu) – Short for Laeʻahi: brow of the ʻahi (fish). See Kaimanahila.

Lealea Pl. (Mililani) – An unidentified star, named for Lea, the goddess of canoe builders.

Lehia St. (Honolulu) – Skilled, expert, as in fishing; deft.

Lehiwa Dr. (Mililani) – Admirable, attractive.

Leho Pl. (ʻAiea) – General name for cowry shell. Cowries were used as food, ornamentals, tools, and octopus lures.

Lehopulu St. (Waipahu) – Earth-clinging rainbow. Literally: wet cowry shell.

Lehua

Lehoʻula Pl. (Waipahu) – The rare, highly prized red cowry (shell).

Lehu St. (ʻEwa Beach) – A variety of sugar cane.

Lehua Ln./St./Rd./Ave. (Honolulu, Wahiawā, Pearl City) – The flower of the ʻōhiʻa tree and also the tree itself, famous in song and legend. Its flowers are used for beautiful leis. Lehua is the flower of Hawaiʻi Island. Its wood was shaped into spears, poi boards, tapa anvils, and images.

Lehuakona St. (Mililani) – Star in the Milky Way, perhaps Antares. Literally: south lehua flower.

Lehulehu St. (Kapolei) – Multitude, crowd, great number, population, legion, the public.

Lehuuila St./Pl. (Kāneʻohe) – Flashes of lightning; to flash.

Lei Rd./Ln. (Honolulu) – Garland, wreath; necklace.

Lēʻia St. (Waipahu) – Abundance; full.

Leialiʻi St. (ʻAiea) – Royal lei, chief's lei, crown.

Leialoalo St./Pl. (ʻEwa Beach, Wahiawā) – Hibiscus lei.

Leialoha Ave. (Honolulu) – Wreath (of) love.

Lei ʻAwapuhi Pl. (Wahiawā) – Wild ginger lei.

Leihaku St. (Waipahu) – Braided lei, as of ferns and flowers.

Leihōkū St. (Waiʻanae) – Lei (of) stars.

Leihua St./Pl. (Waiʻanae) – Fruit lei.

Leihulu Pl. (ʻAiea) – Feather lei, formerly worn by royalty. Figuratively: dearly beloved child, or choice person.

Lei

Leilani St. (Honolulu) – Heavenly lei, royal lei.

Leileho Pl. (Wai'anae) – Lei of cowry shells.

Leilehua Ln./Rd./Ave. (Honolulu, Wahiawā) – Lei of lehua (flower) blossoms. Named for O'ahu land sections.

Leilīpoa Way (Honolulu) – Līpoa (seaweed) lei. Maunalua fishermen offered līpoa leis to Malei (the fishing goddess), in exchange for good luck at fishing.

Leiloke Dr. (Honolulu) – Lei of rose blossoms.

Leima'o Pl. (Kapolei) – Ma'o flower lei.

Leimomi Pl. (Wahiawā) – Pearl necklace.

Leinani Pl. (Waipahu) – Beautiful lei.

Leiole St. (Kapolei) – Pumice stone used for medicine and for polishing.

Leipapa Way (Kapolei) – Flat lei, as for a hat; any lei on a flat surface, especially a feather lei.

Leipūpū Pl. (Wai'anae) – Shell lei.

Leke Pl. ('Aiea) – Lady (nobility title).

Lekeona St. (Kailua) – Legion; a large number.

Lēkō Pl. (Waipahu) – Watercress.

Lele St. (Honolulu) – To leap, jump.

Leleaka St./Pl. (Mililani) – Milky Way. Literally: light wind-blown rain or mist.

Lelehu St./Pl. (Waipahu) – Dusk; sleepy.

Lelehua Pl. (Waipahu) – A good thinker, planner.

Lele

Lelehuna St. (Waipahu) – Fine wind-blown rainspray, dust mist; to fall as fine rain.

Lelehune Pl. (Honolulu) – Fine wind-blown rain spray, dust, mist; to fall as fine rain.

Leleiona St. (Mililani) – Milky Way.

Lelekepue Pl. (Honolulu) – Hard volcanic rock, used for adzes.

Lele'oi St./Pl. ('Ewa Beach) – Excessive, very great.

Lelepau Pl. (Honolulu) – To trust completely.

Lelepua St./Pl. (Waipahu) – Flower altar.

Leleu Pl. (Mililani) – An unidentified fruitful tree.

Leleua Way/Lp./Pl. (Kāne'ohe) – Wind-blown rain.

Leleuli St./Pl. (Kahuku) – A gusty, wintry wind.

Lelewalo St. (Mililani) – Loud, distant cry.

Leleuli

Lemi St. (Wahiawā) – Lemon.

Lemiwai St. (Wahiawā) – A kind of water lemon or sweet granadilla (passion fruit), with orange or purple color.

Lena Pl. (Wahiawā) – Yellow, yellowish.

Leoiki St. (Waipahu) – A low voice; to speak softly. Literally: small voice.

Leokāne St. (Waipahu) – Male voice, bass. Literally: male voice.

Leokū St. (Waipahu) – Song sung to an audience. Literally: standing voice.

Le'olani St./Pl. (Mililani) – Lofty, tall; chiefly, height, rank.

Leoleo St. (Waipahu) – To speak loudly, angrily, vociferously; to wail, for the dead.

Leolua St. (Waipahu) – Duet; to sing in twos; two voices.

Leomana Way/Pl. (Waipahu) – Voice of authority.

Leomanu Pl. ('Aiea) – Voice of birds.

Leomele St. (Pearl City) – Song tune; notes on the scale.

Leomele

Leonui St. (Waipahu) – Loud voice; to speak loudly.

Leo'ole St. (Waipahu) – Uncomplaining, agreeable; considerate of feelings of others; giving generously. Literally: no voice.

Leowaena St. (Waipahu) – Second treble, middle or alto voice.

Leowahine St. (Waipahu) – Soprano, feminine voice, falsetto.

Lepeka Ave. (Wai'anae) – Rebecca.

Lepelepe Cir. (Wahiawā) – Perhaps short for Lepelepeamoa: all species of Selaginella, small club mosses used for leis.

Lewa Pl. (Wahiawā) – Sky, atmosphere, space, upper heavens.

Lewalani Dr. (Honolulu) – Highest level of the heavens.

Lewanu'u St./Pl. (Mililani) – Level in the heavens lower than the lewalani, atmosphere reached by birds. See Lewalani.

Leowahine

Li'a Way (Wahiawā) – Strong desire; amorous yearning; to wish for ardently, crave.

Līanu Pl. (Waipahu) – Cool chill.

Līhau St. (Kapolei) – Gentle cool rain, considered lucky for fishermen; moist and fresh, as plants in the dew or rain; cool, fresh, as dew-laden air.

Lihi Way (Wahiawā) – Edge, rim, border, boundary.

Lihikai Dr. (Kāne'ohe) – Seashore.

Lihimauna Rd. (Ka'a'awa) – Mountain edge.

Lihipali Pl. (Honolulu) – Edge of a cliff.

Lihiwai Rd. (Kailua) – Edge of a stream.

Liho St. (Mililani) – Choice, precious.

Liholiho St. (Honolulu) – Very hot, fiery, glowing. Named for Alexander Liholiho, crowned as King Kamehameha IV. See Kamehameha IV.

Līhu'e St. (Wai'anae) – Cold chill. Named for a Kaua'i district and town.

Li'i-Ipo St. ('Aiea) – Should be Ipoli'i: little sweetheart.

Likeke Pl. (Kāne'ohe) – Richards. Named for the Rev. Theodore Richards (1867-1948). Kamehameha School teacher and principal (1893-1898), and hymn book publisher. He founded Kokokahi YWCA here (1927).

Likelike Hwy./St. (Honolulu, Kāne'ohe) – Similar. Named for Miriam

Likelike (1851-1887). Sister of King Kalākaua and Queen Lili'uokalani. Mother of Princess Ka'iulani.

Likini St. (Honolulu) – Rigging.

Liko Ln. (Honolulu) – Leaf bud; newly opened leaf. Figuratively: a child or descendant, especially of a chief.

Liku St. (Kailua) – Should be Liko. See Liko.

Lile Pl. (Mililani) – Bright, shiny, dazzling, sparkling.

Līlia Ct./Pl. (Honolulu, 'Aiea) – Any kind of lily.

Līlia

Liliana St. (Wai'anae) – Lillian.

Liliha St./Pl./Ct. Ln. (Honolulu) – Very rich, of fatty oily food. Named for High Chiefess Liliha (?-1842). Daughter of Maui Governor Hoapili. Wife of Boki (see Poki). Succeeded her husband as O'ahu governor, but lost her property and was forced to resign after planning a revolt against Ka'ahumanu and other Christian chiefs. She lived nearby.

Lili'i Pl. (Mililani) – Tiny, dainty, fine.

Liliko'i Way/Pl./Ct. (Honolulu, 'Aiea, Wahiawā) – Passion fruit, purple water lemon, or purple granadilla, a vine.

Līlīlehua St. (Mililani) – The Texas sage plant.

Lilinoe Pl. (Honolulu) – Fine mist, rain. Possibly named for Līlīnoe (goddess of mists), sister of Poliahu (goddess of snow).

Lilipuna Rd./Pl. (Kāne'ohe) – Definition not known. Named for an O'ahu land section.

Lili'uokalani Ave. (Honolulu) – Smarting pain of the chiefess. Named for Queen Kamaka'eha Lili'uokalani (1839-1917), the last Hawaiian monarch (1891-1893). Her desire to restore monarch's power (lost after 1887 "Bayonet Constitution"), led to 1893 revolution. Surrendered throne in face of "America's superior force." Imprisoned 9 months in 'Iolani Palace for "treason" (1895). Composer, musician, and author. When a princess, she wrote song, "Aloha 'Oe" (1877). Established the Lili'uokalani Trust (1917) to help orphaned and destitute Hawaiians. Her home, Washington Place, is the official governor's residence. She owned land here.

Lilo Pl. (Honolulu) – Busy, absorbed, occupied, engaged, engrossed.

Līloa Rise (Honolulu) – A long time ago. Name of ancient Hawai'i Island king, father of King 'Umi-a-Līloa, founder of the Royal House of Keawe.

Lima St. (Honolulu) – Arm, hand.

Limahana St./Pl. (Waipahu) – Labor, laborer, worker, employee; industrious, busy.

Limakōkua Pl. (Wai'anae) – Helping hand.

Limu Pl. (Honolulu) – A general name for all kinds of plants living in fresh and salt water; also mosses, liverworts, and lichens.

Limahana

Limukele St. (Kapolei) – Moss growing on trees in rain forests.

Linakola St. (Wai'anae) – Lincoln. Possibly named for Lincoln

McCandless (1859-1940). Territorial legislator (1898-1906). A nine-time losing Democratic candidate for U.S. Congress before he finally won an election as a Congressional Delegate (served from 1932-1934). He and brothers James (Kimo) and John got rich drilling 700 artesian water wells to irrigate plantations. Known as Eliwai ("well digger"). He owned 4,000 acres of land. A brother Frank (Palani) lived on the mainland.

Linapuni St. (Honolulu) – Ring around.

Lino Pl. (Waipahu) – Bright, shiny, shining with splendor, dazzling, brilliant.

Linohau Way (Honolulu) – Dressed to perfection, beautifully decorated, ornamented.

Liʻoliʻo Pl. (Kapolei) – Bright, dazzling.

Liona St. (Honolulu) – Lion.

Liona

Liopolo St. (Waiʻanae) – Leopold. Usually: Leopolo. See Palakamana.

Lipaki Pl. (ʻEwa Beach) – Liberty.

Līpalu St./Pl. (Kāneʻohe) – An edible, green, soft, slippery seaweed.

Līpeʻepeʻe St. (Honolulu) – Some native species of edible red seaweeds. Literally: hiding seaweed.

Lipioma Way (Honolulu) – Small rounded adze or chisel.

Lipo St. (Kapolei) – Name of a star in the southern skies.

Līpoa Pl. (ʻAiea) – Edible brown seaweed with many branches. It has a unique aroma and flavor.

Liʻulā St./Pl. (Kāneʻohe) – Twilight, dusk; mirage, hallucination.

Liuliu Pl. (ʻEwa Beach) – Prepared, ready.

Līwai St. (Honolulu) – Possibly named for an early 1900s Kona family, descended from a Hawaiʻi Island chief.

Loaʻa St./Pl. (Waipahu) – To find, get, obtain, gain, succeed; success, solution.

Loala St. (Lāʻie) – To praise, extol, as a chief.

Loea St./Pl. (Mililani) – Skill, ingenuity, cleverness.

Lohe Pl. (Wahiawā) – To hear.

Lohea Pl. (ʻAiea) – Heard; minded, obeyed; audible.

Lohiʻehu St./Pl. (Kāneʻohe) – Faint sparkle.

Lohilani St. (Honolulu) – Heavenly sparkle.

Loho St. (Kailua) – Origin not known.

Loʻi St. (Honolulu) – Irrigated terrace, for taro and rice.

Loke

Lōʻihi St./Pl. (Kāneʻohe) – Length, height, distance; long.

Loʻi Kalo Pl. (Honolulu) – Irrigated taro terrace.

Loina Pl. (Honolulu) – Rule, custom, code, precept, law.

Lōkahi St. (Honolulu) – Unity, agreement, accord; agreed, in unity.

Lōkālia St./Pl. (Mililani) – Coral plant.

Loke Ct./Pl. (Honolulu) – Rose.

Lōkea Pl. (Kāneʻohe) – Long European knife with a white handle.

Lokelani St. (Honolulu) – The common, small red rose. Substitutes for the double pink rose, now rare, as the flower of Maui. Literally: heavenly rose. Named for the Oʻahu subdivision.

Lokelau Pl. (Kailua) – The green rose.

Lōkihi St. (Mililani) – Length, height.

Loko Dr./Pl. (Wahiawā) – Pond, lake, pool.

Loku

Lokoea Pl. (Haleʻiwa) – Rising fishpond. Named for an Oʻahu land section and former fishpond.

Lokowai St./Pl. (ʻAiea) – Fresh-water pond or lake; fountain.

Loku Pl. (Waipahu) – Downpour of rain; blowing of wind.

Lola Way/Pl. (Kailua) – Laurie.

Lolelau St. (Mililani) – Thatching and trimming, of a house.

Lolena St./Pl. (Honolulu) – Inefficient, unproductive, idle, sterile, faded.

Lolopua St./Pl. (Kāneʻohe) – Zenith.

Lomi Pl. (Kāneʻohe) – To rub, press, squeeze, massage, rub out.

Lono Pl. (Honolulu) – God of the Makahiki harvest festivities, of agriculture and fertility. One of the four major Hawaiian gods. (The other three major gods were Kanaloa: god of the ocean; Kāne: god of creation, ancestor of chiefs and commoners; and Kū: god of war and fishing).

Lonomea St. (Waipahu) – A native tree.

Lopaka Way/Pl. (Kailua) – Robert.

Lopeka Pl. (Honolulu) – Roberta.

Lopikane St. (Waiʻanae) – Robinson.

Loulu St./Pl. (Honolulu) – All species of native fan palms. Its leaves were used for thatching; its juvenile leaves were shaped into hats and fans.

Louluhiwa Pl. (Kapolei) – A small native fan palm.

Loululeo Pl. (Kapolei) – A native fan palm.

Luahine

Luaʻehu St./Pl. (Mililani) – Many and colorful.

Luahine St. (ʻEwa Beach) – Old woman, old lady.

Luahoana St. (ʻEwa Beach) – Halo or rainbow around the sun or moon.

Luahoʻomoe Pl. (Mililani) – An unidentified star.

Luaka St. (Waipahu) – Definition not known. Named for original awardee.

Luakaha St./Pl. (Honolulu) – Enjoyable, pleasant, as a place one is attached to; to while away the time enjoyably.

Luakini St./Pl. (Honolulu) – Temple, church, cathedral, tabernacle; a large heiau where ruling chiefs prayed, and human sacrifices were offered.

Lualaʻi St. (ʻEwa Beach) – To be at leisure, enjoy pleasant surroundings and associates, live in comfort and ease, enjoying oneself, relax, be content.

Lualei Pl. (Waiʻanae) – Definition not known.

Lualualei Homestead Rd./Naval Rd. (Wai'anae) – Definition not known. Named for an O'ahu land division.

Luana Pl. (Kāne'ohe) – To be at leisure; to enjoy pleasant surroundings and associates, live in comfort and ease, enjoy oneself, relax, be content.

Luanaiki St. ('Ewa Beach) – To pause a moment; to enjoy oneself.

Lua'ole St./Pl. (Honolulu) – Superior, incomparable, unequalled, second to none, unique, unsurpassed.

Luapele Dr./Pl. (Honolulu) – Volcano, crater.

Luawa Ct. (Wahiawā) – Probably should be Kuawa or Puawa: guava.

Luawai St./Pl. (Honolulu, Kunia) – Well, pond, reservoir.

Lua'ole

Luawainui St. (Kapolei) – Great deep fresh water spring.

Luehu St./Pl. (Pearl City) – A soft, porous stone that breaks easily.

Lūhau St. (Kāne'ohe) – Shaking down of dew or rain drops from tree branches by a breeze; scattered dew, dew-laden.

Luhi Pl. (Honolulu) – Tedious, tired. Named for a Kaua'i beach.

Luhiehu Way (Kāne'ohe) – Beautiful, attractive, festooned.

Luika Pl. (Kailua) – Louise or Louisa.

Luinakoa St. (Honolulu) – Brave sailor.

Luka St. (Honolulu) – 1) Ruth. 2) Luke.

Lukahi'u Pl. ('Ewa Beach) – Son of Kuhaimoana, who with his brother Kupiapia, came to the aid of Ka'ahupahau, the shark goddess of 'Ewa.

Lukānela St. (Waimānalo) – Lieutenant.

Lukela Ln. (Honolulu) – Luther.

Lukepane Ave. (Honolulu) – Frances Lucy. Named for Frances Lucia James, wife of Frank James, an importer-exporter and realtor who subdivided the area (1926). Adjacent streets are named for his daughter, Mary (Makaleka); son, Francis (Palani); and his real estate partner and future Territorial Governor Samuel (Kamuela) Wilder King (1953-1957).

Lūkini Pl. ('Ewa Beach) – Perfume.

Lūlani St./Pl. (Kāne'ohe) – Scattered in the sky.

Lulu St./Pl. ('Aiea) – Calm, peace, shelter, lee, protection, shield, cloak; to lie at anchor; to be calm; to shield.

Luluka St./Pl. ('Ewa Beach, Waipahu) – Peace, calm.

Luluku Rd./Pl. (Kāne'ohe) – Destruction. Named for an O'ahu land section.

Lumaha'i St./Pl. (Honolulu) – Definition not known. Named for a Kaua'i land division.

Lumi St./Pl. (Waipahu) – Room.

Lumi'āina St. (Waipahu) – Dining room.

Lumi'alani St. (Waipahu) – Orange room.

Lumi'au'au St. (Waipahu) – Bathing room, bathroom.

Lumi'au'au

Lumihoʻāhu St./Pl. (Waipahu) – Store room.
Lumiholoi St. (Waipahu) – Laundry room.
Lumiiki St. (Waipahu) – Small room.
Lumikuke Lp./Pl. (Waipahu) – Kitchen. Literally: cooking room.
Lumikula St. (Waipahu) – School room.
Lumiloke St. (Waipahu) – Rose room.
Lumimaʻo Pl. (Waipahu) – Green room.
Lumimoe St. (Waipahu) – Bedroom. Literally: sleeping room.
Lumipolū St./Pl. (Waipahu) – Blue room.
Lumiponi Pl. (Waipahu) – Purple room.
Luna Pl. (Honolulu) – High, upper, above, over, up.
Lunaʻai St./Pl. (Kailua) – Food inspector.
Lunaʻānela St./Pl. (Kailua) – Archangel.
Lunaʻāpono Pl. (Kailua) – Censor, approving officer.
Lunaawa Pl. (Kailua) – Harbor master.

Lumimoe

Lunahaʻi Pl. (Kailua) – Confessor, as a Catholic priest.
 Literally: speaking superior.
Lunahana Pl. (Kailua) – Overseer, foreman, anyone in charge of work.
Lunahaneli Pl. (Kailua) – Centurion. Literally: overseer of hundred.
Lunahelu St./Pl. (Kailua) – Census taker. Literally: counting supervisor.
Lunahōʻoia Pl. (Kailua) – Auditor. Literally: proving officer.
Lunahoʻokō Pl. (Kailua) – Executive officer. Literally: officer who
 accomplishes.
Lunalilo Fwy./St./Home Rd. (Honolulu) – Very high (of royalty). Named
 for King William Lunalilo (1833-1874). The first elected Hawaiʻi
 monarch (1873-1874). Tried to abolish property requirement for voting,
 but failed. Established Lunalilo Home (1877) to help poor and sick
 Hawaiians. He owned land in Makiki.
Lupe St. (Waimānalo) – Name of the chief of the village where the
 legend occurred.
Lupea St. (ʻAiea) – Pleasing, attractive, as plants.
Lupenui Pl. (Waialua) – Large kite.
Lupo St. (Kāneʻohe) – Wolf.
Lūpua Pl. (Mililani) – Flower scattering. Name of a wind associated with
 Wainiha, Kauaʻi.
Maʻakua Rd. (Hauʻula) – Definition not known. Named for an Oʻahu
 gulch.
Maʻalaea Rd. (Honolulu) – Red color, red earth color. Named for a Maui
 land section.
Maʻalahi St./Pl. (Honolulu) – Contentment, simplicity, ease; to be easy,
 simple.
Maʻalewa St. (Mililani) – Aerial root or vine; swinging.
Maʻalili Pl. (Kapolei) – Cooled, of what has been hot, as food; abated,
 calmed, of anger, love, passion.

Mā'ana St. ('Ewa Beach) – Beginning.

Mā'alo St. (Wahiawā) – To pass along, by, or alongside; to pass through, as land.

Ma'aloa St. (Wai'anae) – A low native shrub, related
to māmaki. Its strong bark yielded afiber that was
pounded into tapa.

Māaniani Way/Pl. (Waipahu) – Gentle blowing of the
wind. Figuratively: tranquility.

Ma'awe

Ma'awe St. (Waipahu) – Fiber, thread; strand, as of
a spider web; faint footprint; to tread, track, follow, as a trail.

Māealani Pl. (Mililani) – To get up, rise.

Mā'eha Pl. (Kāne'ohe) – Hurt, in pain, painful; pain, injury, suffering.

Ma'ema'e Ln. (Honolulu) – Clean, pure, attractive.
Named for an O'ahu land section.

Maha Pl. (Honolulu) – Temple, side of the head.

Mahailua St. (Waimānalo) – Perhaps short for Mahaiulua:
a variety of ulua (fish). Named for an O'ahu land section.

Mahakea Rd. (Kāne'ohe) – Once uncultivated land, for
bananas, sweet potatoes, or taro. Named for original
awardee.

Mā'eha

Mahalani Cir./St./Pl. (Kāne'ohe) – Royal twins. Named
for an O'ahu land section.

Mahalo St. (Honolulu) – Thanks, gratitude; to thank.

Mahamoe St. ('Ewa Beach) – Attractive, sleek, as a plump animal.

Mahana St. (Honolulu) – Warmth, heat; warm. Named for original
awardee.

Māhani Lp. (Honolulu) – Dull (not sharp). Named for an O'ahu land
section.

Mahao'o Pl. (Honolulu) – Mature in wisdom; wise; wise person. Literally:
mature temple.

Mahapili Ct./St. (Mililani) – Name of twin stars, probably short for
Māhana-pili: clinging twins. The twin stars are probably Castor and
Pollux.

Mahau Pl. (Mililani) – Definition not certain. Possibly: twins, referring to
the constellation Gemini.

Maha'ulu Ln. (Hale'iwa) – Grove or group of breadfruit trees.

Māhea St. (Mililani) – Hazy, as moonlight.

Māhealani Pl. (Kailua) – Sixteenth night of the ancient
Hawaiian lunar month, just after the night of the full
moon.

Mahele St./Lp. (Wahiawā) – Portion, division, zone,
category. Land division of 1848 was called the "Great
Mahele."

Māhelu

Māhelu St./Pl. (Mililani) – To dig, rake, scratch the earth.

Mahi Pl. (Honolulu) – To cultivate, farm. Possibly named for a Hawaiian who owned much of Mō'ili'ili.

Mahi'ai St./Pl. (Honolulu) – Farmer, planter. Named for Chiefess Keali'imahi'ai. Daughter of Nāhaku'elua. See Nāhaku.

Māhie St./Pl. (Honolulu) – Delightful, charming, pleasant.

Mahikō Pl. ('Aiea) – Sugarcane plantation.

Mahikū Pl. (Waimānalo) – To clear land for planting.

Māhiloa Pl. (Kailua) – Distant, far.

Mahimahi St./Pl. (Honolulu) – Dolphin, a deep sea game fish, and a popular meal.

Mahimahi

Mahina Ave. (Honolulu) – Moon, month; moonlight.

Mahina'ai St. (Waialua) – Farmer, planter; to farm, cultivate.

Mahina'au Rd. (Wai'anae) – Should be Mahina'ai: farmer, planter; to farm, cultivate.

Māhinahina St. (Waipahu) – Pale moonlight.

Mahinahou St./Pl. (Mililani) – New moon, new month.

Mahinui Rd. (Kāne'ohe) – Great champion. Named for an O'ahu land section.

Mahiole St./Pl. (Honolulu) – Feather helmet, helmet.

Mahipua St. ('Aiea) – Flower garden or patch; horticulture.

Mahina

Māhoa Pl. (Mililani) – To travel together in company, as canoes.

Māhoe St./Pl. (Waipahu) – Twins.

Mahola Pl. ('Aiea) – To spread out; to extend, expand.

Māhua Pl. (Waipahu) – Increase, growth; to increase, thrive, multiply, flourish.

Māhukona St. (Honolulu) – Leeward steam. Named for a Hawai'i Island land division.

Māhuli St./Pl. (Mililani) – To seek.

Mai Pl. (Honolulu) – Pronunciation and definition not known.

Mai'a St. (Wai'anae) – All kinds of bananas, introduced by the Hawaiians.

Mai'a'eka Pl. (Waimānalo) – A Hawaiian banana variety. Literally: discolored banana.

Mai'aiholena Pl. (Wai'anae) – A Hawaiian banana variety, with salmon-pink skin. One of the few bananas that ancient Hawaiian women were allowed to eat before the kapu was abolished (1819). Literally: yellow-cored banana.

Mai'a

Maiakū St./Pl. (Mililani) – Stars in the belt of Orion constellation: Mintaka, Alnilam, and Alnitak.

Maiao Pl. (Mililani) – An unidentified star, used for navigating.

Mai'a'ohe Pl. (Mililani) – An ancient Hawaiian banana variety. Literally: bamboo banana.

Maiapilo Way (Kāne'ohe) – A low shrub with vinelike branches.

Mai'apōlua Pl. (Wai'anae) – An ancient Hawaiian banana variety.

Mai'aponi Pl. (Kāne'ohe) – A Hawaiian variety of mountain banana. Literally: purple banana.

Maiau St. (Waipahu) – Neat and carefrul in work; skillful, ingenious, expert.

Maiele Pl. (Waipahu) – Eloquence, skill in speaking.

Ma'iha Cir./Pl. (Pearl City) – Energetic, persevering.

Maihua Pl. (Kāne'ohe) – A variety of taro.

Maika Way/Pl. (Hale'iwa) – Ancient Hawaiian game suggesting bowling; also, the stone used in the game.

Maika'i St./Pl. (Waipahu) – Good, excellent; good-looking, handsome, beautiful.

Māiki Pl. (Pearl City) – Little, small, wee.

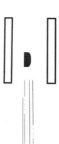

Maika

Māikoiko St. (Waipahu) – A common variety of sugar cane, **used** for chewing; named for maiko, a fish.

Mailani St. ('Ewa Beach) – To extol, praise, treat as a chief or great favorite, indulge, spoil.

Maile Way (Honolulu) – A native twining shrub, with shiny fragrant leaves. See Ala Le'ie.

Mā'ili St./Lp. (Wahiawā) – Pebble; pebbly, full of pebbles.

Mā'ili'ili Rd. (Wai'anae) – Pebbly. Named for an O'ahu hill and stream.

Mā'ilikūkahi Walk (Honolulu) – Perhaps: pebble standing alone. Named for an O'ahu chief who lived 13 generations before Kamehameha. See Haka.

Mā'i'o St. (Mililani) – An unidentified star.

Ma 'Iola St./Pl. (Wai'anae) – To cure sickness. Named for a god of healing.

Ma'ipalaoa Rd. (Wai'anae) – Whale genitals. Named for an O'ahu stream.

Maipela St. (Wai'anae) – Maybelle, Mabel.

Ma'ipuhi St./Pl. ('Ewa Beach) – The bathing place of Ka'ahupahau, the shark goddess of 'Ewa.

Māi'u'u Rd. (Wai'anae) – Toenail or fingernail, hoof, claw.

Māi'u'u

Maka St./Pl. (Kāne'ohe, Honolulu) – 1) Eye. 2) Beloved one. 3) Point. 4) Mesh of a net.

Māka'a St./Pl. (Honolulu) – Clear and open, as a view; a clearing.

Maka'āinana St. (Waimānalo) – Commoner, populace, people in general.

Maka'ala St. (Honolulu) – Alert, vigilant, watchful, wide awake.

Maka'āloa St./Pl. ('Ewa Beach) – A small reddish crab found on mud flats.

Makaaloha St. (Waipahu) – Loving eyes.

Maka'amo'amo Pl. (Mililani) – An unidentified star or constellation in the Milky Way. Literally: twinkling eye.

Maka'aoa St./Pl. (Honolulu) – A shellfish. Named for a demigoddess who lived in Maunalua.

Mākaha Valley Rd. (Wai'anae) – Fierce. Named for an O'ahu land division.

Makahaiku St./Pl. (Kapolei) – Name of a star, in the Southern skies, perhaps Venus when seen in the morning.

Makahani St. (Kapolei) – To step lightly, touch lightly, to skim lightly.

Makahiki Way (Honolulu) – Ancient festival, beginning about mid-October and lasting four months. Festival included sports and religious activities, and a kapu on war.

Makahinu St. (Kāne'ohe) – Bright face, cheerful look.

Makahī'ō St. (Kāne'ohe) – Eyes that dart in every direction, as if looking for mischief; a mischievously alluring look.

Maka'ike St. ('Ewa Beach) – To see clearly and with keen powers of observation.

Makaholowa'a Pl. (Mililani) – Name of a star, perhaps another name for the North Star.

Makahou St./Pl. (Kapolei) – Beginning, new start.

Makahū'ena Pl. (Honolulu) – Possibly: eyes overflowing with heat (very angry). Named for a Kaua'i promontory.

Makaiau Pl. (Kahuku) – Name of a former Kahuku Plantation employee.

Māka'ika'i St. (Mililani) – To visit, see the sights.

Māka'ikoa St. (Honolulu) – Military police. Literally: soldier police.

Maka'imo'imo St. (Mililani) – A constellation in the Milky Way. Literally: blinking eyes, twinkling eyes.

Maka'ina Pl. ('Ewa Beach) – Guard, watchful.

Maka'iolani St. (Mililani) – An unidentified star. Literally: eye (of the) royal hawk.

Makaipooa Rd. (Kāne'ohe) – Definition not known. Named for original awardee.

Makaiwa St. (Honolulu) – Mother-of-pearl eyes, as in an image, especially of the god Lono. Literally: mysterious eye.

Maka'ina

Makakalo St. (Waimānalo) – Taro source. Name of an O'ahu land section.

Makakilo Dr. (Kapolei) – Observant, watchful eyes; to watch with great attention. Named for an O'ahu crater.

Makakoa Lp. (Waipahu) – Bold, unafraid, fierce.

Makalani St. (Kāne'ohe) – Heavenly face.

Makalapa Dr. (Honolulu) – Ridge features. Named for an O'ahu crater.

Makalapua Pl. (Honolulu) – Handsome, beautiful; to blossom forth. Name given to Lili'uokalani in the song "Makalapua."

Makalauna Pl. ('Ewa Beach) – Friendly, having many friends and associates; sociable.

Makaleʻa St./Lp. (ʻEwa Beach) – Twinkle-eyed, happy-eyed, mischievous.

Makaleha St. (Kāneʻohe) – To look about, as in wonder or admiration, to glance.

Makalehua Pl. (Mililani) – Lehua flower petals; Figuratively: attractive, as young girls.

Mākālei Pl. (Honolulu) – Fish trap.

Makaleka Ave. (Honolulu) – Margaret. See Lukepane.

Makalena St. (Honolulu) – Unfriendly, suspicious glance from under the eyelid. Said to be named for Solomon Makalena, a 1920s policeman who lived here.

Makaliʻi Pl. (Kailua) – Tiny, very small, fine, wee.

Makalika Ct. (Honolulu) – Marguerite, daisy.

Makalike Pl. (Honolulu) – Uniform, in color, style, clothes. Literally: similar face.

Makaloa St. (Honolulu) – A sedge (plant). Cloth-like makaloa was woven to make Niʻihau mats, clothing and bedding items.

Makalu Lp. (Mililani) – A variant of Makulu: the planet Saturn.

Makamae St. (Kāneʻohe) – Precious, of great value, highly prized, darling.

Makamai Lp./Pl. (Kapolei) – Should be Makamae: precious, of great value, highly prized, darling.

Makamaka Pl. (Waipahu) – Intimate friend that one is on terms of receiving and giving freely; pal, buddy; host.

Makamua St./Pl. (Pearl City) – First, beginning, commencement. Literally: first end.

Makana Rd. (Haleʻiwa) – Gift, present; reward, prize; to give a gift.

Makanale St. (Haleʻiwa) – Definition not known.

Makanani Dr. (Honolulu) – McInerny. Named for the McInerny brothers who subdivided this area. Jim (1867-1945), chairman, Hawaiʻi Tourist Bureau, and clothing store owner. William (1867-1947), a Territorial Senator and shoe store owner.

Makana

Makani Ave. (Wahiawā) – Wind, breeze.

Makaniʻolu Pl. (Honolulu) – Cool wind.

Makanui Pl. (Honolulu) – Big eyes.

Mākao Rd. (Hauʻula) – Definition not known. Named for an Oʻahu land division.

Makaoe Ln. (Honolulu) – Should be Makaʻoi: piercing, penetrating, sharp eyes.

Makaonaona St. (ʻEwa Beach) – A sweet, lovely, or tender expression of face or eyes.

Makapipipi St./Pl. (Mililani) – Tiny, twinkling stars.

Makapuʻu Ave./Lighthouse Rd. (Honolulu) – Bulging eyes.

Name of a demigoddess who lived at Makapuʻu Point, Maunalua.

Makau St. (Waiʻanae) – Fishhook.

Makauliʻi Pl. (Honolulu) – Saving, economical, thrifty, provident; miserly, avaricious.

Makaʻunulau St./Pl. (Mililani) – An unidentified star used for navigating. Literally: eyes drawing many.

Makawai Pl. (Waipahu) – Small outlets for water through banks of taro patches.

Makau

Makawao St. (Kailua) – Forest beginning. Named for an Oʻahu land section.

Makaweli St./Pl. (Honolulu) – Fearful features. Named for a Kauaʻi land division.

Makaweo Ave. (Wahiawā) – Red eye.

Makeaupeʻa Pl. (Mililani) – An unidentified star or constellation.

Makeʻe Rd. (Honolulu) – Covetous, greedy, desirous to have; to prize.

Mākeke St. (Kapolei) – Black mustard, a weed in Hawaiʻi, but formerly cultivated for the seeds, which are the main source of table mustard.

Ma Ke Kula St./Pl. (ʻEwa Beach) – At school.

Makena St./Pl. (Kāneʻohe) – Calm, of sea, atmosphere.

Makepono St. (Honolulu) – Profitable.

Māki St. (ʻAiea) – To march.

Makiki St./Pl./Hts. Dr. (Honolulu) – A stone used for adzes, and as a weight for octopus lures. Named for an Oʻahu land section.

Makini St. (Honolulu) – Probably: Martin.

Makoa St. (Waipahu) – Fearless, courageous, aggressive.

Mākohilani St. (Mililani) – An unidentified star. Literally: heavenly digging.

Mākua

Mākolu St. (Pearl City) – Thick, heavy, deep, as of clouds.

Makona St. (Waiʻanae) – Mason.

Makou Pl. (Waipahu) – All native and introduced species of buttercups. They are herbs with small yellow flowers.

Mākua St. (Kailua) – Parents.

Mākua Valley Rd. (Waiʻanae) – Parents. Named for an Oʻahu land division.

Makuahine St./Pl. (Honolulu) – Mother, aunt, female cousin of parents' generation.

Makuakāne St./Pl. (Honolulu) – Father, uncle, male cousin of parents' generation.

Makule Rd. (ʻEwa Beach) – Aged, old, of people.

Makulu Pl. (Mililani) – The planet Saturn.

Makuʻu Lp. (ʻAiea) – Should be Mākuʻe: a native fern.

Makalu

Māla St. (Wahiawā) – Garden, plantation, cultivated field.

Māla'ai St. (Honolulu) – Taro patch, food garden or plantation.

Māla'e Pl. ('Aiea, Kāne'ohe) – Clear, calm; serene, as a cloudless sky.

Mālaekahana Rd. (Kahuku) – Definition not known. Named for an O'ahu land division.

Mālahuna Lp./Pl. (Kapolei) – Hidden garden.

Mālakō St./Pl. ('Ewa Beach) – Sugar plantation.

Mālakole St. (Kapolei) – Spent garden, weak plantation.

Malama Pl. (Honolulu) – Light, month, moon.

Mālana Pl. (Mililani) – An unidentified star.

Malanai St./Pl. (Honolulu) – Name of a gentle breeze associated with places on several islands.

Mālapua Pl. (Honolulu) – Flower garden.

Maleko St. (Kailua) – Mark.

Mali St. (Waipahu) – To flatter, speak gently.

Malia St. (Honolulu) – Mary.

Mālie Pl. (Honolulu) – Calm, quiet, still, gentle; calmly, slowly, quietly.

Mālielie St./Pl. (Mililani) – Calm, quiet, serene.

Māliko St. ('Ewa Beach) – To bud, as leaves.

Malina Pl. (Kāne'ohe) – Calming, soothing.

Malino Pl. (Honolulu) – Calm, quiet, pacific, as the sea; peaceful, as one's spirits.

Mali'o St./Pl. ('Ewa Beach, Kāne'ohe) – Dawn light, twilight, especially as it pierces the shadows of night.

Maliona St. (Wai'anae) – Marion.

Maliu St. (Honolulu) – To heed, give attention, listen, look upon with favor, turn toward.

Mālolo St. (Waimānalo) – General term for Hawaiian flying fishes, a popular food,frequently eaten raw.

Malo'o Pl. (Honolulu) – Dry, dried up, evaporated; drought, dryness.

Malu Pl. (Honolulu) – Shade, shelter, protection, peace, control, strength.

Mālua Dr. (Honolulu) – Depression or cavity, planting hole.

Mālualua St./Pl. ('Aiea) – Rough, bumpy, uneven, full of ruts or puddles.

Māluawai St. (Pearl City) – Watery depression.

Maluhia St. (Honolulu) – Peace, quiet, serenity; safety; peaceful, restful.

Malukai Pl. (Kāne'ohe) – Sea shelter.

Malulani St./Pl. (Kāne'ohe) – Royal protection.

Malulu Pl. (Wahiawā) – Pool that never dries up.

Malumalu Pl. (Kāne'ohe) – Shade or protection of any kind, often humble.

Maluna St. (Honolulu) – Above, over.

Maluniu Ave. (Kailua) – Coconut shade.

Malu'ōhai St. (Kapolei) – Shade of the 'ohai.

Māmaki St. (Honolulu) – Small native trees. Their smooth, light-brown bark has a fibrous inner layer, formerly used for making tapa.

Māmalahoa Pl. (Honolulu) – Club stroke. A law guaranteeing safety to all travelers, promoted by Kamehameha.

Māmalu St./Pl. (Honolulu) – Protection, defense, shade, covering; protected, shaded.

Māmane Pl. (Honolulu) – A native tree. Its hard wood was shaped into spades and sled runners.

Mamao St./Pl. (Hale'iwa) – Far, distant, remote, high in rank; distance.

Mamo Ln. (Honolulu) – Safflower or false saffron, an ornamental, branching annual herb, grown for its flowers, which are yellow like the feathers of the mamo bird.

Mamoali'i Way/Pl. (Wai'anae) – Descendant of a chief.

Mamolani Pl. (Mililani) – Descendant of a chief.

Mamua Pl. (Waialua) – Before; previously. Named for original grantee.

Mana St. (Wai'anae) – Supernatural or divine power, mana, miraculous power; to have mana, power, authority.

Mana Pl. (Honolulu) – Supernatural or divine power, mana, miraculous power; to have mana, power, authority. Named for a Matson ship (purchased 1926).

Mana'e St. (Kailua) – To the east.

Mānaiakalani Pl. (Wai'anae) – Name of Maui's famous fish hook, which he used in his attempt to unite the Hawaiian islands into one land mass.

Manaiki Pl. (Honolulu) – Small branch. Named for the Kalihi Stream usually called Kamanaiki.

Manakō St./Pl./Rd. ('Aiea, Wahiawā) – Mango.

Manakū Pl. (Mililani) – An unidentified star.

Manakuke St. ('Ewa Beach) – Mongoose.

Mānalo St. (Honolulu) – Sweet, potable, of water that one may drink but it is not deliciously cool.

Manakuke

Manamana Pl. (Honolulu) – Branching. Named for an O'ahu land section.

Mānana St. (Waimānalo) – Buoyant. Named for Rabbit Island (Mānana).

Mananai Pl. (Honolulu) – A pleasant breeze.

Mana'o St. (Waipahu) – Thought, idea, belief, opinion, theory, meaning; to think, estimate.

Mana'olana St. ('Ewa Beach) – Hope, confidence, expectation.

Mana'opa'a St. ('Ewa Beach) – Conviction, determination, firm intention.

Manauea Pl. (Kapolei) – A variety of taro.

Manauwea St. (Honolulu) – A small red seaweed, used for making gelatin, and for cooking with octopus.

Manawa Pl. (Waipahu) – Time, season.

Manawahine Pl. (Mililani) – An unidentified star. Literally: female power.

Manawai St. (Kapolei) – Water power. Refers to the water source where the 'Ewa plain gets its artesian water; also an old 'Ewa place. Literally: stream branch.

Manawaiola St. (Honolulu) – Supernatural power (of the) water (of) life.

Manawaleʻa St. (ʻEwa Beach) – A generous heart, charity, alms, donation.

Mānele St. (Honolulu) – The native soapberry, a shrub. Its brown or black seeds are used for leis.

Manena Pl. (Honolulu) – A small native tree in the Citrus family, related to the mokihana tree (see Mokihana).

Manini Way (Honolulu) – Very common reef surgeonfish, also called convict tang. Named for a Matson ship (purchased 1928).

Maniniholo St. (Honolulu) – Traveling manini (fish). Named for a Kauaʻi dry cave.

Manino Pl. (Waipahu) – Calm, quiet, pacific, as the sea; peaceful, as one's spirits.

Manō Ave. (Waiʻanae) – General name for the shark.

Mānoa Rd. (Honolulu) – Vast. Named for an Oʻahu valley.

Manōkihikihi Way (ʻEwa Beach) – Hammerhead shark.

Manō

Manono St. (Kailua) – Species of endemic shrubs or small trees in the Coffee family.

Manu St. (Honolulu) – Bird.

Manuā St. (Wahiawā) – Man-of-war, warship.

Manuʻaihue St./Pl. (Waiʻanae) – Partridge. Literally: thieving bird.

Manu-Aloha St. (Kailua) – Love bird.

Manukai St. (Honolulu) – Sea bird.

Manukapu Pl. (Honolulu) – Sacred bird.

Manukū St. (Waiʻanae) – Dove; rock or wild pigeon. Literally: coo bird.

Manu-Laiki St. (Kailua) – Rice bird.

Manulani St./Pl. (Kailua) – Heavenly bird.

Manulele Pl. (Honolulu) – A native variety of sugar cane, used medicinally and in love sorcery. Literally: flying bird.

Manukū

Manuliʻiliʻi Pl. (Waiʻanae) – English sparrow. Literally: little bird.

Manu-Mele St. (Kailua) – Songbird, especially canary.

Manuoioi Pl. (Waiʻanae) – Should be Manuʻioʻio: swallow (bird).

Manunūnū St. (Waiʻanae) – Dove. Literally: cooing bird. family with yellow flowers. Its seed cases contain brown cotton.

Manu-ʻŌʻō St. (Kailua) – ʻŌʻō bird. See ʻŌʻō.

Manuʻū St. (Waiʻanae) – Crane. Literally: groaning bird.

Manuʻulaʻula St. (Waiʻanae) – Cardinal, redbird.

Manuwā Dr. (Honolulu) – Man-of-war, warship.

Maʻo Ln. (Honolulu) – The native cotton, a shrub in the Hibiscus family.

Maʻohaka Way/Pl. (ʻEwa Beach) – A Hawaiian flower raised and used by Kōīhala to string leis daily for her granddaughter, Kaʻahupahu, the shark queen of ʻEwa.

Māʻohu Pl. (ʻAiea) – Misty.

Māʻoi Pl. (Honolulu) – Bold.

Māono Pl./Lp. (Honolulu) – A gray basalt rock used for pounders.

Māpala Pl. (Waipahu) – Marble.

Māpele Rd./Way/Pl. (Kāneʻohe) – 1) Thatched heiau (temple) for the worship of the Hawaiian god Lono and the increase of food. (The offerings were of pigs, not people). 2) A shrub.

Māpu Ln. (Honolulu) – Fragrance, especially wind-blown fragrance; bubbling, splashing, as water. Figuratively: surging, as emotion.

Māpuana St./Pl. (Kailua) – Fragrance, especially wind-blown fragrance.

Māpumāpu Rd. (Kāneʻohe) – Fragrance, especially wind-blown fragrance.

Māpunapuna St./Pl. (Honolulu) – Bubbling spring. Named for an Oʻahu land section and former fishpond.

Maui

Mauele St. (Waipahu) – To clear, as brush.

Maui St. (Honolulu, Wahiawā) – Definition not known. Named for the island. Perhaps the island was named for Māui, a trickster demigod who lassoed the sun and permitted it to rise slowly across the sky, lengthening the day so his mother could dry her tapa.

Mauikupua Pl. (Waiʻanae) replaced by Waiolu.

Maukuku Pl. (Mililani) – An unidentified star near the Pleiades.

Mauli Pl. (Kāneʻohe) – Twenty-ninth night of the ancient Hawaiian lunar month. The night before the new moon.

Maulihiwa St. (Kapolei) – Choice or precious life.

Mauliola Pl. (Honolulu) – Breath of life, power of healing. Name of a god of health.

Mauloa Pl. (Kapolei) – Eternal, everlasting, forever, endless.

Māulukua Rd./Pl. (Haleʻiwa) – Upland forest.

Maumauluukaa St. (Kaʻaʻawa) – Definition not known. Possibly a garble for Maulukua: upland forest.

Mauna Pl. (Honolulu) – Mountain, mountainous region.

Maunahilu Pl. (Honolulu) – Quiet mountain. Probably should be Maunakila: majestic mountain.

Mauna

Maunaʻihi Pl. (Honolulu) – Sacred mountain.

Maunakea St. (Honolulu) – White mountain. Named for a Matson ship (purchased 1934), which was named for the Hawai'i Island mountain (13,796 feet).

Maunalaha Rd. (Honolulu) – Flat mountain.

Maunalani Cir. (Honolulu) – Heavenly mountain. Modern name of an O'ahu land area.

Maunalanikai Pl. (Honolulu) – Heavenly mountain near the sea.

Maunalei Ave. (Honolulu) – Lei mountain.

Maunaloa Ave. (Honolulu) – Long mountain. Named for a Hawai'i Island volcano (13,680 feet).

Maunalua Ave. (Honolulu) – Two mountains. Named for an O'ahu land section.

Maunanani St. (Honolulu) – Beautiful mountain.

Mauna 'Olu St. (Wai'anae) – Cool mountain.

Maunawai Pl. (Honolulu) – Water mountain.

Maunawili Rd./Cir./Lp. (Kailua) – Twisted mountain. Named for an O'ahu land section.

Mawa

Māunuunu St. (Kahuku) – Name of a strong blustering O'ahu wind.

Mawa St. (Waipahu) – Time.

Māwae Pl. (Honolulu) – Cleft, crack, fissure; to crack, split, cleave.

Mawaena St. (Kāne'ohe) – Between, in the midst of.

Mawaho St. (Waipahu) – Outside, beyond, out, outer, outward, exterior.

Meaa'ala St. ('Aiea) – Perfume, fragrance, incense.

Meahala St. (Waipahu) – Sinner. Probably a garble for Meahale: homeowner. Named for original awardee.

Meahale St./Pl. (Waipahu) – Homeowner. Named for original awardee.

Meahou St. (Mililani) – News, new.

Meakanu Pl. (Honolulu) – Plants, crops.

Meakaua St. (Kāne'ohe) – Weapon, warlike person, thing pertaining to war.

Meahou

Meakia'i Pl. (Waipahu) – Guard, preserver, protection.

Meakino St. (Mililani) – Tangible thing with form.

Mealele St. (Kāne'ohe) – Aviator.

Meanui St. (Mililani) – Beloved person or thing.

Meaulu Rd. (Wai'anae) – Vegetable, growing plant.

Mehame Pl. (Waipahu) – Hot, heat.

Mehana St. (Kāne'ohe) – Warmth, heat; warm.

Mehani St./Pl. (Kapolei) – Hot, heat.

Mehe Pl. (Waipahu) – Like, as though, as if.

Meheanu Lp./Pl. (Kāne'ohe) – As though cold. Named for the guardian spirit of He'eia fishpond.

Meheu St. (Mililani) – Track, footprint, tracing, trail, clue.

Mēheuheu Pl. (Waipahu) – Custom, beaten path.

Meheu

Mehe'ula Pkwy. (Mililani) – Path of the sun. Literally: with a redness.
Mei Pl. (Kailua) – May (the month).
Mekeaupe'a Pl. (Mililani) – An unidentified star.
Meki Pl. (Waipahu) – Pit.
Mekia St. (Waimānalo) – Major (military title).
Mekila St. (Kapolei) – Handsome.
Mele St./Pl. (Waipahu) – Song, anthem, or chant
of any kind; poem; to sing, chant.
Meleana Pl. (Honolulu) – Singing.
Meleinoa Pl. (Waipahu) – Name chant; chant
composed in honor of a person, or of a chief.

Meli

Meleka'i St./Pl. (Mililani) – Procession song; chant
while dancers come out before the audience.
Melekomo St./Pl. (Waipahu) – Welcoming song.
Melekula Rd. (Kāne'ohe) – Should be Melekule. See Melekule.
Melekule St. (Wahiawā) – Pot marigold, grown for its showy flowers.
Melemele Pl. (Honolulu) – Yellow, blonde.
Meli Pl. (Kāne'ohe) – Bee, honey.
Melia Ct./Pl. (Wahiawā, Honolulu) – All
species and varieties of plumeria. Their
fragrant white, yellow, pink and rose colored
flowers are commonly used for making leis.

Melia

Melokia St. (Mililani) – Melody.
Menehune Ln. (Honolulu) – Legendary midgets
who energetically built roads, fish-ponds, and
heiau (temples). Their ancient projects were
completed in one night, or they were left unfinished.
Mie Pl. (Wahiawā) – Origin not known. Perhaps a garble for Mei: May.
Miha St. (Kāne'ohe) – Silent, quiet.
Mikahala Way (Honolulu) – Mr. Hall. Named for an inter-island steamship
(launched in Honolulu in 1887). One of several steamships built by the
Hall Brothers of Washington State for Hawai'i waters.
Mikalemi St. ('Aiea) – Pephaps: Mr. Lemon.
Mīkana St. (Wai'anae) – The papaya.
Miki Pl. (Kāne'ohe) – Quick, active, prompt, alert,
fast and efficient in work.
Miki'ala St./Pl. ('Ewa Beach) – Alert, prompt;
early on eand.

Mikihana St. ('Ewa Beach) – Should be Hanamiki:
to work fast; fast work.
Mikihilina St. (Kāne'ohe) – Most beautiful, of
dress, finery, ornaments.

Mīkana
Milikana

Mikilana Pl. (Waipahu) – The Chinese rice flower,
a shrub or small tree in the Mahogany family.

Grown for its handsome leaves and fragrant flowers, which are tiny, round, and yellow.

Mikimiki Pl. (Wahiawā) – Energetic, efficient.

Mikinolia Pl. ('Aiea) – Magnolia (tree).

Mikioi Pl. ('Aiea) – Dainty and neat in craftsmanship, or in doing anything; well-made, as a result of workmanship.

Mikiola Dr. (Kāne'ohe) – Active and alive. Named for an O'ahu land section.

Miko St. (Honolulu) – Seasoned with salt; salted, tasty.

Mikohu St. ('Ewa Beach) – Good-looking, attractive, becoming.

Mīkole St. (Honolulu) – Persevere.

Milia St./Pl. (Mililani) – The beloved flower or child.

Milikami St. (Wai'anae) – Origin not known. Probably a Hawaiianized name.

Milikana Pl. (Wahiawā) – The papaya.

Mililani Mem. Pk. Rd./St. (Honolulu, Waipahu) – To praise, exhalt. Named for the home of ali'i statesman, John 'Ī'ī, formerly located near the state Judiciary Building. He received Waipi'o, O'ahu in the 1848 Great Mahele. Name of the home refers to Princess Victoria Kamāmalu, raised from infancy by John 'Ī'ī. See 'Ī'ī.

Milo Ln./Pl. (Honolulu) – A native tree, related to the hau tree. The tree was used for medicine, dye, oil, gum, and making calabashes. Formerly a common shade tree near homes. The Waikīkī home of Kamehameha I was surrounded by milo trees.

Miloiki St./Pl. (Honolulu) – Small milo tree.

Milokai St./Pl. (Kailua) – Seaward milo (tree). Probably should be: Kaimilo: curling, twisting sea.

Miloli'i St./Pl. (Honolulu) – Fine twist (as sennit cord or rope). Named for a Hawai'i Island land division.

Mimo Pl. (Kāne'ohe) – Gentle, of upright character, quiet; capable and deft but unassuming.

Mino'aka

Mimoka Ct. (Honolulu) – Mimosa, a Biblical name.

Mino'aka Pl. (Waipahu) – Smile; to smile. Literally: laughing dimple.

Mio Pl. (Kailua) – To disappear swiftly; to move swiftly, as a stream of water; to make off with quickly; current.

Miomio Lp. (Kāne'ohe) – To dive into water without splashing.

Miula St. ('Ewa Beach) – Mule. Formerly the primary method of transporting sugar cane in the fields.

Moa St. (Honolulu, Kunia) – Chicken, red jungle chicken, fowl, brought to Hawai'i by Polynesians.

Moa'e Pl. (Wahiawā) – Trade wind.

Moa'elehua St. (Wai'anae) – Trade wind.

Moa'e
Moa'elehua

Moaka St. (Kapolei) – Clear, plain, intelligible; clarity.
Mōakāka Way/Pl. (Kāneʻohe) – Clear, plain, intelligible; clarity.
Moʻala Pl. (Wahiawā) – The sentinel crab. Found in ponds, and in shallow water.
Moamahi Way (Kāneʻohe) – To cherish and cultivate.
Moana St. (Lāʻie) – Ocean, open sea, lake.
Moanalua Lp./Rd. (Honolulu, ʻAiea, Pearl City) – Two encampments. Named for an Oʻahu land division.
Moanalualani Pl./Ct./Way (Honolulu) – Heavenly Moanalua.
Moanawai Pl. (Honolulu) – Fresh-water lake, sea.
Moani St. (Honolulu) – Light or gentle breeze, usually associated with fragrance.
Moaniʻala St./Pl. (Honolulu) – Fragrant breeze.
Moaniani St./Pl. (Waipahu) – Light or gentle breeze, usually associated with fragrance.
Moaʻula St. (Mililani) – Name of a waterfall on Molokaʻi.
Moauli St. (Waiʻanae) – Dark blue sea.
Moea St. (Mililani) – To press onward, go straight toward.
Moehā St. (Waiʻanae) – Striped, of four colors of about the same width and lying parallel.
Moekaʻa Pl. (Waiʻanae) – Trundle bed.
Moekahi St. (Waiʻanae) – To sleep alone.
Moekolu St. (Waiʻanae) – Striped, of three colors of about the same width and lying parallel.
Moelehua Pl. (Mililani) – Rain name.
Moelima St./Pl. (Waiʻanae) – Striped, of five colors of about the same width andlying parallel.

Moekahi

Moelola Pl. (Honolulu) – Striped tapa; an outer, striped sheet for bed covers.
Moelua St. (Waiʻanae) – Striped, of two colors of about the same width and lying parallel.
Moe Moe Pl. (Wahiawā) – To sleep, lie down.
Moena Pl. (Waipahu) – Resting place, position of anything lying down.
Moenamanu St. (Mililani) – Bird resting place.
Mōhā St. (Mililani) – Fully developed as a flower; of fine physique, as a person.
Mōhaʻi (Mililani) – An unidentified star.
Mohala Pl./Way (Wahiawā, Honolulu) – Unfolded, as flower petals; blossoming, opening up; blooming, as a youth just past adolescence.
Mōhalu St. (Waipahu) – At ease, unrestrained, at liberty; comfortable.
Mōhihi St./Pl. (Waiʻanae) – A variety of sweet potato.
Moho St. (Honolulu) – Hawaiian rail, an extinct flightless bird, hunted for sport by chiefs with bow and arrow.
Mōhonua Pl. (Honolulu) – Perhaps should be Moʻohonua: ridge.

Moi Way (Honolulu) – Threadfish, a popular and delicious food.

Mōkapu Blvd./Rd./Saddle Rd. (Kailua, Kāneʻohe) – Kapu district. Named for an Oʻahu promontory.

Mokauea St. (Honolulu) – Definition not known. Named for an Oʻahu land section.

Mokiawe St. (Waiʻanae) – A variety of sweet potato.

Mokihana St./Pl./Lp. (Honolulu, Wahiawā) – A native tree in the Citrus family, found only on Kauaʻi. Its small fragrant fruits represent Kauaʻi in the leis of Hawaiʻi.

Mōkōlea

Mōkōlea Dr. (Kailua) – A rock islet. Possibly literally: cut plover (bird) or plover island.

Moku Pl. (Honolulu) – Island, district. Perhaps named for original awardee.

Mokuahi St. (Waipahu) – Steamship. Literally: fire ship.

Mokuea Pl. (Honolulu) – Airplane.

Mokuhano St./Pl. (Honolulu) – Majestic island. Named for a Maui rock islet.

Mokukaua St. (Waipahu) – Battleship, cruiser, warship.

Mokulama St. (Waimānalo) – Lama grove. Named for an Oʻahu land section.

Mokulele Dr./Pl. (Kāneʻohe) – Airplane, flying ship.

Mokulua Dr. (Kailua) – Two adjacent islands. Named for an Oʻahu land section and two islets.

Mokumanu Dr. (Kailua) – Bird island. Named for two Oʻahu islets.

Mokumoa St. (Honolulu) – Chicken island. Named for a former islet, now joined to Oʻahu.

Mokuna Pl. (Honolulu) – Division, boundary; chapter, section, as a book.

Mokunoio Pl. (Honolulu) – Tern (a bird) islet. Named for a Maui rock islet.

Mokuola St. (Waipahu) – Island of health, healing island.

Mokulele

Mokuone St. (Honolulu) – Sand island. Named for a Kauaʻi valley and stream.

Mokupeʻa Pl. (ʻEwa Beach) – Sailing vessel, yacht.

Molakea St. (Mililani) – Clear, clarity.

Molale St./Pl. (Waipahu) – Clear, plain, unobstructed.

Mōlehu Dr. (Honolulu) – Twilight, dusk; tipsy.

Mōlina St. (Honolulu) – Strip, as of cloth or wood; tape used for trimming clothes; any border used for trimming.

Molo St. (Kailua) – To turn, twist, spin; to interweave and interlace, as roots; to tie securely.

Moloaʻa St. (Honolulu) – Matted roots. Named for a Kauaʻi land division.

Moloalo St. (Waipahu) – Main stream into which branches enter.

Moloka'i St. (Wahiawā) – Definition not known. Named for the island.

Molokini St. (Wahiawā) – Many ties. Named for the crescent-shaped islet(150 feet elevation), located between Maui and Kaho'olawe.

Mololani Pl. (Kāne'ohe) – Well-kept, well-nursed. Named for an O'ahu crater peak.

Momi Way (Honolulu) – Pearl (of an oyster).

Momōlio Ln. (Honolulu) – Taut, tight.

Momona Pl. (Wai'anae) – Fat; fertile, rich, as soil.

Mona St. (Honolulu) – Fertile, rich, as soil.

Monehā Pl. ('Ewa Beach) – Far, distant.

Mo'oheau Ave. (Honolulu) – Definition not known. Possibly named for Hawai'i Island High Chief Ka'ai'awa'awa I Mo'oheau (the bitter food of Mo'oheau). Son of Ho'olulu who hid Kamehameha's bones.

Momi

Mo'ohele St./Pl. (Mililani) – Trail, road.

Mo'oiki St. (Waimānalo) – Small strip of land. Named for an O'ahu land section.

Mo'okāula St. (Honolulu) – A variety of gray lizard. Literally: prophet lizard.

Mo'okua St. (Kailua) – Lizard god.

Mō'ole St. (Waimānalo) – Without lizards. Named for an O'ahu land section and stream.

Mo'olelo St. (Waipahu) – Story, tale, history, tradition, legend.

Mo'omuku Pl. (Honolulu) – Mutilated lizard.

Mo'onui St. (Honolulu) – Big lizard, dragon, alligator, crocodile.

Mo'owa'a St. (Honolulu) – Side planks fitted to the middle section on each side of a canoe hull, technically called gunwale strakes.

Mo'olelo

Mōpua Lp. (Waipahu) – Melodious, pleasant, of a voice.

Moua St. (Wai'anae) – Should be Mouo: buoy; float, as on a fishing net.

Mount Ka'ala Rd. (Waialua) – Definition not known. Named for the highest mountain on O'ahu (4,040 feet).

Mowai St. (Kailua) – Perhaps a garble for Mowa'e: trade wind.

Mua Pl. (Mililani) – Before, ahead, forward, in advance, future.

Mui Pl. (Kāne'ohe, Waipahu) – Assembled, gathered together, an assembly.

Muiona St. ('Ewa Beach) – A kind of worm.

Muku Pl. (Kāne'ohe) – A measure of length from fingertips of one hand to the elbow of the other arm, when both arms are extended to the side.

Mūlehu St. (Mililani) – One of the three stars in a triangle, the others being Polo'ula and Poloahilani. According to one legend, Mūlehu is Venus.

Muliwai Ave./Ln. (Wahiawā, Honolulu) – River; pool near mouth of a stream, as behind a sandbar; estuary.

Munu St. (Kapolei) – A goat fish.

Mūʻolea Pl. (Honolulu) – Definition not known. Named for a Maui land division.

Nāʻai

Mūʻolo St. (Waiʻanae) – First name of Princess Kahanu's mother, Muʻolo Laʻanui.

Muʻumuʻu Pl. (ʻEwa Beach) – A loose gown, without yoke and sometimes with short sleeves. This popular dress originated as a more modern and fashionable version of the holokū (see Holokū).

Nāʻai St. (Honolulu) – The foods. Named for original awardee.

Nāākawelolā St. (Waiʻanae) – Reflections of the sunset.

Nāʻākea St./Pl. (Honolulu) – The canoe outer hulls. Named for a Kauaʻi promontory.

Nāʻale St. (Honolulu) – The waves.

Nāaliʻi St./Pl. (ʻAiea) – The chiefs.

Naʻaualiʻi Pl. (Mililani) – Kind, thoughtful, forgiving, loving.

Naʻauao Pl. (Waipahu) – Learned, enlightened, intelligent, wise.

Nāhaku Pl. (Honolulu) – The masters. Named for High Chiefess Mary Nāhakuʻelua Pua (?-1922), the original grantee. See Pua and Mahiʻai.

Nahawele St. (ʻEwa Beach) – A bivalve shellfish.

Nahele St./Pl. (ʻAiea) – Forest, grove, wilderness; trees, shrubs, vegetation.

Nahenahe Pl. (Wahiawā) – Soft, sweet, melodious, as music or a gentle voice; softly blowing, as a gentle breeze; gentle-mannered, soft-spoken.

Nahewai St./Pl. (Kāneʻohe) – Murmuring stream.

Nāhiku St./Pl. (Kāneʻohe) – The Big Dipper, a constellation. Literally: the seven.

Nāhiku

Nahiolea St. (ʻAiea) – A variety of taro.

Nahoa St. (Waialua) – Bold, daring. Named for original grantee.

Nāhōkū Pl. (Honolulu) – The stars.

Nāhōkūpā St./Pl. (Mililani) – An unidentified constellation of five stars forming a circle, said to be near the Big Dipper. Literally: the enclosure stars.

Nāholoholo St. (Mililani) – The planet Venus.

Nāhua St. (Honolulu) – The fruits. Named for a Hawaiian chiefess who owned property here.

Naika Pl. (Mililani) – Knight.

Naʻina Pl. (ʻEwa Beach) – Conquering, endeavoring.

Naio St. (Honolulu) – The bastard sandalwood, a native tree with sandalwood-like fragrance. During the sandal-

Naika

wood trade era (1810-1830), naio was a substitute for 'iliahi (true sandalwood) when 'iliahi became scarce.

Nākālele St. (Honolulu) – The leaning. Named for a Maui promontory.

Nā Kao Pl. (Kāne'ohe) – Belt and sword in Orion, the constellation. Literally: the darts.

Nakeke Pl. (Wahiawā) – Rattling, as a window; rustling, as paper.

Nakele St. (Honolulu) – Soft, boggy, slippery, yielding, sinking in.

Nakili Pl. (Waipahu) – To glimmer through, as light through a small opening; to twinkle.

Nākini St./Pl. (Waimānalo) – Perhaps: the multitudes.

Nākiu Pl. (Honolulu) – The spies.

Nākolo Pl. (Honolulu) – Rumbling, roaring, as of surf or thunder; reverberating.

Nāko'oko'o St. (Honolulu) – The canes (staffs or rods). Named for original awardee.

Nāku'i Pl. ('Aiea) – To rumble, roar, thump; beating, as the heart; thrilled.

Nākuina St. (Honolulu) – The stitching together. Named for Emma Kā'ili Metcalf Beckley Nākuina (1847-1929). Author, and expert on ancient Hawaiian land and water rights, mele (song or chant), folklore, and fishing methods. Fluent in seven languages. First curator of the Hawaiian National Museum (1880), and Commissioner of Private Water Rights (1902). Married first to Fred Beckley, then to the Rev. Moses Nākuina who was descended from the original grantee. She lived here. See Kā'ili.

Nākula St. (Wahiawā) – The plains.

Nakulu'ai St./Pl. (Kāne'ohe) – Praiseworthy, upright.

Nakumanu Pl. (Kāne'ohe) – Should be Nukumanu: a variety of taro. Literally: bird's beak. (The taro corm is pointed like a bird's beak).

Nālānui

Nālani St. (Honolulu) – The heavens.

Nālani'ehā St. (Honolulu) – The four chiefs. Probably named for Alexander Liholiho, Kamehameha IV. See Kamehameha IV.

Nālānui St. (Honolulu) – The holidays.

Nale St. ('Ewa Beach) – Clear, bright.

Nālei Pl. (Waialua) – The leis. Named for original grantee.

Nāleialoha Pl. (Honolulu) – The leis (of) love.

Nāli'i St./Pl. (Waipahu) – The chiefs. Named for original awardee.

Naliiko Pl. (Kāne'ohe) – Should be Naliliko'i: a variety of taro.

Nālimu Rd. (Hale'iwa) – The seaweeds.

Nalomeli Pl. ('Ewa Beach) – Honeybee. Literally: honey fly.

Nalomeli

Nalopaka Pl. ('Aiea) – Tick; ensign fly. Literally: lean fly.

Nalu St. (Waimānalo) – Wave, surf; full of waves; to form waves; wavy, as wood grain.

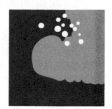

Nāluāhi St. (Waialua) – The mighty. Named for original grantee.

Nalulu Pl. (Honolulu) – Dull headache; dull pain in the stomach, queasy.

Nāmāhana St. (Honolulu) – The twins. Probably named for Nāmāhana (?-1829). Wife of High Chief Ke'eaumoku I. Mother of Ka'ahumanu.

Nalu

Nāmāhealani Pl. (Honolulu) – The Mahealanis (the 17th night of the ancient Hawaiian lunar month. The night after the full moon).

Nāmāla Pl. (Kailua) – The gardens.

Nāmau'u Dr. (Honolulu) – The grasses. Possibly named for John Nāmau'u, a student with Liholiho and John 'Ī'ī in the first English language class taught by missionaries in 1820s.

Nāmilimili St. (Honolulu) – The favorite ones. Named for original awardee.

Nāmōhoe St./Pl. (Kapolei) – The constellation Gemini.

Nāmoku St./Pl. (Kāne'ohe) – The ships.

Nāmoku'ēha St. (Honolulu) – The four islands. Named for original awardee.

Nana Pl. (Kāne'ohe) – Name of an ancient Hawaiian lunar month.

Nānā-Honua St. (Honolulu) – Earth-gazing.

Nānahu St. (Kapolei) – A variety of sugar cane, the red variation of 'akilo 'ula 'ula.

Nānāikalā St./Pl. (Wai'anae) – Look at the sun.

Nānāikeola St. (Waipahu) – Looking to health.

Nānaina Pl. (Honolulu) – General appearance, view, aspect, panorama, sight, scenery.

Nānākai St./Pl. (Pearl City) – Observing seaward.

Nānākuli Ave. (Wai'anae) – Look at knees. Named for an O'ahu land division.

Nānāloko Pl. (Kailua) – Lake view.

Nānāmoana St./Pl. (Kāne'ohe) – Ocean view.

Nānāikalā

Nānāmua Pl. (Mililani) – Castor, a star. Literally: look forward.

Nānāwale Way/Pl. (Kailua) – Just to look, especially to look on without helping.

Nanea St./Ave. (Honolulu, Wahiawā) – Repose, leisure, tranquility.

Nani Pl. (Kāne'ohe) – Beautiful, glory, splendor; beautiful, pretty.

Naniahiahi St./Pl. (Wai'anae) – The four o'clock, a shrubby herb with fragrant red, white, yellow, or striped flowers. Literally: evening beauty.

Naniali'i St. (Kailua) – Allamandas, climbing shrubs grown for their showy yellow flowers. Literally: chiefly beauty.

Nanihale Pl. (Honolulu) – Should be Halenani: beautiful house.

Nanihōkū Way (Kāneʻohe) – Starry beauty.

Nani ʻĪhi Ave. (Wahiawā) – Majestically beautiful.

Nanilani Way (Kāneʻohe) – Heavenly beauty.

Nanilihilihi St. (Waipahu) – Slightly beautiful.

Naniloa Lp. (Lāʻie) – Very beautiful.

Nanimauloa Pl. (Honolulu) – An everlasting or strawflower. Literally: everlasting beauty.

Nāpali

Nāniu Pl. (Honolulu) – The coconuts. Perhaps short for Nāniuʻapo. Named for an Oʻahu land section.

Naniwahine Way (Kāneʻohe) – Feminine beauty.

Nānū St./Pl. (Honolulu, ʻAiea) – Native species of gardenia, shrubs and trees with tubular, white, single flowers.

Nāʻohe St. (Honolulu) – The bamboos. Named for a Kauaʻi land division.

Nāʻōiwi Ln. (Haleʻiwa) – The native sons.

Nāone St. (Honolulu) – The sands. Named for original awardee.

Nāʻōpala Ln. (Honolulu) – The rubbish. Named for original awardee.

Napala St. (Waipahu) – Definition not known. Named for original awardee.

Nāpali Pl. (Honolulu) – The cliffs.

Nape Pl. (Waipahu) – Bending and swaying, as coconut fronds.

Nāpēhā Pl. (Mililani) – An unidentified star.

Napehe Pl. (Mililani) – Should be Nāpēhā: an unidentified star.

Nāpoko Pl. (Honolulu) – The short ones.

Napoʻo St. (Kapolei) – The going down or setting of the sun.

Napoʻonalā Pl. (Haleʻiwa) – Sunset.

Nāpuaʻa Pl. (Honolulu) – The pigs. Named for original grantee.

Napoʻonalā

Nāpuanani Rd./Pl. (ʻAiea) – The beautiful flowers.

Naʻu Pl. (Kapolei) – Mine, belonging to me.

Nāuahi St. (Waialua) – The wisps (of smoke). Named for original awardee.

Nāukana St. (Waialua) – The baggage. Named for original grantee.

Naukewai Pl. (ʻAiea) – Perhaps a garble for Nauewai: a variety of sweet potato.

Nāulu Pl. (Honolulu) – Sudden shower; showery; to shower.

Naupaka St./Pl. (Lāʻie, Honolulu) – Native shrubs, having white or light-colored flowers that look like half-flowers.

Nāwaʻakoa St./Pl. (Waipahu) – The koa (wood) canoes.

Nāwahine Lp. (Kāneʻohe) – The ladies.

Nāwele St. (Waipahu) – Fine, threadlike, small.

Naupaka

Nāwenewene Cir. (Mililani) – Unidentified stars.

Nāwiliwili St. (Honolulu) – The wiliwili (trees). Named for a Kauaʻi land division.

Neʻemua Pl. (Kāneʻohe) – To advance, go forward, progress.

Neʻepapa Pl. (Kāneʻohe) – To move as a whole or unit; moving or working together in unison; combined, united.

Neʻepū Pl. (Kāneʻohe) – To move together.

Nehe St./Ln. (Honolulu) – Native shrubs and herbs in the Daisy family, with yellow flowers, commonly found at seashore.

Nehoa St./Pl. (Honolulu) – Bold, defiant, daring.

Nehu Pl. (Honolulu) – Anchovy, an edible large-scaled fish used as a baitfish for aku.

Nehupala Pl. (ʻEwa Beach) – Yellowfish anchovy fish.

Neki St. (ʻAiea) – Great bulrush (plant). It grows near fresh or brackish water marshes.

Neleau Pl. (Mililani) – The native Hawaiian sumach, a shrub or small tree in the Mango family. It has light, soft, tough wood.

Nemo St. (Kapolei) – Smooth, smoothly polished, slick.

Nēnē St. (Honolulu) – The endemic Hawaiian goose, the state bird of Hawaiʻi. An endangered upland bird, with webbed feet, now claw-like, adapted to living in a lava environment.

Nēnēhiwa Pl. (Kāneʻohe) – Prized, beloved, precious.

Nēnēleʻa St. (Kapolei) – Joyous, gladness.

Nēnē

Nenewai St. (Waiʻanae) – A variety of sweet potato.

Nenue St./Pl. (Honolulu, Waimānalo) – Chub fish, also known as rudder or pilot fish. It is popularly eaten raw.

Newa St./Pl. (Kapolei) – A constellation, probably the Southern Cross. Literally: war club.

Newe Pl. (Mililani) – Southern Cross, a constellation.

Nīʻau St. (Waipahu) – Midrib of coconut leaf or frond. Named for original awardee.

Niele Pl. (Honolulu) – To keep asking questions; inquisitive, curious, asking frivolous questions (used to discredit a "busy-body" who asks about things that do not concern him or her).

Nihi St. (Honolulu) – Edge, brink, rim, border.

Nihina Pl. (Kāneʻohe) – Edge, brink, rim, border.

Ninihua St. (Honolulu) – Resentment; resentful.

Nihipali Pl. (Honolulu) – Cliff edge.

Nihiwai Pl. (Wahiawā) – Edge of the water.

Niho St. (Waialua) – Tooth. Named for original grantee.

Nihopeku St. (Kapolei) – Bud shooting from the ground.

Niʻihau St. (Wahiawā, Waiʻanae) – Definition not known. Named for the island.

Niho

Nikolo St. (Honolulu) – Nicholas. With a companion street, Noela (Noël), this street is named for St. Nicholas.

Nilu St. (Kāneʻohe) – Admirable, fine.

Ninihua St. (Honolulu) – Resentment; resentful.

Niniko Pl. (Honolulu) – Named for Ninito (1838-1898). She was related to a royal Tahiti family. Wife of John Sumner (a Honolulu businessman). She lived here. Niniko is Hawaiianized Tahitian.

Ninini Way/Pl. (Honolulu) – Pour. Named for a Kauaʻi promontory.

Nipo

Nīoi Pl. (Honolulu) – 1) Any kind of hot red pepper. Figuratively: a controversial or important problem. 2) A tree, endemic to Molokaʻi, said to have poisonous wood only from trees at Mauna Loa, Molokaʻi.

Niolo St. (ʻEwa Beach) – Upright, straight; stately.

Niolopā Pl. (Honolulu) – Definition not known. Named for an Oʻahu land section.

Niolopua Dr. (Honolulu) – Handsome. Named for Mrs. Rowena Niolopua Dowsett Turner of the Dowsett family. See Kimopelekane.

Nipo St. (Honolulu) – To yearn for; to be in love with; to love, desire, long for.

Niu St./Pl. (Honolulu) – The coconut, the world's best-known palm. Hawaiians used all parts of the tree for food, fiber, oil, and building materials. Its leaves were used for fans, baskets, brooms, and musical instruments. Its husk was used for containers and hula rattles. Its milk and meat were forbidden to ancient Hawaiian women. Official tree of Hawaiʻi Territory (1930-1959).

Niuhi St. (Honolulu) – A large, gray, man-eating shark. Catching niuhi was a dangerous sport, a game for chiefs.

Niuhiwa Pl. (ʻEwa Beach) – A variety of coconut, with husk of dark green fruit and a black shell.

Niu

Niuiki Cir. (Honolulu) – Little niu. Named for an Oʻahu valley.

Niukahiki Pl. (ʻEwa Beach) – Date palm.

Niulelo Pl. (ʻEwa Beach) – A variety of coconut with reddish fruit and yellow shell; trees found at the Manager's House and Plantation Administration Building.

Niuliʻi St. (Waipahu) – Small coconut. Named for original awardee.

Niumaloʻo Pl. (Waialua) – Copra, dry coconut meat.

Niumalu Lp. (Honolulu) – Shade (of) coconut trees. Named for a Kauaʻi land division.

Niuʻula Rd. (Haleʻiwa) – Red coconut.

Noe St. (Honolulu) – Mist, fog, vapor, rain spray; to form a mist; misty.

No'eau St. (Honolulu) – Clever, skillful, dexterous, wise, artistic, talented.

Noela St./Pl. (Honolulu) – Noël. Named for the Christmas carol.

Noelani St./Pl. (Pearl City) – Heavenly mist.

Noelo St. ('Ewa Beach) – To delve, seek, as for knowledge.

Nohea Pl. (Kāne'ohe) – Handsome, pretty, lovely, of fine appearance.

Noheaiki St./Pl./Way (Waipahu) – Small beauty.

Nohi Pl. (Kapolei) – Bright-colored, vivid, as the rainbow.

Nohili St. (Honolulu) – Tedious, slow. Named for a Kaua'i promontory.

Noho Way/Pl. (Wahiawā) – Seat, chair, stool, bench.

Nohoali'i St. ('Aiea) – Throne, reign, tenure as chief, to rule; to reign, as a chief.

Nohoali'i

Nohoaloha Pl. ('Ewa Beach) – On friendly terms, dwelling in peace; friendly relationship.

Noho'ana Pl. ('Ewa Beach) – Conduct, bearing, deportment.

Nohoaupuni Pl. ('Aiea) – To rule; a reign, ruler.

Nohohale St. (Kapolei) – House occupant, owner, sitter.

Nohoiho'ewa Pl./Way ('Ewa Beach) – Name of one of two stones, now destroyed, that once marked the boundary between the chief's land and that of the commoners in 'Ewa.

Nohokai Pl. (Kāne'ohe) – To live by the sea.

Noholike St./Pl. ('Ewa Beach) – To live in unity, with equal rights.

Noholio Rd. (Wai'anae) – Saddle.

Noholoa Ct./Lp. (Mililani) – Polaris, the North Star. Literally: long staying.

Nohomalu Pl. (Kāne'ohe) – Peaceful living.

Nohona St./Pl. (Kapolei) – Residence, dwelling, seat, mode of life, existence.

Nohonani Pl. (Kāne'ohe) – Sitting pretty.

Nohonani St. (Honolulu) – Sitting pretty. A poetic name of Queen Lili'uokalani. A phrase in the song, "E Lili'u e."

Nohopa'a St. (Kapolei) – To live permanently; to settle down; to be established.

Nohopono St. (Kapolei) – Sitting properly, behaving well; moral behavior; morality.

Nohu St. (Honolulu) – Scorpionfish or stonefish, a poisonous fish. It preys on smaller fish attracted to its appendages, which resemble algae.

Nohua Pl. ('Aiea) – Perhaps should be Nūhou: news.

Noi'i Pl. (Kāne'ohe) – To seek knowledge or information.

Noio St. (Honolulu) – The black or white-capped or lesser noddy, a marine bird. Many feed at Kāne'ohe Bay and in brackish ponds nearby.

Noke St. (Kailua) – To persist, continue, repeat, persevere; perseverance, persistence.

Nola St. (Pearl City) – Nora.

Nolupē St. (Waipahu) – Graceful bending, swaying, as shrubs.
Nomilo St./Pl. (Honolulu) – Should be Nōmilu: definition not known. Named for a Kauaʻi valley and fishpond.
Nona Lp. (Kāneʻohe) – Nona.
Nonanona Pl. (Honolulu) – Ant.
Noninui Pl. (Kailua) – A soft, pinkish porous stone, used for polishing.
Nonohe St./Pl. (Wahiawā) – Attractive, beautiful.
Nonohina Pl. (Waipahu) – White blossoms of the olopua tree.
Nonokiʻo St. (Waimānalo) – Pool seepage. Named for an Oʻahu land section.
Nonou St. (Honolulu) – Should be Nounou: Throwing. Named for a Kauaʻi mountain peak (now called "Sleeping Giant").
Nopu Pl. (Kapolei) – To swell; sprouting, plump. figuratively: to spring up in the mind, as a thought or desire.
North Circle Makai St. (Wahiawā) – Makai: seaward.
North Circle Mauka St./Pl. (Wahiawā) – Mauka: mountainward.
Noʻū St. (Kapolei) – Moist and fragrant, as a flower in the rain or dew.
Noulu St. (Kapolei) – Native fan palms.
Nowela Pl. (Kailua) – Noel, Nowell.
Nowelo Pl. (Mililani) – To delve, seek, as for knowledge.
Nōweo Pl. (Kāneʻohe) – Bright, shiny.
Nū Pl. (Honolulu) – New.
Nuʻao Pl. (Waipahu) – Porpoise. Ancient Hawaiians believed it was related to the shark.
Nuhōlani Pl. (Honolulu) – All species of Eucalyptus trees. Grown for ornament and reforestation. Literally: New Holland.
Nui Ave. (Wahiawā) – Big.
Nui St. (Mililani) – An unidentified star.
Nūkea St./Pl. (Waiʻanae) – White-billed ʻalae bird.
Nūkoki Pl. (Kāneʻohe) – Snub-nosed, homely, of facial features; pug-nosed.
Nukuawa St. (Kailua) – Entrance to a harbor.
Nukumomi Pl. (Kāneʻohe) – A kind of jackfish. Literally: pearly snout.
Nukupuʻu St./Pl. (Kāneʻohe) – Group of Hawaiian honeycreepers (birds), now extinct on Oʻahu.
Nukuwai Pl. (Kāneʻohe) – Stream mouth.
Numana Rd. (Honolulu) – Neumann. Named for attorney Paul Neumann. He was Attorney General for King Kalākaua and Queen Liliʻuokalani. He defended Queen Liliʻuokalani at her 1895 trial for treason.
Nuna St./Pl. (Honolulu) – Same as Luna: high, upper, above, over, up.
Nūnū St. (Kailua) – Introduced rock pigeon or wild pigeon; dove (bird).

Nonanona

Nuʻao

Nuʻuanu Ave. (Honolulu) – Cool heights. Named for an Oʻahu valley.
Nuʻuanu Pali Dr. (Honolulu) – Cliff Nuʻuanu. Named
for an Oʻahu cliff.
Nuʻuolo St./Pl. (Honolulu) – Definition not known.
Named for a Kauaʻi valley. Usually called Nuʻalolo.
ʻOā St. (ʻAiea) – Split, cracked, burst; to split, crack.
ʻŌaheahe Way/Pl. (Kapolei) – To blow gently, as
a breeze.

ʻŌahi Pl. (Kapolei) – Rough stone or pumice,
as used for polishing surfboards or bowls, or for
scraping bristles of a pig.

ʻOā

Oʻahu Ave./St. (Honolulu, Wahiawā) – Definition not known. Named for
the island.
Oama St./Pl. (ʻEwa Beach, ʻAiea) – Young of the weke (goatfish).
ʻŌaniani St. (Kapolei) – Very slight stir of air, a breeze.
Oea Pl. (Kapolei) – Name of a star.
Oeoe Way (Honolulu) – Bull-roarer, made of
kamani nut or coconut shell, on a long string.
Blowing into it creates a whistling sound.

Oha St. (ʻEwa Beach) – Spreading, as vines;
thriving; to grow lush.
ʻŌhā Pl. (Honolulu) – Native lobelias (flowers).
Ōhāhā St./Pl. (Kāneʻohe) – Flourishing, fully
developed, plump, healthy.

Oʻahu

ʻOhai Ln./St./Pl. (Honolulu, Wahiawā) – Monkeypod
or rain tree, an impressively large symmetrical shade
tree with pink flowers. It grows up to 80 feet tall. Its wood is shaped into
handmade planters and bowls. Its seeds are used for leis.
ʻOhai Aliʻi Ct. (Wahiawā) – The pride of Barbados, a thorny, handsome
flowered shrub used for hedges. Literally: royal ʻohai.
ʻOhaiʻula Pl. (ʻAiea) – The royal poinciana, an ornamental tree with a
bright-red canopy of flowers. It grows to 40 feet tall.
ʻŌhala St./Pl. (Kāneʻohe) – Green, immature, as fruit.
ʻOhana St. (Kailua) – Family, clan, kin group; related.
ʻOhana Nui Cir. (Honolulu) – Large family.
ʻŌhāpali St. (Waipahu) – A kind of lobelia (plant).
Ohapueo Pl. (ʻAiea) – An unidentified fruit
tree.
ʻŌhāwai Pl. (Honolulu) – Native lobelias.
They arewoody plants, shrubs, and small
trees.
ʻOhe St. (Honolulu) – All kinds of bamboo,
woody shrubs or trees. Its stem was shaped
into bamboo rattles and nose flutes.

ʻOhana

'Ohe'ala Pl. (Mililani) – Sweet cane. Literally: fragrant bamboo.

'Ohekani Lp./Pl. ('Aiea) – Flute. Literally: playing bamboo.

'Ōheke Pl. (Honolulu) – Somewhat modest, shy.

'Ōhelo Ln. (Honolulu) – A small, native shrub bearing red or yellow berries. Considered sacred to goddess Pele.

'Ōhelokai Rd. (Ka'a'awa) – A small, spreading shrub with shiny red berries. It grows near salt marshes and among rocks near the sea.

'Ōhelopapa Pl. ('Aiea) – A native Hawaiian strawberry. A primary food of the nēnē goose.

'Ōhelo

'Ohemauka Pl. (Wai'anae) – A small tree, found only on O'ahu. Literally: upland bamboo.

'Ohenānā Lp./Pl. ('Aiea) – Spyglass, telescope, microscope. Literally: tube for looking.

'Ohe'ohe St. (Wai'anae) – A variety of sweet potato.

'Ohepi'o Pl. (Waipahu) – Siphon. Literally: bent, bamboo.

'Ohi St. (Mililani) – To gather, harvest.

'Ohi'aha St. (Mililani) – Native tree related to the mountain apple.

'Ōhi'akea St. ('Aiea) – An 'ōhi'ā-'ai (mountain apple) or 'ōhi'a-lehua with white blossoms. See Lehua.

'Ōhi'akū St./Pl. ('Aiea) – A native, filmy fern which grows on trees in damp forests. Literally: standing (on) 'ōhi'a.

'Ohenānā

'Ōhi'aloke St. (Honolulu) – The rose apple, a tree bearing round, crisp, edible fruits with a rose-like odor. Literally: rose 'ōhi'a.

'Ōhi'alomi Pl. ('Aiea) – The common table tomato, sometimes used in lomi salmon.

'Ōhiki Pl. (Kailua) – Ghost crabs, common on sandy beaches.

'Ohilau Pl. (Waipahu) – Bundle of leaves.

'Ohina Pl. (Honolulu) – Gathering, collecting; selection.

Ohiohi Pl. (Wai'anae) – To grow vigorously, flourish, of plants.

Ohiula Ct. (Wahiawā) – Should be 'Ōhi'a'ula: a mountain apple tree with red fruit.

Ohohia St. (Honolulu) – Enthusiastic, delighted, pleased; enthusiastic acclaim.

'Ohu St. (Honolulu) – Mist, fog, vapor, light cloud on a mountain.

'Ōhua Ave. (Honolulu) – Servants. Refers to servant quarters formerly adjacent to the home of Queen Lili'uokalani.

'Ōhi'alomi

ʻOi Pl. (Kapolei) – 1) Sharp. 2) Best, superior.

ʻOihana St./Pl. (Kapolei, ʻAiea) – Occupation, trade, profession, job.

ʻŌʻili Lp./Pl. (Honolulu) – To appear, come into view; appearance.

ʻŌʻililua Pl. (Waipahu) – Prominent, conspicuous, clearly seen.

ʻŌʻilipuʻu Pl. (Honolulu) – Appearing. Named for a Maui cinder cone.

ʻŌʻio Dr. (Honolulu) – Ladyfish, bonefish.

ʻŌkaʻa St. (Kapolei) – To revolve, spin.

ʻŌkaikai St. (Waiʻanae) – Rough or raging sea.

ʻOkana Rd./Pl. (Kāneʻohe) – District or subdistrict, usually comprising several ahupuaʻa (land divisions).

ʻOkika Pl. (Honolulu) – All orchids.

Oko St. (Kailua) – To move ahead of others; to try to be better than others, surpass.

ʻOkoʻa St./Pl. (Honolulu) – Whole; entirety.

ʻŌkoholā St. (Waiʻanae) – Whaling; to whale, to harpoon whales. Literally: pierce whales.

ʻOkokomo St. (Waiʻanae) – Filled, as a canoe.

ʻOkika

ʻŌkupe St. (ʻEwa Beach) – A bivalve shellfish.

ʻŌkupu St. (Waipahu) – To sprout, as seeds; to send out shoots; to come forth, as clouds.

Ola Ln. (Honolulu) – Life, health, well-being, livelihood, salvation.

ʻŌlaʻa Pl. (Honolulu) – Definition not known. Named for a Hawaiʻi Island land division.

Ōlaʻi St. (Kapolei) – Earthquake, tremor.

Olakino Pl. (Kāneʻohe) – State of health, constitution.

ʻOlalahina Pl. (Honolulu) – Frail, delicate.

Olaloa St. (Honolulu) – Long life; completely cured or recovered.

ʻŌlani St. (Kapolei) – To toast over a fire, broil, warm in sunlight.

ʻŌlaʻo Pl. (Waialua) – To weed and work the soil, to hoe; to gather, as ʻopihi shells.

ʻŌlapa St. (Honolulu) – Several native species and varieties of forest trees, some very common. Ancient Hawaiians cut poles from ʻōlapa trees, and smeared them with sticky substances to catch birds.

ʻŌlauniu Pl. (Kahuku) – A wind on several islands. Literally: coconut leaf piercing. Figuratively: promiscuous.

Old Kalanianaʻole Rd. (Kailua) – See Kalanianaʻole.

Old Kamehameha Rd. (Wahiawā) – See Kamehameha.

Old Mōkapu Rd. (Kailua) – See Mōkapu.

Old Pālama St. (Honolulu) – See Pālama.

Old Pali Rd./Pl. (Honolulu) – See Pali.

Old Waiʻalae Rd. (Honolulu) – See Waiʻalae.

ʻOleana Ct. (Honolulu) – All kinds of oleander (shrubs), grown for their fragrant white, pink, or red flowers.

ʻOlēhala St. (ʻEwa Beach) – Cheerful singing, as birds in tree-tops.

'Ōlena St./Pl. ('Aiea) – The turmeric, a kind of ginger, once common, now rare. Used medicinally, as a tapa dye, and for purification.

'Ōlepe Lp. ('Aiea) – All kinds of bivalves (shells with two movable pieces), such as clams, mussels or oysters.

'Olepekupe St. ('Ewa Beach) – A bivalve shellfish.

Oli Lp./Pl. (Waipahu) – Chant that was not danced to, especially with prolongued phrases chanted in one breath; to chant thus.

'Oliana Lp./St./Pl. ('Aiea, Waialua) – All kinds of oleander (shrubs), grown for their fragrant white, pink, or red flowers.

'Oliko Pl. (Wahiawā) – Shiny, sparkling, bright.

'Olili Pl. (Honolulu) – Shiny, sparkling, shimmering, as moonlight.

'Oliliko St. (Mililani) – Shimmering.

'Olina St. (Kāne'ohe) – To make merry; joyous; rejoicing, merry-making.

'Ōlino St. (Honolulu) – Bright, brilliant, dazzling; brightness, glare.

'Oliona Pl. (Mililani) – Orion, the constellation.

'Oliwa St. ('Aiea) – The olive tree. Grown ornamentally in Hawai'i, it rarely flowers or yields fruit.

'Oloa Pl. (Kapolei) – A low native shrub with strong bark formerly used for making tapa.

'Olohana St. (Honolulu) – All hands. Hawaiian name for John Young (1749?-1835), a British sailor who visited Hawai'i in 1790. Name refers to the nautical shout, "all hands." A trusted advisor to Kamehameha I, he mounted cannon on large canoes to help Kamehameha attack Hawai'i Island and O'ahu. Married Kuamo'o, niece of Kamehameha I. Governor of several islands, father of John Young II (see Keoniana), and grandfather of Queen Emma.

Olohena St. (Honolulu) – Definition not known. Named for a Kaua'i land division.

Olohi'o St. (Waialua) – To cultivate, weed.

'Olohū Rd. (Ka'a'awa) – Stone used in maika game; to play the 'ulu maika game, suggesting bowling. See maika.

Olokani Pl. (Wahiawā) – To sound.

Olokele Ave. (Honolulu) – 'I'iwi (bird). See 'I'iwi.

Ololani St. ('Ewa Beach) – Acclaimed, as a chief.

'Ololū St. (Mililani) – An unidentified star. Literally: dejected.

Olomana St. (Kailua) – Forked hill. Named for an O'ahu mountain (1,643 feet).

Olomana Ln. (Honolulu) – Forked hill. Named for an O'ahu land section.

Olomea St. (Honolulu) – A native Hawaiian shrub or small tree. Ancient Hawaiians may have produced fire by rubbing the hard olomea wood with soft hau wood.

Olomehani St. (Honolulu) – Dumping ground, refuse or rubbish dump.

Olonā Ln. (Honolulu) – A native shrub, related to māmaki. Its bark was shaped into fishing nets and carrying containers. 19th Century traders bought olonā rope from the Hawaiians for their ship rigging.

'Olopana St. ('Aiea) – Definition not known. Name of a legendary O'ahu chief.

Olopua St. (Honolulu) – A tall, native evergreen tree in the Olive family. Its wood was shaped into spears, adze handles, and digging sticks.

Olowalu Way/Pl. (Honolulu) – Many hills. Named for a Maui land division.

'Olu St. (Honolulu) – Cool, refreshing; pleasant, comfortable; courtesy, kindness.

Olua Pl. (Waipahu) – A native fern.

'Olu'olu St. (Waimānalo) – Cool, refreshing; pleasant, comfortable; courtesy, kindness.

'Ōma'o St. (Kailua) – Green. Named for an O'ahu land section.

'Ōmea Pl. (Honolulu) – Reddish, murky.

'Ome'o Pl. ('Ewa Beach) – To bud, unold, as a blossom.

'Ōmilo Ln. (Honolulu) – To twist, turn. Probably should be 'Ōmilu: an ulua-like fish.

'Ōmilu Pl. ('Ewa Beach) – A kind of ulua fish.

'Ōnaha St. (Honolulu) – Bowlegged, bent over, stooped, bent, arched; curved, crescent-shaped, as the moon.

Onaona Pl. (Kailua) – Softly fragrant; gentle and sweet, as the eyes or disposition; inviting, attractive, alluring, lovely.

'Ōnaha

One St. (Honolulu) – Sand; sandy; poetic name for land.

Oneawa St./Pl. (Kailua) – Milkfish sand, milkfish beach. Named for an O'ahu land section.

Oneawakai Pl. (Kailua) – Oceanside of Oneawa.

One'ele Pl. (Honolulu) – Black sand.

Oneha St. (Waipahu) – Definition not known.

Onekai St. (Kāne'ohe) – Sea sand.

Onekea Dr. (Kailua) – White sand.

Onelua St. ('Ewa Beach) – Two sands.

One'ula Pl. ('Ewa Beach) – Red sand.

'Ōnohi

'Ōnikiniki Pl. ('Aiea) – Flat, smooth, level.

'Ōnini Pl. (Honolulu) – A slight breeze, puff of wind; to gasp for breath.

'Oni'oni St. (Kailua) – To move, stir, shift, fidget.

'Onipa'a St./Pl. (Honolulu) – Fixed, immovable, steadfast, firm, resolute.

'Ono Rd. (Honolulu) – Delicious, tasty; to relish, crave. Named for original awardee.

'Ōnohi St. (Honolulu) – The eyeball; center; setting, as a ring.

'Ō'ō Ln. (Honolulu) – The black honey eater, an endangered bird. Its yellow feathers were prized for feather capes and headdresses.

'Ō'ōhao St. ('Ewa Beach) – Iron tool for digging, plow.

'Ō'ōkala Pl. (Honolulu) – Sharp digging stick. Named for a Hawai'i Island land division.

'O'olā Pl. ('Ewa Beach) – Young of fish.

'Ō'ōmanō Pl. (Honolulu) – Shark spear. Named for a Kaua'i promontory.

'O'opuhue Pl. (Kāne'ohe) – Swellfishes, puffers, balloon fishes, globefishes. A poisonous fish which some people eat (carefully).

'O'opuola St. (Hale'iwa) – A stroke in lua fighting. Literally: live 'o'opu (fish).

'Ōpae Rd. (Hale'iwa) – General name for shrimp.

'Opaehuna St. ('Ewa Beach) – An indigenous shrimp, almost transparent, found in brackish ponds. Literally: small shrimp.

'Ōpae

'Ōpaeka'a St. (Honolulu) – Rolling shrimp. Named for a Kaua'i stream and waterfalls.

'Ōpae'ula Rd. (Hale'iwa) – Snapping shrimps, small reddish shrimp. Literally: red shrimp. Named for an O'ahu land section and stream.

'Ōpakapaka St. (Kapolei) – Blue snapper fish.

'Opeha St. (Honolulu) – A native fern.

'Opihi St. (Honolulu) – Limpets and forms with similar shells. The most commonly eaten shellfish in Hawai'i.

'Opihikao Way/Pl. (Honolulu) – Named for a Hawai'i Island valley. Probably formerly called 'Opihikāō: crowd (gathering) limpets.

'Ōpio Pl. (Kapolei) – Youth, juvenile; youngster.

'Opo Pl. (Waipahu) – To lay a foundation, as of stones.

Opoi St. (Honolulu) – Definition not known. Perhaps Hawaiianized: "oh, boy!"

'Ōpua St. (Honolulu) – Puffy clouds, banked up near the horizon; cloud bank.

'Ōpuaki'i Pl./Way (Kapolei) – Cloud bank containing images.

Ōpuhe St. (Wai'anae) – Three species of endemic trees related to the olonā. Its bark was shaped into fishing nets.

Ōpūhea Pl. (Kāne'ohe) – Quiet, tranquil, calm, disinclined to work, lazy.

Opukea St. ('Aiea) – A large, strong, superior sugar cane variety.

'Ōpuku St. (Kapolei) – Name of one of two drums that announced the birth of Kākuhihewa.

'Ōpule St. (Kapolei) – A wrasse fish.

'Owakalena St. (Kapolei) – Flash of yellow.

'Owāli'i Cir. (Wahiawā) – Maidenhair spleenwort, a fern found on Hawai'i Island mountains. It has wiry, narrow fronds.

Owāwa St. (Honolulu) – Valley, ravine, gulch.

ʻŌwena St. (Honolulu) – A faint glow.

ʻOwene Ln. (Honolulu) – Owen. Possibly named for Owen Holt. His sons James and George lived nearby.

Pā St. (ʻEwa Beach) – Mother-of-pearl shell.

Paʻa St. (Honolulu) – Firm, solid, steadfast, permanent.

Paʻaʻāina St./Pl. (Pearl City) – Landholder; to hold land.

Paʻahana St. (Honolulu) – Industrious, busy, hardworking; workman, laborer.

Paʻahihi St. (Waialua) – Spread here and there.

Pāʻaila Pl. (Kāneʻohe) – The castor-oil plant. Rubbing its leaves on the face relieves fever.

Paʻailalo St. (Mililani) – The earth below.

Paʻailuna Way (Pearl City) – Heavens above.

Paʻakai St./Pl. (Kapolei) – Salt.

Paʻakāmaʻa

Paʻakāmaʻa St. (Pearl City) – Pair of shoes.

Paʻakea Rd. (Waiʻanae) – Limestone, coral beds, found on the leeward sides of the islands. Literally: white hardness.

Paʻakikī Pl. (Kailua) – Hard, tough; compact, difficult, stubborn.

Paʻaliʻi St. (Mililani) – A morning glory, when used in medicine.

Paʻakō St. (Kailua) – Dry lowland plain.

Paʻala Lp./Pl. (Kapolei) – Named for an Oʻahu land district.

Paʻalaʻa Rd. (Haleʻiwa) – Sacred firmness. Named for an Oʻahu land division.

Paʻalaʻa Uka-Pūpūkea Rd. (Haleʻiwa) – Upland Paʻalaʻa; white shell. Named for two Oʻahu land districts.

Paʻaleʻa St. (Honolulu) – Pleasure loving. Named for original awardee.

Paʻaloha St. (ʻEwa Beach) – Keepsake, memento, souvenir.

Paʻalua St. (ʻEwa Beach) – A banana variety.

Pāʻaniana

Pāʻani St. (Honolulu, Kunia) – To play, sport; joking, amusing, playful.

Pāʻaniana St. (ʻEwa Beach) – Playing games or sports.

Pāʻao Pl. (Mililani) – An unidentified star, possibly one of a large group resembling a double canoe. Pāʻao was an ancient priest who reputedly led people from Raʻiātea, Society Islands to Hawaiʻi.

Paʻaono St. (Waipahu) – Hexagon.

Paʻapū St. (Honolulu) – Solid.

Paʻauilo Pl. (Honolulu) – Definition not known. Named for a Hawaiʻi Island village.

Paʻawalu St. (Waipahu) – Octagon.

Paʻea St. (Mililani) – A variety of taro.

Paehiʻa Pl. (Mililani) – To fasten sticks to thatching of a house.

Paʻaono

Paeheu Pl. (Mililani) – Large bundle.

Paeheʻulu St. (ʻEwa Beach) – Row of breadfruit trees.

Paekiʻi St. (ʻEwa Beach) – Row of clouds, on the horizon. Literally: row of images.

Paekō St. (ʻEwa Beach) – Cultivation of sugar cane growing along a border.

Pāʻeli Pl. (Mililani) – To dig the earth, as to plant a taro patch.

Paeloahiki Pl. (Mililani) – 1) An unidentified star. 2) The Milky Way. Literally: eastern long row.

Paemoku

Paemoku Pl. (Mililani) – Group of islands, archipelago.

Paeoki Dr. (Honolulu) – Definition not known.

Paepae St. (Mililani) – A support, prop, stool, pavement, house platform.

Paepuʻu St. (Kāneʻohe) – Row or cluster of hills.

Paʻewalani Pl. (Kāneʻohe) – Heavenly mistake; royal error.

Paha Pl. (Waipahu) – To improvise a chant; an improvised or conversational chant.

Pahaku St./Pl. (Mililani) – Name of a design on Niʻihau mats.

Pāhala Pl. (Mililani) – A method of making mulch soil by placing pandanus (hala) branches and leaves in holes in rocky soil containing mulch, and then burning the hala for fertilizer.

Pāhano Lp. (Waiʻanae) – Distinguished enclosure.

Pāhau Pl. (ʻEwa Beach) – Striped flatfish.

Pahē St. (ʻEwa Beach) – Soft-spoken, soft-mannered.

Pāheahea St. (ʻEwa Beach) – To call, especially to invite someone to eat; hospitality.

Pāheʻeheʻe Rd./Pl. (Waiʻanae) – Slippery. Named for an Oʻahu mountain ridge.

Pahelehala Lp. (Kahuku) – A wind at Waiʻanae, Oʻahu. Literally: pandanus ensnarement.

Pahemo St./Pl. (ʻAiea) – Loosened, slipping off; to loosen, get loose.

Pāhiʻa Rd. (Kāneʻohe) – A slipping, falling down. Named for original awardee.

Pahikā St. (ʻEwa Beach) – Cane knife, machete.

Pahikaua St./Pl. (Kāneʻohe) – Sword. Literally: war knife.

Pahikā

Pāhiki St. ('Ewa Beach) – To pass quietly, go lightly, touch gently.

Pahikoli Pl. (Kāne'ohe) – Carving knife.

Pāhiku Pl. (Mililani) – Seven fold, by sevens; seven times; to distribute to seven or divide by seven.

Pāhili Rd. (Honolulu) – To blow strongly, as a wind, especially a veering wind; to lash, as a storm.

Pahiolo St. ('Aiea) – A saw (tool); to saw.

Pahu

Pahipahi'ālua St. (Kahuku) – Definition not known. Named for an O'ahu land division.

Pāhoa Ave. (Honolulu) – Short dagger; sharp stone, used for a weapon; kapu sign. Named for an O'ahu land section.

Pāhoe Rd. (Hale'iwa) – To paddle; to drive fish into a net by beating the paddles rhythmically against the canoe; paddler.

Pāhoehoe Pl. (Honolulu) – Smooth, unbroken type of lava.

Pāhōlei St. (Kāne'ohe) – Legendary name for kawa.

Pāhounui Dr. (Honolulu) – Big Pāhou (hou fish enclosure). Named for a former Kalihi fishpond.

Pahu St. (Waipahu) – Box, drum, cask, chest, barrel, trunk, tank.

Pāhuhu St./Pl./Way ('Ewa Beach) – Name of the famous pearl fishhook owned by Hino'oleki, the mighty fisherman who became a ruling chief of Wai'anae.

Pahukui St. (Honolulu) – Hypodermic injection. Literally: needle piercing.

Pahukui

Pahukula Pl. (Honolulu) – Chest (of) gold.

Pahulu St. (Honolulu) – Nightmare (named for a Lāna'i chief of evil spirits).

Pahumele Way/Pl. (Kailua) – Should be Pahumeli: beehive.

Pahupa'i Way (Honolulu) – Small sharkskin hula drum. Literally: beating drum.

Pahuwai Pl. (Kāne'ohe) – Water tank. (A water tank converted into a home is at the end of this Place).

Pai Cir. (Wahiawā) – A native fern, growing on trees at high altitudes.

Pai'ā St./Pl. (Mililani) – Bracken, a stiff, weedy native fern with creeping underground stems.

Pa'iaha Pl. (Kapolei) – A variety of taro.

Pai'ea St. (Honolulu) – A reddish crab with hard shell and short legs. A name Kamehameha I earned as a youth for his steadfastness in athletic games with Hawaiian wariors. Figuratively: a star athlete.

Pā'ihi St. ('Aiea) – A small weed related to watercress. Used medicinally, and as a tapa dye.

Pahukula

Paikau St. (Honolulu) – To march, drill, parade, pass to and fro; to practice firearms.

Paikauhale St./Pl. (Mililani) – An unidentified star. Literally: to go gadding about (to roam or wander) from house to house.

Paikō Dr. (Honolulu) – Named for Joseph Paikō, Jr. (?-1947), a landowner here. He gave land and money from his estate to benefit St. Francis Hospital.

Paila St. (Honolulu) – Pile, heap.

Pailaka Pl. (Kāneʻohe) – Pilot.

Pailani St. (ʻEwa Beach) – To praise.

Pailolo Pl. (Waipahu) – A variety of sugar cane.

Paina St. (Honolulu) – Pine trees and all kinds of conifers; ironwood.

Paʻiniu Pl. (Kapolei) – Some native Hawaiian lillies with long narrow silvery leaves forming rosette-shaped plants.

Paioa Pl. (Waipahu) – Tall, slim.

Paiʻoluʻolu Way (Honolulu) – Lift gently. Named for an Oʻahu promontory on the south side of Hanauma Bay.

Paionia St./Pl. (ʻEwa Beach, Mililani) – Pioneer.

Paʻiua Pl. (Mililani) – Fine, white tapa.

Pāiwa St./Pl. (Waipahu) – Nine times, nine at a time. Named for an Oʻahu land section.

Pākāhi Pl. (Honolulu) – Singly, once, one at a time, one by one, apiece, individually.

Pakai Pl. (Kāneʻohe) – Two amaranths (tropicalherbs resembling spinach). They are the spleen aramanth and the slender amaranth. Eaten as green vegetables.

Pakaiea St. (Waipahu) – A variety of sugar cane.

Pākalā St. (Honolulu) – The sun shines. Named for a Kauaʻi promontory and village.

Pakalana St./Pl. (ʻAiea, Honolulu) – The Chinese violet, a vine. Its fragrant yellow-green flowers are used in leis.

Pākanu St./Pl. (Honolulu) – Garden, cultivated field. Literally: planting enclosure.

Pākau St. (Mililani) – To place; table, stand.

Pakaua St. (Mililani) – Raindrops.

Pākau

Pāka'uwili Dr. (Wahiawā) – To turn, twist, suffer in pain.

Pakaweli St. (Kapolei) – A variety of sugar cane, with different names on different islands.

Pākeke St. (Wai'anae) – A variety of sweet potato.

Pākela St. (Waipahu) – To exceed, surpass, excel.

Pakelo Pl. (Lā'ie) – To slip out, as an animal from a trap or a fish through the hand; slippery, slick.

Pākī Ave. (Honolulu) – Overplentiful. Named for High Chief Abner Pākī (1808-1855). Supreme Court Judge, House of Nobles, and Acting O'ahu governor. Father of Bernice Pauahi Bishop.

Pākīkō Way/Pl. (Kāne'ohe) – Stone adze.

Pākini St. (Honolulu) – Tin pan, pan, basin.

Pakohana St. (Honolulu) – Nude, naked, alone, by itself. Named for original awardee.

Pākolu Pl. (Honolulu) – By threes, three at a time, three times, threefold.

Pākōnane Pl. ('Aiea) – To shine brightly, of the moon.

Pākū Pl. (Kāne'ohe) – Curtain, screen, partition, veil.

Pakualua Pl. (Kāne'ohe) – Probably should be Pākualau: pearl-shell lure, dark-colored inside. Literally: showery lure.

Pāku'i St. (Honolulu) – To splice or add on, annex. Named for original awardee.

Pala St. (Honolulu) – A native fern. The frond stem base was baked and eaten during famines. Used medicinally, and in heiau ceremonies.

Pāla'au St. (Honolulu) – Wooden fence, hedge.

Palahi'a St./Pl (Kapolei) – To glide.

Palahinu Pl. (Honolulu) – Polished, bright.

Pāla'au

Palai St. (Waipahu) – A native fern. See Ala Le'ie.

Palaiali'i Way/Pl. ('Aiea) – A variety of palai (fern). Literally: royal palai.

Palaiki St. (Waipahu) – Sound of a stone falling into the water; to fall with a sound.

Palailai St./Pl. (Kapolei) – Young of the lai (fish).

Palakamana St. (Wai'anae) – Perhaps: Blackman. Possibly named for Leopold Gilbert Blackman (1874-1951). Military aide to several Hawai'i governors. 'Iolani School principal (1900-1901), Bishop Museum librarian (1902-1907), and president of Territorial Teachers Association. Commissioner and Superintendent of Public Instruction. He owned land here (1928).

Pālala St. (Kapolei) – Gift or tax given to a chief at the birth of a child; to honor a child with a gift; house-warming feast; to have such a feast.

Pālama St. (Honolulu) – Lama (wood) enclosure. Short for Kapālama: an O'ahu land division.

Palamea Ln. (Honolulu) – Plump.

Pālāmoa St. (Mililani) – Thick, dense, as clouds.

Pālāmoi St. (Pearl City) – Second or third growth stage of the moi (fish).

Palanehe Pl. (Honolulu) – Noiseless, quiet, dainty, deft; to move in a dainty fashion.

Palani St. (Wai'anae) – Frank. Possibly named for Frank McCandless, a Tacoma, Washington businessman. See Linakola.

Palani Ave. (Honolulu) – Frank. Named for Francis Peter James. See Lukepane.

Palaoa Pl. (Honolulu) – Sperm whale; ivory, especially whale tusks used for the highly prized lei palaoa; whale-tooth pendant.

Palaoa

Pala'ole Pl. (Honolulu) – Perfect, flawless. Literally: without a daub.

Palapala Pl. (Honolulu) – Document of any kind; writing of any kind; printing on tapa or paper; formerly the Scriptures, or learning in general.

Palapalai Cir. (Wahiawā) – A native fern. See Ala Le'ie.

Palapū St. (Kailua) – Wound, flesh injury. Named for an O'ahu land section and stream.

Palawiki St. (Kailua) – Should be Pālawaiki: neat, dainty, having good taste in clothes and the like.

Palea Way (Honolulu) – Brushed aside. Named for an O'ahu promontory on the north side of Hanauma Bay.

Pālehua Rd. (Kapolei) – Lehua (blossom) enclosure. Named for an O'ahu land section and mountain peak.

Paleka Rd./Pl. (Kāne'ohe) – Parker. Named for the Rev. Benjamin Parker (1803-1877). A missionary, he came to Hawai'i with the 6th Missionary Company. Stationed in Kāne'ohe (1833-1863).

Palekaiko St. (Pearl City) – Paradise.

Palekana St. (Lā'ie) – Safe, saved, rescued; defense, savior, safety.

Palekaua St./Pl. (Honolulu) – War defense, shield, defensive armor.

Palekona St. (Honolulu) – Falcon.

Palena St./Pl. (Honolulu) – Boundary, border, margin.

Pāleo Way ('Aiea) – To converse, chat; to talk loudly; chatting.

Pali Dr./Hwy. (Honolulu, Kailua) – Cliff, precipice.

Pali'āhina Pl. (Honolulu) – Gray cliff.

Pali'i St. (Mililani) – Micro chips. Literally: having the quality of being made small or tiny.

Paliiki Pl. (Kāne'ohe) – Small cliff.

Palikea St./Pl. (Wai'anae) – A kind of sweet potato.

Palikilo Rd. (Kāne'ohe) – Observation cliff; spying cliff.

Palikū St. (Honolulu) – Vertical cliff. Named for a Kaua'i promontory.

Pāleo

Pālima Pl. (Honolulu) – Five times, in fives, fivefold.

Palimalu Dr. (Honolulu) – Shady cliff.

Pali Momi St. ('Aiea) – Pearl cliff. Probably intended: Pearl Ridge.

Palione Pl. (Kailua) – Steep hill (of) sand.

Palipaʻa Pl. (Honolulu) – Cliff.

Paliuli St. (Honolulu) – Dark cliff. Name of the legendary Puna, Hawaiʻi Island garden where the Princess Lāʻieikawai lived in a garden of paradise, plenty and joy.

Pāloa Pl. (Waimānalo) – Long fence or enclosure.

Pālolo Ave./Pl./Ter. Pl. (Honolulu) – Sticky clay. Named for an Oʻahu valley.

Pālua Pl. (Honolulu) – Two by two, double, twofold, twice.

Pālūlā Way (ʻAiea) – Tranquil, serene, calm.

Pāmāʻele St. (Kailua) – An unidentified star.

Pāmakani Pl. (Honolulu) – A native hibiscus, having fragrant flowers.

Pana

Pāmoa Rd. (Honolulu) – Chicken enclosures. Named for an Oʻahu land section.

Pāmoho Pl. (ʻAiea) – A creeping fern.

Pana Pl. (Honolulu) – To shoot, as marbles, arrows, bow; bow and arrows.

Panalāʻau St. (Honolulu) – Colony, dependency, territory, province.

Panaleʻa Pl. (Honolulu) – Dexterous, gleeful, quick, as in danger.

Pānānā St. (Honolulu, Kapolei) – Compass. Named for Harriet Pānānā Napela (1852-1901), a part-Hawaiian descendant of Maui kings. She managed Maunaʻolu Seminary on Maui. Wife of Samuel Parker, owner of Parker Ranch. Possibly the Hawaiian name of the Jacobean lily, an herb, named for the chiefess.

Panapanapuhi St. (ʻEwa Beach) – A kind of shellfish.

Paneʻe St. (Pearl City) – To move along; pushed forward.

Panekai Pl. (Kailua) – To move in, as the tide.

Pāneki St./Pl (Honolulu) – Pansy, a plant in the violet family.

Pānini

Panepoʻo Pl. (Wahiawā) – Pinnacle, summit; topmost, most important. Literally: hind part (of) head.

Pānini Lp. (Honolulu) – The prickly pear, a cactus. Its fruit was eaten raw, or made into liquor. Literally: fence wall.

Paniʻo St. (Honolulu) – Smooth.

Paniolo Pl. (Honolulu) – Cowboy. Literally: Spain (España).

Pānui St. (Honolulu) – Large enclosure. Possibly named for Kimokeo Pānui, a 1900s diver employed at Lyle's Marine Railway.

Paoa Pl. (Honolulu) – Literally: strongly odoriferous. Named for original awardee. One of his descendants was Duke Paoa Kahanamoku, the world-famous surfer, champion Olympic swimmer, and Hawaii's good-will ambassador, who lived here.

Paniolo

Paoakalani Ave. (Honolulu) – The royal perfume. Named for one of the homes of Queen Liliʻuokalani.

Paokano Lp./Pl. (Kailua) – Definition not known.

Pāoʻo St. (Honolulu) – Name of several varieties of sea ʻoʻopu (fish), also called rockskipper. Paoʻo love the rough seas and rocky coasts, where they leap from pool to pool.

Pāʻopua Lp./Pl. (Kailua) – An unidentified star.

Papa Cir. (Waialua) – Native-born. Named for original awardee.

Pāpaʻa St. (Kapolei) – A red sugar cane with light-brown fibers; it has an odor similar to burned sugar, hence its name.

Papahehi Pl. (Honolulu) – Footboard, used for dancing; treadle. Literally: board to step on.

Pāpahi Pl. (ʻEwa Beach) – To decorate, honor, confer honors.

Pāpaʻi St. (Honolulu) – General name for crabs.

Papaiāula Ave. (Kapolei) – To blow or rise as a breeze.

Pāpaʻi

Pāpaʻiloa Rd. (Haleʻiwa) – Long crab.

Papakū Pl. (Honolulu) – Foundation or surface, of the earth; floor, of the ocean; bed, of a stream; bottom.

Pāpala St. (Honolulu) – Several shrubs and small trees belonging to the Amaranth family. Hawaiians used this light, inflammable wood for fireworks, throwing burning pieces from Kauaʻi cliffs.

Papalalo Pl. (Honolulu) – Lower floor of a house, valley bottom, lower layer.

Papalani St. (Kailua) – Heavenly layer, heaven and all the spiritual powers; upper heavens, firmament.

Pāpalealiʻi St. (ʻAiea) – Crown.

Pāpalealiʻi

Papali St./Pl. (Honolulu) – Small cliff or slope, along a ravine.

Papapuhi Pl. (ʻEwa Beach) – The eel companion of Awāwelēʻī.

Pāpipi Dr./Pl./Rd. (ʻEwa Beach) – The prickly pear, a cactus. Its fruit was eaten raw, or made into liquor. Literally: cattle fence or fence wall. Same as Pānini.

Pāpolohiwa St. (Mililani) – An unidentified star, said to have been observed by priests.

Pāpū Cir. (Honolulu) – Fort. Derived from pā (enclosure) and pū (gun).

Paʻū St./Ln. (Honolulu) – Moist, damp. Named for an Oʻahu land section in Waikīkī. Refers to former Waikīkī duck ponds and taro patches. Also possibly Pau: finished. Said to refer to canoe races that ended here, but the street name pre-dates the Ala Wai canal.

Paua

Paua Pl. (ʻEwa Beach) – A bivalve, clam.

Pauahi St. (Honolulu) – Destruction by fire, burn. Probably named for Bernice Pauahi Bishop (1831-1884). Hawaiian chiefess and philanthropist. She inherited over 400,000 acres (11% of Hawai'i land area). Daughter of Abner Paki and Konia. Wife of Charles Bishop. She refused the offer of dying King Kamehameha V to succeed him as monarch. Her will provided money to establish Kamehameha Schools (Boys School, 1887; Girls School, 1894). Her husband founded Bishop Museum in her memory (1889). Bernice was named for an aunt, Kalani Pauahi, who was saved from a fire as a child.

Pauahi

Pauahilani Way/Pl. (Kailua) – An unidentified star.

Pāu'i Pl. (Honolulu) – Beautiful fence, beautiful enclosure.

Paukikī St. (Honolulu) – Fast, speedily; speed; to do with great speed.

Paukū St. (Kailua) – Section; verse; small land section.

Paula Dr. (Honolulu) – Paula.

Paulele St. (Kailua) – Faith, confidence, trust; to believe implicitly.

Pauloa Pl. (Honolulu) – All, everything, to have all.

Pāuma Pl. (Honolulu) – Large curved needle, used in sewing burlap sacks.

Paumaka Pl. (Honolulu) – An unidentified star, said to be an omen for chiefs.

Paumakua Way/Pl. (Kailua) – An unidentified star.

Paumalū Pl. (Hale'iwa) – Taken secretly. Named for an O'ahu land division.

Pauoa Rd. (Honolulu) – Definition not known. Named for an O'ahu valley.

Pau'ole Pl. (Honolulu) – Always.

Pā'ūpahapaha Pl. (Waimānalo) – When Kauholokahiki came ashore, she was covered only by a skirt of green pahapaha seaweed. Literally: skirt of the pahapaha seaweed. See Kauholokahiki.

Pauwala Pl. (Mililani) – An unidentified star, the companion of Ululoa.

Pawa Way (Mililani) – An unidentified star.

Pāwa'a Ln. (Honolulu) – Canoe enclosure. Named for an O'ahu land section.

Pāwaina St./Pl. (Honolulu) – Vineyard.

Pāwale Pl. (Honolulu) – Native dock, a vinelike plant belonging to the Buckwheat family.

Pāwehe Pl. (Waialua) – Generic name for colorful geometric motifs, as on mats, bowls and gourds. Named for original awardee.

Pe'a St. (Waialua) – Possibly: cross. Named for original awardee.

Pe'ahi St. (Waialua) – Possibly: fan. Named for original awardee.

Peawini Pl. (Kahuku) – Fair wind.

Pe'eone Pl. ('Ewa Beach) – Sand crab that buries itself backwards in wet sand. Literally: sand hiding.

Pehu St. (Honolulu) – Swollen. Named for original awardee.

Peke Ln./Pl. (Waipahu) – Becky.

Pekelo Pl. (Wahiawā) – Peter.

Pekunia Pl. (Honolulu) – Petunia.

Pelanaki St. (Waiʻanae) – Perhaps: Bernard.

Pele St. (Honolulu) – Lava flow, volcano, eruption. Named for the volcano goddess.

Peleiake Pl. (Kapolei) – The cluster of stars known as Peiades.

Pele

Pelekane Dr. (Honolulu) – British. Named for James (Kimo) Isaac Dowsett, Jr. See Kimopelekane.

Pelu Pl. (Honolulu) – To fold, turn over or under, bend.

Penakiʻi Way/Pl. (Waipahu) – To paint pictures; picture painter.

Penekū Pl. (Honolulu) – To reside at a place for several generations.

Pepeʻekeo St./Pl. (Honolulu) – Named for a Hawaiʻi Island mill and promontory. Said to be formerly called Pepeʻekeō, literally: the food crushed (as by warriors in battle).

Pia St./Pl. (Honolulu) – Polynesian arrowroot, an herb grown for its starchy tubers, used primarily for food and medicine.

Pihana St. (Honolulu) – Fullness. Named for a Maui heiau.

Pihapono Pl. (ʻEwa Beach) – Completely full, complete.

Pihi St. (ʻEwa Beach) – Badge or identification button assigned to plantation workers.

Piʻikea St./Pl. (Honolulu) – To become light, as the day.

Piʻikoi St./Pl. (Honolulu) – To claim to be of higher rank than one is. Named for Chief David Kahalepouli Piʻikoi (1843-1884), the original awardee. Father of David Kawānanakoa and Jonah Kūhiō Kalanianaʻole.

Penakiʻi

Piʻimauna St./Pl. (Honolulu) – Mountain climber.

Piʻipiʻi St. (ʻEwa Beach) – Bubbling forth, as water.

Pīkai St. (Haleʻiwa) – To sprinkle with sea water or salted fresh water to purify or remove a kapu.

Pīkaiʻōlena St. (Waiʻanae) – To sprinkle with sea water or salt water with a bit of ʻōlena root, to purify or remove taboo.

Pīkake Ct./Pl./Way (Wahiawā, Honolulu, Pearl City) – The Arabian jasmine, a shrub or climber from India. Its small, white, fragrant flowers are used for leis. Princess Kaʻiulani was fond of these flowers and also her peacocks (pīkake), so the same name was given to the flowers.

Piki St./Pl. (ʻAiea) – Peach.

Pīkoiloa Pl. (Kāneʻohe) – Long tripping club. Pīkoi: tripping club, of wood or stone, with a rope attached. It was hurled at the foe to encircle his arms or legs, and render him helpless.

Pikokea St. (Mililani) – A native variety of taro widely planted.

Pīkoni Pl. (Honolulu) – Cord attaching floats to a fishing net. Named for a Kauaʻi place.

Piku Way/Pl. ('Aiea) – Fig.

Pila Pl. (Honolulu) – Fiddle; any string instrument.

Pīla'a Pl. (Honolulu) – Sacred sprinkling. Named for a Kaua'i land division.

Pili Pl. (Honolulu) – Tanglehead, a pleasant-smelling brown grass used as a thatch.

Pilialo St. (Honolulu) – Bosom friend, beloved wife.

Pilialoha Pl. (Honolulu) – Close friendship, beloved relative or companionship; to have a loving or tender relationship, to be in a bond of love.

Pilina

Pili'ana St. ('Ewa Beach) – Connection.

Pilikai St. (Honolulu) – Two vines in the Morning-glory family, one of them is the wood rose.

Pilikana Way (Wai'anae) – Relation, kin, family.

Pilikino St. (Honolulu) – Personal, private.

Piliko'a St. ('Aiea) – Hawkfish, a large-eyed fish that waits motionlessly among coral for prey. Literally: coral clinging.

Pililā'au Ave. (Wai'anae) – Edge of a forest.

Pililani Pl. (Honolulu) – Close to heaven.

Pililua Pl. (Mililani) – Two unidentified stars, appearing same time as 'ōpelu fish. Literally: a close companionship of two.

Pilimai St./Pl. (Waipahu) – A native sugar cane variety, used in hana aloha (love sorcery), with the prayer for love to cling and hold fast.

Pilina Way/Pl. (Kāne'ohe) – Association, relationship, meeting, joining.

Piliokahi Ave./Pl./Way (Wai'anae) – Should be Piliokahe: clinging to Kahe. Named for an O'ahu hill.

Pilipa'a St. (Kāne'ohe) – Sticking firmly together, associating constantly, living in harmony.

Pilipili'ula Pl. (Kapolei) – A variety of grass used for making mats.

Pilipono St. (Kapolei) – Well-suited, well-matched; close fitting, as clothes; to refer exactly or concisely.

Pilipū Pl. (Kailua) – To unite, join, cling to; hard-pressed, as in danger.

Piliuka Way/Pl. (Wai'anae) – A stiff, clumpy, native grass. A good forage grass, growing only at high altitudes.

Piliwai St. (Honolulu) – Close to water.

Piliwale Way (Honolulu) – To cling. Named for an O'ahu chief who lived 11 generations before Kamehameha. See Haka.

Pilokea St. (Wai'anae) – A small native tree or shrub in the Orange family.

Pinana St. (Honolulu) – To climb; a climb.

Pinao St./Pl. (Honolulu) – Dragonfly.

Pinao'ula St./Pl. (Honolulu) – A variety of dragonfly. Literally: red dragonfly.

Pi'o Pl. (Honolulu) – Arch, arc; bent, arched, curved.

Pi'o

Pi'ohi'a Pl. (Waimānalo) – Small endemic trees. According to an old belief, eating the fruit of these trees aided fertility.

Piowa St. (Waipahu) – Named for original awardee.

Pīpā Pl. (Honolulu) – Alongside, as of a road, sidewalk, or river; to go along the side; sidewalk.

Pipi Cir. (Wahiawā) – Clumpy, green, leafless plants, used medicinally, and for a children's game.

Pīpīlani Pl. (Hau'ula) – Some kinds of green seaweeds.

Pō'aha Pl. ('Aiea) – Circle, of flowers.

Pō'ailani Cir./Pl. (Waipahu) – Horizon. Literally: sky circle.

Pohā

Pō'alima St./Pl. (Waimānalo) – Chief's plantation where the people worked on Friday's. Literally: Friday.

Poamoho St./Pl. (Waialua) – Name of a stream, trail and camp in the Wahiawā area.

Po'e Pl. (Waipahu) – People, persons, population, assemblage.

Poelua St./Pl. (Honolulu) – Should be Pe'elua: caterpillar.

Poepoe Pl. (Honolulu) – Round. Possibly named for Joseph Moku'ōhai Poepoe (1852-1913). Lawyer, Territorial House member (1913), and editor of Hawaiian language newspapers.

Pohā Ln. (Honolulu) – The cape gooseberry, a perennial herb in the Tomato family. They are eaten raw, or used in making jam and jelly.

Pōhāhāwai St./Pl. ('Ewa Beach) – Bubble.

Pōhai Pl. ('Aiea) – Circle, group, as of people, trees; gathering; as to gather about in a circle.

Pōhākea Pl. (Wai'anae) – White stone, as limestone.

Pōhaku St./Pl. (Honolulu) – Rock, stone; rocky, stony.

Pōhakulana Pl. (Honolulu) – Mooring rock for anchoring canoes.

Pōhakulepo St. ('Ewa Beach) – Adobe, brick; describes the soil at 'Ewa Villages. Literally: dirt rock.

Pōhaku

Pōhaku Loa Way (Hale'iwa) – Long stone.

Pōhakunui Ave. (Wai'anae) – Large stone.

Pōhakupalena St. (Wai'anae) – Boundary stone. Refers to the stone thrown by the gods Kane and Kanaloa to mark the Wai'anae and 'Ewa district boundaries.

Pōhakupili Pl. ('Ewa Beach) – A legendary supernatural stone that belonged to the gods, Kāne and Kanaloa, who divided the lands of 'Ewa.

Pōhakupuna Rd./Pl. ('Ewa Beach) – Round coral piece, used for polishing or rubbing; concrete. Literally: coral rock.

Pōhina St./Pl. (Honolulu, Mililani) – An unidentified star.

Pohoiki Pl. (Honolulu) – Small depression. Named for a Hawai'i Island land division.

Pohu Pl. (Waipahu) – Calm, quiet; to calm down, become quiet.

Pōhue St./Pl. ('Aiea) – General name for gourd plant.

Pōhuehue Rd. (Ka'a'awa) – The beach morning-glory plant, a strong vine growing on sandy beaches. Used for driving fish into nets.

Pohukaina St. (Honolulu) – Definition not known. Named for an O'ahu land section.

Pōhuli St. ('Aiea) – Sucker, sprout, shoot; to sprout, usually of bananas.

Po'ike'o St. (Waipahu) – White cover, white lid.

Pōiki St. (Waipahu) – Early in the morning, rise in the early morn.

Po'ipū Dr./Pl. (Honolulu) – To cover over entirely, as clouds or engulfing waves. Named for a Kaua'i land division.

Pōkā St./Pl. (Honolulu) – Bullet, cannon ball, shot, shell, pellet.

Pōka'ī Bay St. (Wai'anae) – Night (of) the supreme one. Named for an O'ahu bay.

Pōkāpahū Pl. (Honolulu) – Bomb, bullet, mine. Literally: bursting bullet.

Poke'o St. (Waipahu) – Child, childhood; pre-adolescent.

Poki St. (Honolulu) – Boki. Named for Boki Kamaulele (?-1830). Younger brother of Kalanimoku, cousin of Ka'ahumanu, and husband of Liliha. O'ahu governor, and chief counselor to Kamehameha III. Broke religious kapu (1819) after baptized a Catholic on a French ship. Feuded with Ka'ahumanu for political power: he supported British, she preferred Americans. Active in many businesses, and got into debt when drunk. Sailed to New Hebrides for sandalwood, but lost at sea with ship (1830). The name Poki is derived from variation of Poki ("Boss"), favorite dog of Kamehameha I, and a popular name for dogs, including guardian dog.

Pōki'i Pl. (Wai'anae) – Younger sister or brother, or closely related younger cousin, often spoken affectionately.

Pokiwai Way/Pl. (Hau'ula) – A drink of either warm or cold water, with sugar and cream.

Poko Rd./Pl. ('Aiea) – Short.

Pōkole St./Way (Honolulu, Kailua) – Short.

Pōlale Pl. (Mililani) – Clear, bright.

Pōlani St. (Waipahu) – Handsome, beautiful, clean, pure.

Polapola Pl. (Mililani) – An unidentified star, paired with Melemele. They are said to be twin stars: Melemele is the male star, and Polapola is the female star.

Pōkāpahū

Polea St. ('Ewa Beach) – Name of a former konohiki or headman of an ahupua'a land division in 'Ewa.

Poli'ahu Pl. (Kāne'ohe) – To caress. Named for the Mauna Kea snow goddess.

Poli'ala St. (Waimānalo) – Fragrant breast.

Poli'e Pl. (Mililani) – Shining, gleam; a gleam, flash of light.

Polihale Pl. (Honolulu) – Bosom (of the) house. Named for a Kaua'i mountain ridge, spring, and heiau.

Poli Hiwa Pl. (Honolulu) – Garble for Polohiwa: glistening black.

Polina Pl. (Waipahu) – Resplendent, shiny black.

Polinahe Pl. (Waipahu) – Soft and gentle, as low music or a breeze.

Pōlinalina Rd. (Kaʻaʻawa) – An aromatic beach shrub.

Poloʻai Way (Waipahu) – To summon, command to appear, invite.

Poloahilani St. (Mililani) – An unidentified star.

Polohi Pl. (Honolulu) – Smooth, as skin.

Polohilani Pl. (Honolulu) – Same as Poloahilani: an unidentified star.

Polohīnano Pl. (Honolulu) – White male pandanus bloom with its stem.

Polohiwa Pl. (Honolulu) – Dark, glistening black, as clouds or tapa.

Polohuku St./Pl. (ʻEwa Beach) – Rich, prosperous.

Poloke Pl. (Honolulu) – A large herb with large red or red-and-yellow flowers. Its round black seeds are worn in leis or placed in laʻamia shells for hula rattles. Commonly called: Aliʻipoe. Named for an Oʻahu land section.

Pololei Pl. (Honolulu) – Straight, upright, correct, right, accurate.

Pololia St. (ʻEwa Beach) – Jellyfish.

Poloʻula Pl. (ʻEwa Beach) – Same as Poloahilani: an unidentified star.

Polū Way (Waialua) – Blue. Named for original grantee.

Poluhi Way (Waipahu) – Long spear.

Polūlani Pl. (Honolulu) – Sky blue.

Poma Pl. (Honolulu) – Apple.

Pōmahina Pl. (Kailua) – Moonlight night.

Poma

Pōmaikaʻi Pl. (Kāneʻohe) – Good fortune, blessedness, prosperity; prosperous, fortunate.

Pomelaiki Pl. (Honolulu) – Should be Pomelaike: pomegranate, a shrub grown ornamentally for its flowers and fruits.

Pōnaha Pl. (Kāneʻohe) – Circle, of flowers.

Pōnahakeone Pl. (Waiʻanae) – Name of the fishing ground located off Ulehawa, Waiʻanae, where Maui lowered his fish hook to try and unite the Hawaiian islands into one land mass.

Poni St. (Honolulu) – To anoint, consecrate, crown, ordain, inaugurate.

Poni Mōʻī Rd. (Honolulu) – The carnation, with showy white to red or purple fragrant flowers. Used for leis. The Hawaiian name resulted from confusing the English word "carnation" with "coronation."

Pono St. (ʻAiea) – Goodness, uprightness, morality, moral qualities, correct or proper procedure.

Ponohale St. (ʻAiea) – Furniture, household goods.

Ponohana Lp./Pl. (ʻAiea) – Tools.

Ponokaulike St. (ʻAiea) – Equal rights.

Ponohana

Ponokīwila St./Pl. ('Aiea) – Civil rights.

Ponopono Pl. (Honolulu) – Neat, tidy, in order, arranged, attended to.

Poʻo Pl. (Honolulu) – Head, summit.

Poʻohaili St. (Lāʻie) – Indistinct depression. Said to be the name of an Oʻahu land section.

Poʻohōlua Dr. ('Aiea) – Hōlua (sled) depression.

Poʻohuku Way (Waipahu) – Top of a hill, ridge.

Poʻokela St./Pl. (Kāneʻohe) – Foremost, best, superior; champion; to excel.

Poʻolā St./Pl. (Honolulu) – Stevedore.

Poʻolau Way (Waipahu) – Leaf base.

Poʻoleka St. (Honolulu) – Postage stamp. Literally: letter head.

Poʻomaʻū St. (Kāneʻohe) – Damp depression.

Poʻopaʻa Pl. ('Aiea) – Several hawkfishes, having blue, red, and brown blotches with white vertical bars. Literally: hard head.

Poʻopoʻo Pl. (Kailua) – Depression, cavity.

Poʻowai Pl. ('Ewa Beach) – Water source or head, dam.

Pōpōhau Pl. (Waiʻanae) – The hydrangea, a shrub with large, rounded or flat-topped clusters of pink, white, or blue flowers.

Popoʻi Pl. ('Ewa Beach) – To catch between cupped hands, as a small bird or butterfly; to pounce, as a cat on a mouse; to snatch.

Popoiʻa Rd. (Kailua) – Fish rot. Named for an Oʻahu islet.

Pōpoki

Pōpoki St./Pl. (Kāneʻohe) – Cat. Possible Hawaiianization of expression, "poor pussy" (cat).

Pōpolo Pl. ('Aiea) – The black nightshade, a common weed with small, black, edible berries. It was eaten as vegetables, and used medicinally.

Pouhala Rd. (Waipahu) – Perhaps same as Pouhana: post set in the middle of each end of the house, supporting the ridge pole. Named for an Oʻahu land section.

Pouhana St./Way/Lp. (Waipahu) – Post set in the middle of each end of the house, supporting the ridge pole. Figuratively: support, mainstay, as of a family.

Pouhānuʻu Way/Pl. (Kāneʻohe) – An unidentified star. Literally: low post.

Pouli Rd. (Kailua) – Dark; darkness, dark night.

Princess Kahanu Ave. (Waiʻanae) – Named for Princess Elizabeth Kahanu Kalanianaʻole, a commissioner of the Hawaiian Homes Commission, and the wife of Jonah Kuhio Kalanianaʻole.

Pua Ave. (Waiʻanae) – Flower.

Pua Ln. (Honolulu) – Flower. Named for David William Pua (1836-1896). Member, House of Nobles (1890-1893). Married High Chiefess Mary Nāhakuʻelua. He lived here. Great grand-father of former Honolulu City Clerk Raymond Pua. See Nahaku.

Pua

Pua'a'ē Rd./Pl. (Kāne'ohe) – Foreign pig. Named for an O'ahu land section.

Puaahi Pl. (Mililani) – An unidentified star. Literally: fire flower.

Pua'ala Ln. (Honolulu) – Fragrant flower.

Puaali'i St./Pl./Way ('Aiea) – Descendant of a chief.

Pua Alowalo St. (Kāne'ohe) – Hibiscus flower. Usually: Pua Aloalo.

Pua'a'ē

Pua'anuhe St. ('Aiea) – Butterfly weed. Literally: caterpillar flower.

Pua'āpiki St. ('Aiea) – A name of the 'ilima flower.

Pua'ena Pl. (Honolulu) – To glow brightly.

Puahala St. ('Ewa Beach) – Bright yellow base of a pandanus (hala) that may be used for leis.

Puahau Pl. ('Aiea) – Hau (tree) blossoms.

Pūaheahe St. (Mililani) – To blow gently.

Puāhi St. (Waipahu) – To glow like fire. Also spelled Pua ahi.

Puahia Pl. (Honolulu) – Spry, quick.

Puahio St. ('Ewa Beach) – To come and go swiftly, as a puff or gust of wind.

Puahōkū Pl. ('Aiea) – The star-of-Bethlehem, a poisonous herb with starlike white flowers. Literally: star flower.

Pū'ahu'ula Pl. (Kāne'ohe) – Feather cape spring. Named for an O'ahu land section.

Pua'ilima St./Pl. ('Aiea) – 'Ilima flower.

Pua'ina St. ('Ewa Beach) – Flowing, bubbling, boiling.

Pua 'Inia St. (Kāne'ohe) – Pride of India flower.

Puakai Pl. (Mililani) – Red of tapa; or malo dyed with noni juice.

Puakala Pl. (Honolulu) – A thorny lobelia (flower).

Puakala St. ('Aiea) – The spear thistle, a coarse prickly weed.

Puakea Pl. (Honolulu) – White blossom. Named for Hawai'i Island land sections.

Puakenikeni Rd. (Ka'a'awa) – A shrub or small tree. Its fragrant, white blooming, color-changing flowers are used for leis. Literally: ten-cent flower. The flowers used to sell for 10¢ each.

Puakīkā Pl. ('Aiea) – Cigar flower.

Pua Kīkā Pl. (Honolulu) – Cigar flower.

Puakō Way (Kailua) – Stem and tassel of sugar cane. The stem was used in making hats.

Puakolū St. (Wai'anae) – Kolū flower. See Kolū.

Puakukui Pl. ('Aiea) – Kukui (tree) blossoms.

Pū'ala'a St. ('Aiea) – Heap of small taro tubers.

Pualalea St./Pl./Way (Kahuku) – Clear, bright.

Pualani Way (Honolulu) – Descendant of a chief. Literally: royal flower.

Pualei Cir. (Honolulu) – Flowers for leis; cherished blossom or child.

Pualeilani St. (Wai'anae) – Name of the Waikīkī beach home of Prince Jonah Kūhiō Kalaniana'ole. Literally: wreath of heaven.

Pualele Pl. (Honolulu) – The sow thistle, a weedy herb, sometimes fed to pigs. Its leaves were eaten by people during famine.

Pū'ali St. (Kāne'ohe) – Warrior, soldier.

Pū'ali Koa Pl. (Kāne'ohe) – Armed forces, troops, regiment, brigade, corps.

Pualoalo Pl. ('Ewa Beach) – Hibiscus flower; found in front yards of 'Ewa Villages homes.

Pualoke Pl. (Honolulu) – Rose flower.

Pualu St. ('Ewa Beach) – All together, in unison, united, cooperative.

Puama'ole St. ('Ewa Beach) – Flower that never fades.

Puamano

Pua Mākāhala St. (Kāne'ohe) – Mākāhala (shrub) flower. Mākāhala: the orange cestrum, a climbing shrub with orange flowers, are used for leis.

Puamale Ct. (Wahiawā) – The stephanotis, a vine in the Milkweed family from Madagascar. It has fragrant, tubular, wax-white flowers. Literally: wedding flower (because the flowers are sometimes worn by brides).

Puamāmane St. (Honolulu) – Māmane (tree) flower. See Māmane.

Puamano Pl. (Waipahu) – Many flowers.

Puamae'ole St. ('Ewa Beach) – Flower that never fades.

Puamōhala St. (Kāne'ohe) – Unfolded flower, blossoming flower.

Puanānālā

Puama'oma'o Pl. (Kapolei) – Ma'o flower.

Puana St. (Waipahu) – Beginning of a song; theme of a song.

Puanakau St. (Honolulu) – Rigel, the guardian star of West Maui.

Puanānālā St. (Pearl City) – The sunflower. Literally: flower looking (at) sun.

Puanane Lp./Pl. (Mililani) – An unidentified star.

Puanani Ln. (Honolulu) – Beautiful flower.

Puanihi St. (Kapolei) – Young taro, taro tops.

Puaniu St. (Kapolei) – Coconut flower.

Puanoho Pl. (Kapolei) – Nohu flower.

Pua'ole Pl. ('Aiea) – A flowerless sugar cane.

Puapākē St. (Kapolei) – Chrysanthemum.

Puapo'o Pl. (Kāne'ohe) – Comb or crest of a bird, as a chicken. Literally: head issue.

Pueo

Puawa Pl. ('Aiea) – Guava.

Puawiliwili Pl. (Wai'anae) – Wiliwili (tree) flower. See Wiliwili.

Pueo St. (Honolulu) – Hawaiian short-eared owl. Often worshipped as an 'aumakua (family god).

Pueohala Pl. (Kailua) – Should be Puʻoihala: definition not known. Named for an Oʻahu land area.

Pueonani St. (Kapolei) – Beautiful Hawaiian owl.

Pūhala Rise (Honolulu) – Pandanus tree. See Hala.

Pūhano St. (Waiʻanae) – To beautify, glorify.

Puhau Way (Waipahu) – Cool spring.

Pūhāwai Rd. (Waiʻanae) – Water hollow. Named for an Oʻahu land section.

Puhikāni St./Pl. (ʻEwa Beach) – Place where the shark goddess, Kaʻahupahau bathed.

Puhikō (ʻEwa Beach) – Burning cane.

Puhilaka St. (ʻEwa Beach) – The tame eel of ʻEwa legend; also a point in ʻEwa.

Puhilaumilo Pl. (ʻEwa Beach) – A variety of eel, considered appetizing.

Puhinalo Pl. (Waiʻanae) – Concealed eel. Named for a legendary Waiʻanae eel.

Puhipaka St. (ʻEwa Beach) – One of the most common of the larger eels.

Pūhuli St. (Hauʻula) – To grow thick, as taro shoots.

Puīa St. (Waipahu) – Sweet-smelling; diffused, as fragrance; permeated with perfume, fragrant.

Pūʻili Pl. (Honolulu) – Bamboo rattles, as used for dancing.

Pūʻiwa Rd./Ln. (Honolulu) – Startled, surprised, astonished. Named for an Oʻahu land section.

Pukalani Pl. (Honolulu) – Heavenly gate.

Pukanalā St./Pl. (ʻEwa Beach) – Sunrise.

Pukanawila Pl. (Honolulu) – Bougainvillea.

Pūkea Rd. (Haleʻiwa) – Perhaps: various fishes with high heads.

Pūʻili

Pūkele Ave. (Honolulu) – Muddy. Named for an Oʻahu land section and stream.

Pūkō St. (Waipahu) – Clump of sugar cane.

Pūkoʻa St. (Kailua) – Coral head.

Pūkōloa St. (Honolulu) – An unidentified star.

Pūkoʻo St./Pl. (Honolulu) – Support hill. Named for Molokaʻi land divisions.

Pūkuʻi Pl. (Waiʻanae) – Hub, of a wheel.

Pula Way (Waiʻanae) – Particle, as dust; particle in the eye, speck.

Pule

Pūlaʻa Ln. (Honolulu) – Sacred triton conch shell. Possibly named for John Pūlaʻa, a 1900s carpenter and painter.

Pūlāʻī St. (Waipahu) – Tī-leaf whistle.

Pūlama Rd./Pl. (Kāneʻohe) – To care for, cherish, treasure, save.

Pulapula Pl. (Waiʻanae) – Seedlings, sprouts, cuttings, of sugar cane.

Pule Pl. (Honolulu) – Prayer; to pray, say grace, ask a blessing.

Pūlehu St. (Honolulu) – Broiled. Named for a Kaua'i mountain ridge.

Pūlehulehu Pl. (Mililani) – Dusk, twilight.

Pulelehua Way (Honolulu) – Butterfly, moth, the Kamehameha butterfly.

Pulelo St./Pl. (Waipahu) – To float, wave, rise, as a flag of fire.

Pūlena Pl. (Honolulu) – Yellow hill. Named for an O'ahu land section.

Pūliki Pl. ('Aiea) – To embrace, hug; to gird on, as a corset; to grip tightly.

Pūloku St. (Waipahu) – Bright, sparkling, as sun or dew.

Pulu Pl. (Kāne'ohe) – Wet, moist, soaked, saturated.

Pulu Cir. (Wahiawā) – A soft, glossy, yellow wool on the base of tree-fern leaf stalks. It was used for stuffing mattresses and pillows. Ancient Hawaiians stuffed their dead with pulu after removing vital organs.

Pūlua Pl. (Waipahu) – Two persons together, as for mutual help.

Puluniu Lp. ('Aiea) – Coconut husk or fiber.

Pūliki

Pūmai'a Way/Pl. (Waipahu) – Banana stalk.

Pumehana St. (Honolulu) – Warm; warmth, affection.

Puna Ln. (Honolulu) – Spring (of water).

Puna St. (Honolulu) – Spring (of water). Named for a Hawai'i Island district.

Punaa St. (Kailua) – Definition not known.

Punahele Pl. (Honolulu) – A favorite or pet; to treat as a favorite.

Punahou St. (Honolulu) – New spring. Named for Punahou College. The school (established in 1841) was named for the land, which was named for the spring, formerly at the school site.

Punakō ('Ewa Beach) – Section between joints or nodes of sugar cane.

Punalau Pl. (Hale'iwa) – Many springs.

Punalē'ī Pl. (Kāne'ohe) – Crowded spring.

Punalu'u Valley Rd. (Hau'ula) – Diving spring. Named for an O'ahu land division.

Pūnana Lp. (Kailua) – Nest, shelter, hive; to nest.

Pūnana'ula St. (Wai'anae) – Red nest. Named for an O'ahu heiau.

Punaulua Pl. (Kahuku) – Ulua (fish) spring.

Pūnāwai St. (Kāne'ohe) – Water spring. Named for an O'ahu land section.

Pūnana

Pūneki St./Pl./Way (Mililani) – To cluster, as leaves.

Puni Pl. ('Ewa Beach) – To be fond of, desire, covet, like, be partial to; devoted; a favorite thing, delight, love.

Pūnihi St. (Honolulu) – Lofty, majestic, dignified.

Puninoni St./Pl. (Wahiawā) – Should be Puninani: fond of beauty.

Pūniu St. (Kailua) – Perhaps: polished coconut shell or bowl.

Puniwai St. (Waipahu) – Surrounded by water; fond of water.

Pūnono St./Pl. (Mililani) – Gorgeously red, filled
with sunshine, ever-beautiful.

Pūnua Way/Pl. (Kailua) – Young bird, fledgling.
Figuratively: young child or sweetheart.

Pū'ōhala St. (Kāne'ohe) – Definition not known.
Named for an O'ahu land section.

Pūpuhi

Puōlani St. (Honolulu) – To place high, or in a lofty
or sacred place.

Pū'olo Dr. (Honolulu) – Bundle, bag, container.

Puoni Pl. (Kāne'ohe) – To save, preserve.

Pū'ou St. (Waipahu) – Protruding top knot (of hair).

Pūowaina Dr. (Honolulu) – Hill of placing (human sacrifices). Hawaiian
name for Punchbowl.

Pūpū St./Pl. ('Ewa Beach) – General name for marine and land
shells.

Pūpuhi St. (Waipahu) – Trumpet, horn, conch shell trumpet.

Pūpūkahi St./Pl. (Waipahu) – United, as in harmonious
cooperation.

Pūpūkea Rd./Pl. (Hale'iwa) – White shell. Named for an
O'ahu land division.

Pūpūkoa'e St. (Waipahu) – A rare land shell. Literally:
tropic-bird shell.

Pūpūkui St. (Waipahu) – Moonshell, a snail. Literally:
pin shell.

Pūpū'ole

Pūpūkupa St. (Waipahu) – A native clam. Literally: native shell.

Pūpūmomi St. (Waipahu) – A small mother-of-pearl shell, a dirty gray,
thick-shelled oyster. Literally: pearl shell.

Pupunohe St. (Waipahu) – Should be Pūpūnoho: an unidentified sea shell.
Literally: sitting shell.

Pūpū'ole St./Pl. (Waipahu) – Large auger shells, with elongated pointed
spires.

Pūpūpani St. (Waipahu) – A violet snail which floats on ocean surface,
using bubbles attached to its foot. Literally: cork shell.

Pūpūpuhi St. (Waipahu) – Sundial shell. Literally: blowing shell.

Pu'u Dr./Pl. (Kunia, Wahiawā) – Hill, peak, cone, mound.

Pu'uahi St. (Lā'ie) – Fire hill.

Pu'u'āinako Pl. ('Ewa Beach) – A plain in
Honouliuli on the way to Pu'uokapolei.

Pu'u 'Alani Way (Pearl City) – Orange hill.

Pu'uali'i Pl. (Honolulu) – Royal hill.

Pu'ualoha St. (Kailua) – Beloved hill.

Pu'uanu St. (Mililani) – Cool hill.

Pu'uehu Pl. (Honolulu) – Dust hill. Named
for a Kaua'i mountain peak.

Pu'u

Puʻu ʻEleʻele Pl. (Honolulu) – Black hill.
Puʻuhala St. (ʻEwa Beach) – Pandanus hill.
Puʻuhale Rd./Pl. (Honolulu) – House knoll. Named for an Oʻahu land section.
Puʻu Hina Pl. (Pearl City) – Gray hill.
Puʻuhonua St. (Honolulu) – Place of refuge, sanctuary, asylum, place of peace and safety.
Puʻuhue Pl. (Honolulu) – Gourd hill.
Puʻuhulu Rd./Pl. (Waiʻanae) – Hulu hill. See Puʻu o Hulu.
Puʻuʻikena Dr./Pl. (Honolulu) – View hill.
Puʻuiki St. (Waialua) – Small hill. Named for an Oʻahu land section.
Puʻukaʻa St. (Mililani) – A course native grass-like plant that grows in Maʻalaea, Maui marshes.

Puʻukani

Puʻu Kākea Pl. (Honolulu) – A cinder cone on the western side of Mānoa Valley, and named for a storm wind associated with Mānoa.
Puʻu Kala St. (Pearl City) – Hill (of) colors.
Puʻukani Pl. (Kailua) – Sweet-voiced, as singing; a singer.
Puʻukapu St. (Honolulu) – Sacred hill.
Puʻu Kipa St. (Pearl City) – Visiting hill.
Puʻukoʻa St. (Mililani) – 1) A coarse native grass-like plant that grows in marshes; 2) A reddish-brown tapa.
Puʻu Kula Dr. (Pearl City) – School hill.
Puʻukū Makai Dr. (Honolulu) – Seaward Puʻukū. Puʻukū: treasurer, steward.
Puʻukū Mauka Dr. (Honolulu) – Inland Puʻukū. Puʻukū: treasurer, steward.
Pūʻula Rd. (Haleʻiwa) – Red conch shell.
Puʻulani Pl. (Honolulu) – Heavenly hill, royal hill.
Puʻulau Pl. (Kāneʻohe) – To increase rapidly in number.
Pūʻulaʻula Lp./Pl. (Honolulu) – Red hill, earth bank.
Puʻulena St. (Kāneʻohe) – Yellow hill. Named for a cold wind at Kailua and Puna, Hawaiʻi Island.
Puʻuloa Cir./Rd. (Honolulu, ʻEwa Beach) – Long hill. It is the Hawaiian name for Pearl Harbor.

Puʻulu

Puʻuloko Pl. (Kāneʻohe) – Inside hill.
Pūʻulu St. (Mililani) – Group, crowd, party.
Puʻuluana St./Pl. (Kahuku) – Comfortable hill.
Puʻuluna Pl. (Kāneʻohe) – Upper hill.
Puʻu Māhoe Pl. (Honolulu) – Twin hill. Named for Maui volcano cones.
Puʻumakani St. (ʻAiea) – Windy hill.
Puʻumalu Pl. (Honolulu) – Peaceful hill, shady hill.
Puʻumele Pl. (Honolulu) – Singing hill.
Puʻu Momi St. (Pearl City) – Pearl hill.
Puʻu Nanea Pl. (Honolulu) – Hill of leisure, enjoyable hill.

Pu'unani Pl. (Honolulu) – Beautiful hill.

Pu'unoa Pl. (Honolulu) – Hill free from restrictions.

Pu'unui Ave. (Honolulu) – Big hill. Named for O'ahu land sections.

Pu'uohāla'i Pl. (Kāne'ohe) – Should be Pu'uokahāla'i: hill of tranquility.

Pu'u'ōma'o St./Pl. (Honolulu) – Green hill.

Pu'uone St. (Waimānalo) – Sand dune or heap.

Pu'u'owa'a St. (Hau'ula) – Furrowed hill.

Pu'u Paka Dr. (Honolulu) – Tobacco hill.

Pu'u Pānini Ave. (Honolulu) – Prickly pear hill.

Pu'upele St./Pl. (Kāne'ohe) – Volcanic mound, hill.

Pu'u Poni St./Pl. (Pearl City) – Purple hill.

Pu'u 'Ula'ula St. (Pearl City) – Red hill.

Pu'uwai St. (Honolulu) – Generous.

Pu'uwepa Pl. (Mililani) – An unidentified star.

Pūwā Pl. (Kailua) – To shine, glitter, reflect brightly, as a
night fire.

Ua

Puwalu St. ('Ewa Beach) – All together in unison, united, cooperate.

Ua Dr. (Honolulu) – Rain; to rain; rainy.

Ua'awa Pl. (Honolulu) – Cold, bitter, drizzling rain. Figuratively: hard
experience.

Uahānai St./Pl. (Kapolei) – Rain that nurtures the earth.

Uahi St./Pl. ('Aiea) – Smoke.

Uakaniko'o St./Pl. (Wahiawā) – A rain that accompanies the Ko'olau wind.

Uakea Pl. (Kāne'ohe) – Mist. Literally: white rain.

Uakoko Pl. (Kāne'ohe) – A low-lying rainbow. Literally: blood rain.

'Uala St. (Wai'anae) – Sweet potato.

'Ualaka'a St./Pl. (Honolulu) – Rolling sweet potato. Hawaiian name for
Round Top, an O'ahu hill.

'Ualakahiki Pl. (Wai'anae) – The white or Irish potato. Literally: foreign
potato.

'Ualakupu St. (Kapolei) – Sprouting sweet potato.

'Ualalehu St. (Mililani) – A variety of sugar cane.

'Ualamaoli Pl. (Wai'anae) – Sweet potato. Literally: native potato.

Ualani Pl. (Kāne'ohe) – Heavenly rain.

Ualēhei St. (Kapolei) – Short for Kaualēheiomakawao: a lua fighting
stroke.

Ualena St. (Honolulu) – A yellow-tinted rain, famous at Hanalei, Kaua'i,
and on Maui.

Ualo St. ('Aiea) – To call out, for help; to resound; a call.

Uāni'i Pl. (Waipahu) – Stiff, as salted fish; stiffness.

'Uao Pl. ('Aiea) – To intercede, arbitrate, reconcile; referee, umpire,
peacemaker.

Uapō'aihala Pl. (Kāne'ohe) – A rain famous at Kahalu'u, O'ahu. Literally:
rain surrounding pandanus.

'Uhaloa St. ('Aiea) – A small, feathery weed. Its bitter leaves and inner root bark were used for tea, or chewed to relieve sore throat. One of the plant forms of the pig demigod Kamapua'a.

Uhi Pl. (Honolulu) – Yam.

Uhilehua St./Pl. (Kāne'ohe) – A variety of yam, grown in Kona, Hawai'i Island, having a tuber with pink fruit.

Uila

'Ūhini Pl. (Honolulu) – Long-horn grasshopper; cricket, locust.

Uhi'uala St. (Kapolei) – A variety of yam, with a tuber like a sweet potato grown on Hawai'i Island. Literally: sweet potato yam.

Uhiuhi St. (Honolulu) – An endemic tree with pink or red flowers. Its heavy, hard wood was shaped into sleds, spears, digging sticks, and used for building homes.

Uhu St. (Honolulu) – The parrotfishes. Colorful blue-green fish with a parrot-like beak and sharp teeth that chew on dead coral. The colors of this fish are so pretty, the fish is sometimes compared to a sweetheart. Commonly seen at Hanauma Bay.

Uila St. (Honolulu) – Lightning, electricity; electric.

Uilama St. (Kailua) – William.

U'ilani Pl. (Honolulu) – Heavenly beauty, royal beauty.

'Uiwi Pl. (Mililani) – A small endemic undershrub.

Ukana

Ukali St. (Honolulu) – The planet Mercury. Literally: following.

Ukaliali'i Pl. (Mililani) – The planet Mercury. Literally: following the chief (i.e., the sun).

Ukana St. (Honolulu) – Baggage, luggage, freight, cargo, supplies.

'Ūke'e St./Pl. (Waipahu) – Crooked, twisted, as the mouth.

'Ūkēkē St. (Waipahu) – A variety of musical bow held against the lips, as the fingers strum the strings. It produces soft sounds, as messages prior to love making.

'Uki'uki Pl. (Honolulu) – Several kinds of native Hawaiian lilies, bearing clusters of small blue flowers. The fruits are the primary attraction of the plant.

Ukuwai St. (Mililani) – Place in the grass house, between the sleeping place and the door, where host and guests visited.

Ula St. (Honolulu) – General name for crayfish or spiny lobsters.

Ulana St./Pl. (Honolulu) – Calm, still.

Ulehawa Rd. (Wai'anae) – Filthy penis. Named for an O'ahu land section and stream.

Ula

'Ūlei Lp. (Wai'anae) – A native spreading ever-green shrub. Its tough wood was shaped into fish spears, digging sticks, and the musical bow.

Ulele Pl. (Kapolei) – To leap at, get into action, do quickly, do at once.

Ulelele Pl. (Kapolei) – A chief's favorite.

Uli'eo St./Pl. (Waipahu) – Fitness, aptitude; preparedness, for running.

Ulihi Pl. (Waialua) – A small endemic shrub in the Mint family.

'Ūlili St. (Honolulu) – Wandering tattler, a migratory water bird.

Uliuli Pl. (Mililani) – An unidentified star.

'Ulu St. ('Aiea) – Breadfruit.

Ulua St. (Honolulu) – Certain species of crevalle, jack, or pompano (fishes).

Ulualana Pl. (Kailua) – Should be Ulu'alani: orange grove.

Uluamahi Pl. (Kailua) – Officer in the hale nauā, a place where genealogy was reviewed to determine if applicants were related to the high chief, and therefore eligible for royal household status.

'Ulu

Ulueki Pl. (Kailua) – Brush, undergrowth, forest.

Ulu'eo St. (Kailua) – An unidentified hardwood tree.

'Uluhaku St./Pl. (Kailua) – Lumpy, as of poi; knotty, bumpy, pimply.

Uluhala St./Pl. (Kailua) – Pandanus grove.

Uluha'o St./Pl. (Kailua) – Rough, jagged, as rocks.

Uluhe Cir. (Wahiawā) – All Hawaiian species of false staghorn fern, weedy, creeping, branching ferns, forming dense thickets.

Uluhui St. ('Ewa Beach) – A type of sugar cane used as a salve in early times.

'Ulukahiki St. (Kailua) – Foreign breadfruit.

Ulukanu St. (Kailua) – Garden patch.

Ulukoa St. (Mililani) – An unidentified star. Literally: soldier's inspiration.

Ulukou St. (Kailua) – Kou (tree) grove.

Ululā'au Pl. ('Aiea) – Forest, grove of trees. Figuratively: a fleet at sea.

Ululani St. (Kailua) – Heavenly growth, royal grove.

Ululoa Pl. (Mililani) – An unidentified star.

'Ulumaika St. (Honolulu) – Stone used in the ancient Hawaiian maika game; to play the 'ulu maika game; bowling, bowling ball.

'Ulumalu St. (Kailua) – Shady breadfruit (tree).

Ulumanu Dr. (Kailua) – Flock of birds.

Ulumawao St. (Kailua) – Growth at forest. Named for an O'ahu mountain peak.

Ulumū St. (Kailua) – Growing quietly.

Ulunahele St. (Kailua) – Wilderness, place of wild growth.

Ulune St./Pl. ('Aiea) – Should be Uluna: probably pillow, cushion.

Uluniu St. (Kailua) – Coconut grove.

Uluniu Ave. (Honolulu) – Coconut grove. Named
for an Oʻahu land section.

Uluʻoa St. (Kailua) – Same as Ulukoa: an unidentified
star.

Uluʻohiaʻa St. (Kapolei) – A grove of ʻohia trees.

Uluʻopihi Lp. (Kailua) – Limpet (shellfish) growth.

Ulupa St. (Kailua) – Should be Ulupō: dark or
dense, as growth. Named for an Oʻahu land
section and heiau.

Ulupiʻi

Ulupaina St. (Kailua) – Pine grove.

ʻUlupalakua St. (Kailua) – Breadfruit ripening (on) backs (of carriers).

Ulupiʻi St./Pl. (Kailua) – To shiver or tremble, with cold or fright.

Ulupono St. (Honolulu) – Successful.

Ulupua Pl. (Honolulu) – Flower garden, growth of flowers.

Ulupuni St. (Kailua) – Overcome with emotion, hysteria, passion, or an
occult influence.

Uluwale St./Pl. (Wahiawā) – To grow easily or without care.

Uluwehi St./Pl. (Wahiawā, Honolulu) – Lush and beautiful verdure (green
vegetation); a place where beautiful plants thrive; festively adorned.
Literally: decorative growth.

ʻŪmalu Pl. (Honolulu) – Brow of a hill or cliff; shade under
cliff or hill.

ʻUmeke Pl. (Waipahu) – Bowl, calabash.

ʻUmena St. (Kapolei) – An attraction, pulling.

ʻUmi St. (Honolulu) – Ten. Named for an Oʻahu land section.

Unahe Pl. (Kāneʻohe) – Light breeze.

10

ʻUmi

Unahipipi Pl. (ʻEwa Beach) – Young pipi shellfish
(Hawaiian pearl oyster).

Unulau Pl. (Honolulu) – A wind on several islands, famous in song.
Perhaps it is the tradewind.

Uouoa St. (ʻEwa Beach) – A fish, known as the false mullet or false
ʻamaʻama.

ʻUpaʻi Pl. (Waipahu) – To flap, as wings, or clothes in the wind.

ʻŪpalu St. (Pearl City) – Gentle, mild, tender, soft-spoken, soft, tender,
fragile.

ʻUpāpalu Dr. (ʻAiea) – The larger cardinal fishes.

ʻUpena St. (Waiʻanae) – Fish net. Figuratively: trap.

Upolo Pl. (Honolulu) – Should be ʻUpolu: definition not known. Named for
a Hawaiʻi Island promontory.

ʻŪʻū Pl. (Kapolei) – Soldier fishes.

ʻUʻuku St. (Wahiawā) – Tiny, small.

ʻUwalu Cir. (Wahiawā) – To claw, scratch, rub, grate, rasp.

ʻUwao St. (Honolulu) – To intercede, arbitrate, reconcile; referee, umpire,
peacemaker. Commonly: ʻuao.

Uwaʻu Dr. (ʻAiea) – Perhaps: to grate, scrape, claw, wear away by friction.

Waʻa St. (Honolulu) – Canoe.

Waʻakaua St. (Honolulu) – War canoe.

Waʻakea Pl. (Kapolei) – Unpainted canoe set to sea after the taboos were lifted during the Makahiki Festival. Literally: white canoe.

Waʻa

Waʻaloa Way/Pl. (Honolulu) – Long canoe.

Waʻapuhi St. (Waiʻanae) – A small, slim canoe used for surfing.

Waʻaʻula St. (Kapolei) – Chief's canoe with red sails.

Waena St. (Wahiawā) – Middle, between, center, central.

Wahamana Pl. (Waipahu) – Voice of authority. Literally: powerful mouth.

Wāhane St./Pl. (Kapolei) – Seed of the loulu native palm.

Wahinani St. (Pearl City) – Beautiful place.

Wahine Pl. (Honolulu) – Woman, lady, wife, female; feminine.

Wahinekoa Pl. (Honolulu) – Brave woman. Probably should be Koawahine: female soldier.

Wahineʻōmaʻo Pl./Way (ʻEwa Beach) – A legendary friend of Hiʻaka (sister of Pele).

Wahinepeʻe St. (Lāʻie) – Hiding woman.

Wahipana St. (Kapolei) – Legendary place.

Waho Pl. (Waipahu) – Outside.

Waia Lp. (Mililani) – An unidentified star. Literally: disgraced.

Wahine

Waiāhole Homestead Rd./Valley Rd. (Kāneʻohe) – Āhole (fish) water. Named for an Oʻahu land division.

Waiahu St. (Waipahu) – Pool of water.

Waiʻaka Rd./Pl. (Honolulu) – Laughing water. Named for an Oʻahu land division.

Waiakamilo Rd. (Honolulu) – Water of the milo (tree). Named for an Oʻahu land section.

Waiākea Pl. (ʻAiea) – A variety of taro also called lehua keʻokeʻo.

Waiʻala St. (Wahiawā) – Perfume, cologne, toilet water.

Waiʻalae Ave. (Honolulu) – Mudhen water. Named for an Oʻahu valley.

Waiʻaleʻale St. (Honolulu) – Rippling water, overflowing water. Named for a Kauaʻi mountain (5,080 feet), the world's wettest place, with 470 inches of rain yearly.

Waialiʻi Pl. (Kapolei) – Chiefly water.

Waialua Beach Rd. (Waialua, Haleʻiwa) – Definition not known. Named for an Oʻahu district.

Wai'anae Ave./Cir./Rd./Valley Rd. (Wahiawā, Honolulu, Wai'anae) – Mullet water. Named for an O'ahu district, and a land division within that district.

Waianiani Pl. (Honolulu) – Crystal-clear water, artesian water.

Waianuhea Pl. (Wahiawā) – Lukewarm water, neither hot nor cold.

Wai'ape Pl. (Kāne'ohe) – 'Ape (plant) water. Named for an O'ahu land section.

Wai'apo Pl. ('Ewa Beach) – Water caught in a taro leaf, often used in ceremonies. It was regarded as pure since it did not touch the ground. Figuratively: a beloved mate, spouse.

Waiau Pl. (Honolulu) – Swirling water of a current. Named for an O'ahu land division.

Wai'au'au Ave. (Pearl City) – Bathing water.

Waiawa Rd. (Pearl City) – Milkfish water. Named for an O'ahu land division.

Waiawī St. (Kāne'ohe) – The yellow strawberry guava.

Waiea Pl. (Wai'anae) – Sea water used for purification.

Waiehu Pl. (Wahiawā) – Spraying water.

Wai'eli St. (Honolulu) – Well water, well. Literally: dug water.

Waihau St. (Wahiawā) – A heiau where hogs, bananas, and coconuts were sacrificed, not people.

Wai'au'au

Waihe'e St. (Honolulu) – Squid liquid, octopus water.

Waihe'e Rd./Pl. (Kāne'ohe) – Squid liquid, octopus water. Named for an O'ahu land division.

Waihili Pl. (Honolulu) – Water obtained by shaking the dew or raindrops from the leaves of plants or trees, as was said to have been done in dry areas.

Waiholo St./Pl. (Honolulu) – Running water.

Waihona St./Pl. (Pearl City) – Depository, vault, file, place for laying up things for safekeeping; treasury.

Waihonu St./Pl. (Wahiawā) – Turtle waters.

Waihou St. (Honolulu) – New water.

Waihua Pl. ('Ewa Beach) – Water drop caught in a taro leaf, much likened for purification and medicine, as it has not touched the earth.

Waihūnā St./Pl. ('Ewa Beach) – One of the principal sources of water for Honouliuli which was later hidden by a powerful kahuna. Literally: hidden spring.

Waiiki St./Pl. (Honolulu) – Little water.

Waikā Pl. (Honolulu) – Cleared water. Named for a Hawai'i Island land division.

Waikahalulu Ln. (Honolulu) – Water (of) the roaring. Named for an O'ahu land section.

Waikahe Pl. (Honolulu) – Stream. Literally: flowing water.

Waikai Ave. (Pearl City) – Brackish or salty water.

Waikalani Dr./Pl. (Wahiawā) – Water (of) the chief.

Waikāloa St. (Waimānalo) – Probably: water (of) Kanaloa.

Waikalua Rd./Pl. (Kāneʻohe) – Water (of) the pit, water (of) the lua fighter. Named for an Oʻahu land section.

Waikalualoko Lp. (Kāneʻohe) – Inland Waikalua. Named for an Oʻahu land section.

Waikanaloa St. (Honolulu) – Water (of) Kanaloa. Named for a Kauaʻi wet cave.

Waikāne Valley Rd. (Kāneʻohe) – Water (of) Kāne. Named for an Oʻahu land division.

Waikapōkī Rd. (Kāneʻohe) – Water (of) the younger brother. Named for an Oʻahu land section.

Waikapū Lp. (Honolulu) – Water (of) the conch. Named for a Maui land division.

Waikele Rd./Pl. (Waipahu) – Muddy water. Named for an Oʻahu land division.

Waikō Pl. (Kapolei) – Water with a strong current.

Waikoaʻe Rd. (Honolulu) – Tropic-bird water. Named for an Oʻahu land section.

Waikolu Way (Honolulu) – Three waters.

Waikuʻi St./Pl. (Honolulu) – Pounding water. Named for original awardee.

Waikūlama St. (Hauʻula) – Definition not known.

Waikupanaha St./Pl. (Waimānalo) – Extraordinary water. Named for an Oʻahu land section.

Wailana Pl. (ʻAiea) – Calm, quiet, as the sea; still water.

Wailani Rd. (Honolulu) – Rain water, used for medicine and purification.

Wailawa St./Pl. (Wahiawā) – Sufficient water.

Waileʻa St. (Waimānalo) – Water (of) pleasure. Named for an Oʻahu land section.

Wailehua Rd./Pl. (Kāneʻohe) – Lehua (blossom) water.

Waileia Pl. (Mililani) – An unidentified morning star.

Wailele St. (Honolulu) – Waterfall, cataract.

Wailele Rd. (Kāneʻohe) – Waterfall, cataract. Named for an Oʻahu land section.

Wailepo St./Pl. (Kailua) – Dirty water.

Wailewa Pl. (ʻEwa Beach) – Coconut water. Literally: hanging water.

Wailoa Lp. (Mililani) – An unidentified star near the Pleiades, said to be a member of the group called Kaulua (double canoe). Literally: long stream.

Wailohia Pl. (ʻEwa Beach) – Sparkling water.

Wailua St. (Honolulu) – Two waters. Named for Kauaʻi land divisions.

Wailupe Cir./Pl. (Honolulu) – Kite water. Named for an Oʻahu valley.

Waimahū'ī Pl. ('Ewa Beach) – An 'Ewa chiefess, so very kapu that even her own children could not eat a portion of any food served for her.

Waimaka St. (Mililani) – Tears. Literally; eye water.

Waimaka

Waimakua Dr./Pl. (Wahiawā) – Parent water.

Waimānalo Rd. ('Ewa Beach, Kapolei) – Potable, drinkable water. Named for an O'ahu gulch.

Waimano Home Rd. (Pearl City) – Many waters. Named for an O'ahu land division.

Waimanu St. (Honolulu) – Bird water.

Waimāpuna Pl. ('Ewa Beach) – Spring water.

Waimea Valley Rd. (Hale'iwa) – Reddish water. Named for an O'ahu land division.

Waimeli Pl. (Wahiawā) – Honey. Literally: bee liquor.

Waimoku Pl. (Wahiawā) – Water breaking loose.

Waimomona Pl. ('Ewa Beach) – Soda water, sweet water.

Wainaku Pl. (Mililani) – An unidentified star, sometimes called the patron star of Hilo.

Waimomona

Wainana St. (Kāne'ohe) – Should be Nānāwai: water view.

Wai Nani Way (Honolulu) – Beautiful water.

Wainiha St. (Honolulu) – Unfriendly water. Named for a Kaua'i land division.

Wainihi St. (Wahiawā) – Water's edge.

Wainohia St./Pl./Way (Kapolei) – Safe, safety.

Wainui Rd. (Waipahu) – A large flow of water; to flow in great quantities.

Waioha Pl. (Mililani) – Joy.

Wai'ōhi'a St./Pl. (Kāne'ohe) – A variety of sugar cane.

Waiohinu Dr. (Honolulu) – All kinds of cultivated dahlias (ornamental flowers), named for a Hawai'i Island town where the plant was first grown. Literally: shiny water.

Waiokeola St. (Waimānalo) – Water of the life.

Waiola St. (Honolulu) – Water (of) life.

Waioleka St. (Mililani) – Fragrant cultivated violets.

Wai'oli St./Pl. (Honolulu) – Joyful water. Named for a Kaua'i land division.

Waiolina St. (Waipahu) – Violin.

Wai'olu St. (Wai'anae) – Cool, pleasant, attractive, soft, gentle, pleasing.

Wai'ōma'o Rd. (Honolulu) – Green water. Named for an O'ahu land section and stream.

Waiolina

Wai'ōmea St. (Kapolei) – Reddish water.

Wai'oni St./Pl. (Wahiawā) – Moving water.

Wai'ōpae St. (Waipahu) – Gulch and fishpond on eastern Lana'i.

Waiopouli Pl. (Honolulu) – Should be Waipouli: dark water. Named for a Kaua'i land division.

Wai'ōpua St./Pl. (Honolulu) – Cloud bank water. Named for a Kaua'i bay.

Waipā Ln. (Honolulu) – Request, prayer, to the gods. Possibly named for Police Captain Robert Parker Waipā, who served during 1890s-1900s.

Waipahē Pl. ('Ewa Beach) – Courteous, gentlemanly, polite, modest, gentle, good natured, easygoing, agreeable, gracious.

Waipahe'e Pl. (Honolulu) – Slippery water.

Waipahu St./Depot St. (Waipahu) – Drum water. Said to have been originally Waipahū: bursting water. Named for an O'ahu land section.

Waipa'ipa'i St. (Kāne'ohe) – Mixed liquid or drink of any kind.

Waipao Pl. ('Aiea) – Scooped water. Named for an O'ahu land section.

Waipi'o Pt. Access Rd. (Waipahu) – Arched water. Named for an O'ahu land division.

Waipi'o Uka St. (Waipahu) – Upper Waipi'o. See Waipi'o.

Waipono St./Pl. (Wahiawā) – Beneficial water.

Waipo'o St. (Wahiawā) – Water (of the) summit.

Waipua Pl. (Kāne'ohe) – Honey from flowers.

Waipuilani Ave. (Pearl City) – Water spout.

Waipuka St./Pl. (Wahiawā) – Issuing water.

Waipuna Ave./Rise (Pearl City, Honolulu) – Spring water. Figuratively: sweetheart.

Waipū'olo Pl. (Wahiawā) – Water in leaves, of taro, that could be carried; coconut water. Literally: bundled water.

Waipa'ipa'i

Waiua Pl./Way ('Aiea) – Rain water.

Waiwai Lp. (Honolulu) – Goods, property, value, estate; costly.

Waka Rd. (Hale'iwa) – Sharp, protruding.

Wākamali'i Pl. (Kapolei) – Childhood.

Wākea St. (Kapolei) – The ancestor of all Hawaiians. Father of Kapo. (Kapo: sister of Pele).

Wākine Pl. (Honolulu) – Joaquin. Possibly named for the Joaquin family, ranchers who lived in area.

Wala'au Pl. (Kapolei) – To talk, speak, converse.

Walea St./Pl. (Wahiawā, Honolulu) – Repose, leisurely, tranquility.

Walea Uka Pl. (Wahiawā) – Upper Walea. See Walea. Named for the land tract.

Wali Pl. (Waipahu) – Smooth, thin, as poi.

Walikanahele Rd. (Hale'iwa) – Definition not known.

Wākamali'i

Walina St. (Honolulu) – Softness.

Waliwali Pl. (Kāne'ohe) – Gentle, easygoing, good-natured, smooth.

Walu Way (Honolulu) – Perhaps: eight.

Wana Pl. (Hale'iwa) – Perhaps: long-spined sea urchins. Named for original awardee.

Wana'ao Rd./Pl. (Kailua) – Dawn, to dawn.

Wanaka St. (Honolulu) – Wanda.

Wānini St./Pl. (Waialua) – A native tree or shrub in the Tea family. Commonly called: Ānini.

Wao'ala Pl. ('Aiea) – Fragrant inland region.

Waokanaka St./Pl. (Honolulu) – An inland region where people may live or occasionally frequent.

Waolani Ave. (Honolulu) – Mountain area believed occupied by gods. Named for an O'ahu valley.

Waonahele Rd. (Honolulu) – Inland forest region, jungle.

Wā'ōpio Pl. (Kapolei) – Youth (time of).

Wauke St. (Honolulu) – The paper mulberry, a small tree or shrub. Its bark was pounded into tough tapa, used for clothing.

Wawau St. (Honolulu) – Definition not known. Named for a Maui promontory.

Wela

Wawe Pl. (Honolulu) – Quickly; fast.

Wehena Pl. (Waipahu) – Opening, unfastening, taking off; solution, as of a problem.

Wehewehe Lp. (Mililani) – An unidentified star.

Wehiwa Way/Pl. (Hale'iwa) – Choice, prized; a choice object.

Wēkiu St./Pl. (Mililani) – Tip, top, topmost, summit; of the higher rank or station.

Wela St./Ln. (Honolulu) – Hot, burned; heat, temperature. Figuratively: lust, passion.

Welehu St./Pl. (Mililani) – Ancient Hawaiian lunar month.

Welelau Pl. ('Aiea) – Tip, top, extremity, end.

Weleweka Pl. (Kāne'ohe) – An ornamental perennial herb or small shrub. Its colorful leaves are red, yellow, green, and purple. Literally: velvet.

Welina Lp. (Waipahu) – A greeting of affection, similar to aloha; to greet.

Welo St. (Kapolei) – Ancient Hawaiian lunar month.

Welona Pl. (Mililani) – To set, as the sun.

Welowelo St. (Kapolei) – To flutter, float, or strain, as in the wind.

Wena St. (Kāne'ohe) – Glow, of sunrise or fire, red.

Wenuka Pl. (Mililani) – The planet Venus.

West Kuilima Lp./Pl. (Kahuku) – To go arm in arm; to hold hands.

Wīka'o St. (Wahiawā) – Strong, hard, rigid, inflexible; dry.

Wikolia Pl. (Wai'anae) – Victoria.

Wili St. ('Ewa Beach) – To wind, twist, crank, turn; mill, drill, wrench; various machines used for turning

Wiliama Pl. (Honolulu) – William.

Wilikī Dr. (Honolulu) – Engineer, turnkey; engineering. Literally: turn key.

Wilikina Dr. (Wahiawā) – Sister, nun (Catholic). Literally: virgin.

Wilikō St. ('Aiea) – Sugar mill, sugar grinder, to grind sugar cane.

Wilikoki Pl. (Kailua) – Wilcox. Site of the former country home of Gaylord Wilcox (1881-1970). Associated with many sugar plantations, vice president of American Factors, and Interisland Steam Navigation Co. Grandson of missionary Abner Wilcox.

Wilikina

Wilinau Rd. (Hale'iwa) – To turn, twist, wriggle, suffer in pain.

Wiliwili St./Cir. (Honolulu, Wahiawā) – A native tree. Its light wood was shaped into surfboards, canoe outriggers, and net floats.

Wiliwilihele Pl. (Kapolei) – Meandering wiliwili trees.

Wīlou St. ('Aiea) – Willow (tree).

References

Birds:

Berger, Andrew J. *Hawaiian Birdlife*. Honolulu: University of Hawai'i Press, 1972.
Shallenberger, Robert J. *Hawaii's Birds*. Honolulu: Hawai'i Audubon Society, 1981.

Plants:

Lamb, Samuel H. *Native Trees and Shrubs of the Hawaiian Islands*. Santa Fe, New Mexico: Sunstone Press, 1981.
Neal, Marie C. *In Gardens of Hawai'i*. Honolulu: Bishop Museum Press, 1965.

Fish:

Titcomb, Margaret, with Mary Kawena Pūku'i. *Native Use of Fish in Hawai'i*. Honolulu: University of Hawai'i Press, 1972.

Marine Invertebrates:

Titcomb, et al. *Native Use of Marine Invertebrates in Old Hawai'i*. Honolulu: University of Hawai'i Press, 1969.

Stars and the Calendar:

Johnson, Rubellite and John Kaipo Mahelona. *Nā Inoa Hōkū*. Honolulu: Topgallant Publishing Co., 1975.
Malo, David. *Hawaiian Antiquities*. Translated by Dr. Nathaniel Emerson, 1898. Honolulu: Bishop Museum, 1951.

Place Names:

Budnick, Rich and Holt-Padilla, Hōkūlani. *Maui Street Names.*
Honolulu: Aloha Press, 1991.
Clere, John. *Bryan's Sectional Maps of Oʻahu.* Honolulu: EMIC
Graphics, 1986.
Coulter, John Wesley. *A Gazetteer of the Territory of Hawaiʻi.*
Honolulu: University of Hawaiʻi Press, 1935.
Honolulu Department of Land Utilization. Documents.
Pūkuʻi, Mary Kawena and Elbert, Samuel H. *Hawaiian Dictionary.*
Honolulu: University of Hawaiʻi Press, 1971, 1986 revised edition.
_____and Moʻokini, Esther T. *Place Names of Hawaiʻi.* Honolulu:
University of Hawaiʻi Press, 1974.
Sterling, Elspeth P. and Summers, Catherine C. *Sites of Oʻahu.*
Honolulu: Bishop Museum, 1978.
Taylor, Clarice B., in collaboration with George Miranda. "Honolulu
Street Names." *Honolulu Star Bulletin*, January-May, 1956.

General History:

Clark, T. Blake. "Honolulu's Streets." *Papers of the Hawaiian
Historical Society*, no. 20, pp. 4-25. Honolulu. 1939.
Daws, Gavan. *Shoal of Time, a History of the Hawaiian Islands.* New
York: Macmillan Co. 1968.
Day, A. Grove. *History Makers of Hawaii.* Mutual Publishing Co. of
Honolulu, 1984.
Hawaiʻi State Library. Documents, *Honolulu Advertiser,* and *Honolulu
Star Bulletin* newspaper clippings.
Kamakau, S.M. *Ruling Chiefs of Hawaii.* Honolulu: Kamehameha
Schools Press, 1961.
*Missionary Album: Portraits and Biographical Sketches of the
American Protestant Missionaries to the Hawaiian Islands, enlarged
from the Edition of 1937.* Honolulu: Hawaiian Mission Children's
Society, 1969.
Mitchell, Donald D. *Resource Units in Hawaiian Culture.* Honolulu:
Kamehameha Schools, 1969.
Mrantz, Maxine. *Women of Old Hawaiʻi.* Honolulu: Tongg Publishing
Co., 1975.
Nellist, George, edited. *The Story of Hawaii and Its Builders.* Honolulu
Star Bulletin, Ltd., 1925.
_____*Men of Hawaii.* Honolulu Star Bulletin, 1921, 1935.
Peterson, Barbara Bennett. *Notable Women of Hawaii.* Honolulu:
University of Hawaiʻi Press, 1984.

Street Notes

About the Authors

Duke Kalani Wise earned his B.A. Degree at the University of Hawai'i in Anthropology, with emphasis in Hawaiian history and language. He taught a class about O'ahu place names at the University of Hawai'i. His great-grandfather, John Wise, was the first teacher of the Hawaiian language at Kamehameha Schools and at the University of Hawai'i, in the 1920s.

Rich Budnick received a B.A. Degree in History and Political Science from UCLA, and a M.A. Degree in Government from California State University, Sacramento. He has worked for Governor Ben Cayetano and Maui Mayor Hannibal Tavares. He has been a government Public Information Officer, Legislative Assistant, and a history teacher. His other books are: **Hawaii's Forgotten History: the Good...the Bad...the Embarrassing**, **Stolen Kingdom: An American Conspiracy**, **Maui Street Names** (translations by Hōkūlani Holt-Padilla), and **How to Get the Job You Want in Hawaii**.